本书系 2016 年度湖南省社会科学成果
评审委员会立项课题成果

人民教育家 徐特立

The People's Educator Xu Teli

中文：梁堂华、彭红霞、刘宏伟

英译：贺龙平

译审：罗宾·史蒂芬·吉尔班克

插图：宋立军

Written By: Liang Tanghua / Peng Hongxia / Liu Hongwei

Translated By: He Longping

Proofread By: Robin·Stephen·Gilbank

Illustrated By: Song Lijun

中央编译出版社
Central Compilation & Translation Press

图书在版编目(CIP)数据

人民教育家徐特立:汉、英 / 梁堂华, 彭红霞, 刘宏伟著;贺龙平译. -- 北京:中央编译出版社, 2022.8
ISBN 978-7-5117-4119-6

Ⅰ.①人… Ⅱ.①梁…②彭…③刘…④贺… Ⅲ.①徐特立(1877-1968)—传记—汉、英 Ⅳ.①K825.46

中国版本图书馆CIP数据核字(2021)第269924号

人民教育家徐特立

责任编辑	杜永明
责任印制	刘　慧
出版发行	中央编译出版社
地　　址	北京市海淀区北四环西路69号(100080)
电　　话	(010)55627391(总编室)　(010)55627310(编辑室) (010)55627320(发行部)　(010)55627377(新技术部)
经　　销	全国新华书店
印　　刷	佳兴达印刷(天津)有限公司
开　　本	787毫米×1092毫米 1/16
字　　数	243千字
印　　张	17.5
版　　次	2022年8月第1版
印　　次	2022年8月第1次印刷
定　　价	98.00元

新浪微博:@中央编译出版社　　微　信:中央编译出版社(ID:cctphome)
淘宝店铺:中央编译出版社直销店(http://shop108367160.taobao.com)(010)55627331
本社常年法律顾问:北京市吴栾赵阎律师事务所律师　闫军　梁勤
凡有印装质量问题,本社负责调换,电话:(010)55626985

徐老是人民的教育家

甘泗淇

目 录

001 第一章
   苦学成才，终身不懈

021 第二章
   舍家办学，教育救国

037 第三章
   爱生如子，培育英才

059 第四章
   "读书不忘救国"

085 第五章
   家风家教，遗泽后人

099 第六章
   一代师表，世之楷模

Contents

119   **Chapter One**
　　　　A Lifetime of Purposeful Hard Study

149   **Chapter Two**
　　　　Sacrificing His Family Life to Run Schools and Saving the Country through the Promotion of Education

169   **Chapter Three**
　　　　Loving the Students as if They Were His Own Children and Nurturing Their Talents

195   **Chapter Four**
　　　　"You Should Study Hard but Never Forget about Our National Salvation"

229   **Chapter Five**
　　　　His Family Style and Education Still Benefit Subsequent Generations

247   **Chapter Six**
　　　　"An Exemplary Teacher of His Generation and a Role Model for the World"

私塾里换了一位姓张的先生,他对学生要求严格,注重做人的道理。

第一章

苦学成才,终身不懈

苦难的童年

1877年2月1日（农历十二月十九日），徐特立出生于湖南省长沙县五美乡荷叶坝一户贫苦农民家庭。母亲心地善良，主要在家料理家务，浆洗织补，一生勤劳节俭；父亲是个老实巴交的农民，没有文化，不善言谈，除了耕种少得可怜的一点土地外，农闲时还要去帮别人打短工，成年累月地干活。祖父也是农民，但读过一点医书，略懂医道，在缺医少药的乡村，经常热情地为邻里乡亲看病。他还爱看《三国演义》《水浒传》等小说。徐特立出生后，祖父翻阅《康熙字典》，给孙子取名"懋恂"。懋，勤勉；恂，诚信。老人希望孙子长大为人，一定要勤勉、诚实。

▲ 今日的五美乡荷叶坝。

徐特立4岁那年，母亲得病去世了。咽气的那天晚上，破旧的屋子里，昏暗的灯光映照着母亲惨白的脸。父亲和哥哥呆呆地坐在一边，姐姐搂着小妹妹，徐特立依偎在母亲的身旁，哭喊着妈妈，可妈妈再也不能应答他一声了。

母亲去世不久，祖父接着也去世了。家里连续遭遇两次丧事，家境愈加窘迫，只剩下50串钱。为了保住这个家，父亲拿着这笔钱和外祖父合买了一块山地、几间茅房，两家住在一起，帮扶度日。

往后的日子越来越艰难，父亲在万般无奈的情况下，把大女儿送给人家做了童养媳，10岁的大儿子跟着自己下地干活。徐特立在家照看妹妹，兄妹俩常常搬一条长板凳放在屋子中间，面对面坐着，互相看着背后，生怕有害人的东西出来。

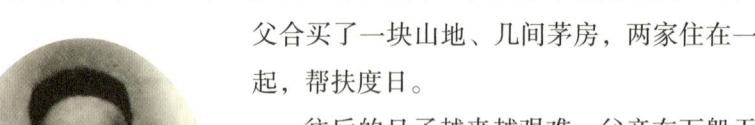

▶ 徐特立的父亲徐树兆（1840—1920）。

8岁那年的除夕夜

徐特立8岁那年,年关到了,北风呼啸,大雪纷飞,有钱人家里杀猪宰羊,准备过节,高墙大院里不断传出"噼啪""噼啪"的爆竹声。可徐特立家里什么年货也没有准备,不懂事的小妹妹一个劲地哭着向父亲要糖果。父亲看着孩子,心里十分难受,他把女儿搂在怀里哄着:"莫哭,莫哭!"泪水湿润了眼眶。可这个年怎么过呢?他忽然记起,年前给颜姓财主做短工,还没有拿到工钱,便站起身说:"大伢子、二伢子,你们在家照顾好妹妹,我去讨笔工钱回来过年。"说完,披上蓑衣,急匆匆地走出了家门。夜深了,北风刮得簌簌的响,大雪还在纷纷扬扬地下个不停,兄妹三个紧紧地坐在一起,眼巴巴地等着父亲回来。

直到大年初一早晨,父亲才拖着疲惫的身子回到家中。年幼的徐特立赶紧上前,帮父亲脱下带雪的蓑衣,焦急地问工钱讨到没有。父亲气得面色铁青,浑身发抖,愤愤地说:"那没良心的财主,仗势欺人,根本不理会这件事,我一等再等,等到天明,他们的管家出来不光不认账,还说我故意在年关时节闹事。"

"这太欺侮人了,咱们就不能找他说理去?"徐特立气愤地说。

"孩子,你不知道,跟他们哪有理讲?"父亲叹了口气:"唉,也怪我不识字,要是当时立张字据,就不怕黑心的财主赖账了。明年借债讨米,也要送你去读书。"

窗外风雪弥漫,虽已天亮,但仍天昏地暗。一家人在悲愤中又冷又饿地迎来了新的一年。

入私塾勤奋读书

徐特立9岁那年,他那吃过没有文化苦头的父亲,东拼西凑地筹了一点学费,送他入蒙馆读书,开始接受传统的启蒙教育。

在偏僻的乡下,教育很落后。乡村蒙馆的教学方式陈旧单一,通常是着青布长袍、戴着老花镜的教书先生站在台前或者端端正正地坐在椅子上,摇头晃脑地领读《论语》之类的古书,别的什么也不讲。学生跟着先生一遍一遍地重复诵读,根本不懂书的含义。年幼的徐特立觉得这样的学习索然无味,对所学内容也不感兴趣。

半年之后,私塾里换了一位姓张的先生。他选用朱柏庐的《治家格言》做课本,注重教学生做人的道理,如"黎明即起,洒扫庭除""一粥一饭,当思来处不易;半丝半缕,恒念物力维艰",等等。徐特立觉得这些话读起来朗朗上口,道理浅显易懂,且对为人处世有用,因此,学起来特别用功。

后来,张先生又教学生朗读明朝忠臣杨椒山的遗嘱。杨椒山因看不惯奸臣严嵩一伙祸国殃民、搅乱朝政,毅然向皇帝写奏章弹劾严嵩,反遭陷害,被捕入狱,判处死刑。这篇文章,就是他在临刑前写给儿子的。文中告诫儿子做人要有志气,不要向邪恶势力低头,要谦虚诚实、光明正大。文章极有感情,徐特立读着读着,感动得泪流满面,心中久久不能平静。杨椒山坚持正义、宁死不屈的形象,深深地印刻他的脑海里。从此,他对读书产生了兴趣。

▼ 徐特立在私塾所读书籍《朱子格言》《椒山遗嘱》。

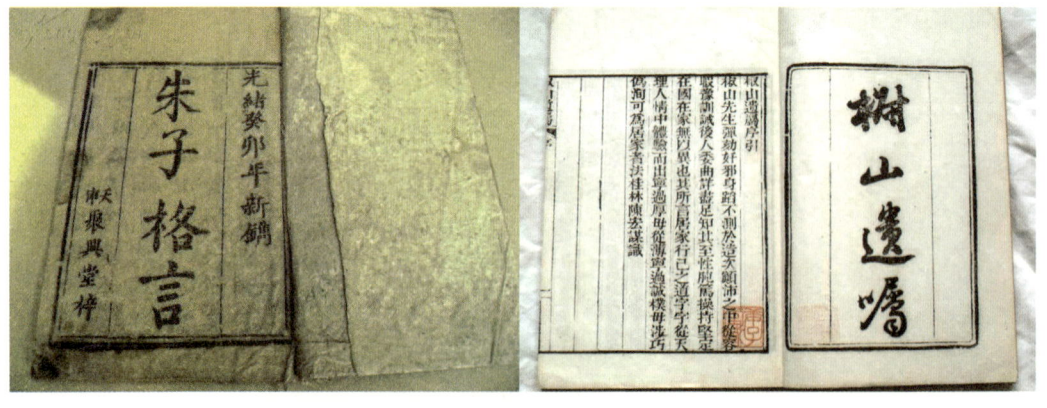

过继给伯祖母为孙

◀ 位于五美乡观音塘的徐特立故居。

徐特立 12 岁的时候，居住在五美乡观音塘的伯祖父病故，伯祖母也已经 60 多岁了，半身瘫痪，跟前没人照料，父亲就把徐特立过继给她做孙子。不久，伯祖母给徐特立娶了一个童养媳，名叫熊立诚，比他小 11 个月。这姑娘年纪虽小，却精明能干，家务活样样都会。徐特立和她兄妹相称，和睦友爱，对伯祖母也非常孝顺，深得伯祖母喜欢。

伯祖母一生勤劳节俭，是个治家能手。虽然瘫痪，行动不便，但是家里大大小小的事情，她都安排得井井有条。家里的木盆木桶，每年擦一次桐油，用了几十年都没有坏。她自己身上穿的围裙也是补丁加补丁，连原来的底布都难以认出来了。

伯祖母的家教很严，为节省灯油，晚上不让徐特立点灯看书，也不许外出串门走户，要他和熊立诚围坐在身旁，听她讲为人处世、勤俭持家的道理以及家族历史故事。每天天刚亮，就催促他起床，让他先打扫庭院，然后大声朗读诗文。这使徐特立养成了勤俭、爱劳动、爱学习的习惯。

"教书兼习科举业"

15岁的徐特立，已是俊秀的少年了，他双目炯炯有神，言谈举止文雅得体，读书习字发奋用功，乡亲们对他称赞有加。可是，这年伯祖母病危，不久便去世了，徐特立只好辍学在家，但这并没有影响徐特立读书，他一面寻找谋生的职业，一面设法找书阅读，增长见识。

一次，他跟一个和尚在庙里做事。那和尚学识渊博，教他静坐，读佛家的禅宗语录，还常教他寒山和拾得的诗歌。寒山和拾得是唐朝两位有学问的和尚，他们用近似白话的文句写了一些诗歌，反映当时的社会现实，富有趣味性。徐特立很喜欢这些生动亲切的诗歌，其中许多篇章他都能倒背如流。在寺庙遇到这样学问高深的老师，甚至使他产生了出家当和尚的想法，但继而又想：家里需要我照顾，怎能这样出家呢？他最终打消了这个念头。

徐特立想像祖父一样行医，给乡亲们看病，便拿来不少医书研读。但当他学切脉时，对脉理究竟怎样分析，总是弄不清楚，又找不到老师指点，自己又不愿当庸医，便放弃了。后来，他还想过学卜卦看风水，看了许多书，照着卜辞去判断，常不灵验。仔细分析这些卜辞，大多是些模棱两可的话语，实在有骗人的嫌疑，于是也放弃了这个打算。

18岁那年，徐特立终于下决心"教书兼习科举业"，一边开蒙馆教书，一边利用空闲时间勤奋读书，这样不仅能够勉强维持生计，还可参加科举考试，或许能谋个一官半职。有一个时期，他潜心练习写八股文章，半年中一连写了11篇，但到底写得怎样，他自己心中也没底。一天，他从写好的文章中，挑出满意的几篇，远行40公里，去长沙城找陈云峰先生求教。陈先生是一位声名远播的举人，作得出很好的诗文，但中举后闲居在家，不肯钻营利禄。陈先生被徐特立虚心求教的精神所打动，不仅告诉他一些学习方法，勉励他发奋读书，不要只盯在八股文上，还送他一把扇子，上面写了几句话："读学贵有师，尤贵有书。乡村无师又无书，但书即师耳。张之洞《书目答问》即买书之门径，《輶轩语》即读书之门径。读此二书，终生受用不尽。"徐特立得到陈先生的指点后，心里豁然开朗，更加勤奋地读书学习。

制定"十年破产读书计划"

按照陈云峰先生的指点，徐特立勤学苦读两年后，收获不小，但很快遇到一个问题：没有书可读了。他家里的藏书本来就很少，在偏僻的乡下想要借书也不容易，除了买书没有别的办法。但对于贫苦人家来说，当时书的价格昂贵，他教书一年可得十来串钱，还不够买一部《十三经注疏》。怎么办呢？他思来想去，想到了伯祖母留给他的那点微薄田产：能不能将教书所得的收入用以维持家庭开支，每年卖一点田产，去买想看、该看的书呢？他估算了一下，这点田产每年卖一点去买书的话，不到十年就会卖光，但是有了十年的勤学苦读，书也应该能够读通了。

思索再三后，他将这计划跟妻子熊立诚说了。熊立诚略犹豫后，马上表示赞同："日子可以节俭点，但这书一定要读。"就这样，徐特立着手实施他的"十年破产读书计划"，卖田产买书读。有人笑他太傻，说谁不知道只有田产才是好东西，哪有变卖了田产来买书的？徐特立不顾讥笑，毫不动摇地按照计划去做。

徐特立读书非常认真，书上的许多篆字不容易记熟，便坚持每天学习两三个字，晚上睡觉时还在掌心上默写，直到写熟练了才入睡。那时候的代数、几何等新知识，很少有人懂得，徐特立学习中碰到不懂的地方全靠自己钻研。他常常把数学书放在衣袋里，先翻看一条定理，边走路边默记，再翻看另一条定理。他读书不仅在书上画满各种记号，在空白的地方写上自己的意见和感想，还把主要内容摘录下来。他常对人说："求学没有偷巧的办法，我用的都是笨方法。我读了书上的每一个字、每一句话以后，就闭着眼睛想想：这儿告诉我一些什么知识呢？弄

▶ 徐特立自学过的部分书籍。

懂了,再读下去。这样读一本懂一本,才能牢牢记住。"

就这样,徐特立坚定不移地努力学习,收获非常大。他不仅把中国古代的经、史、子、集的主要著作都读了一遍,而且还学习了物理、化学、数学等自然科学知识和新的社会科学知识,成了一个知识丰富、很有学问的青年。

参加岳州会试

1905年,"十年破产读书计划"进行到第8年,此时家中经济已濒于破产,徐特立为此深感焦虑,但好运也就在此时来临:岳州城要举行会试啦!学而优则仕,是每个读书人的梦想。参加科举考试,这对28岁满怀壮志的徐特立,无疑是一个难得的机会。如能考取功名,可以施展自己抱负,就是不中,也可检验"破产读书"的效果。

一天晚饭后,徐特立与熊立诚商量:"立诚,我准备去岳州参加会试,你看怎样?""这事好是好,只是考试用的钱到哪里去弄呢?"熊立诚当然知道丈夫的心思,只是赶考的盘缠让夫妻俩犯难了。熊立诚打算找邻居去借,但徐特立不愿妻子去求人,简单凑了几串钱,打起背包,带上干粮,就上了去岳州的路。

到了岳州，前来考试的人很多，许多客栈都住满了考生。其中许多是富贵人家的公子哥，信心十足；也有少数穷人家子弟，虽衣帽破旧，但也踌躇满志。徐特立住的店里，旁边住着位吴姓考生，是个富家公子，徐特立跟他打招呼，他爱搭不理，十分傲慢。

考试开始了，先是初试。徐特立拿到试卷后，一看题目十分晦涩。地理题目是"汉之安息即今波斯条支即今亚拉伯辨"，历史题目是"张居正毁天下书院论"。徐特立根据汉唐史书以长安为中心描述西域位置的相关知识，估计安息和条支大概是在葱岭之西、红海之东，距长安若干里，等等，这样分析一通完成了第一份答卷。第二份答卷，徐特立虽然不知道张居正毁天下书院的具体史实，但知道张居正是明朝的大宰相，当时宦官专权、士大夫之间竞争激烈，于是便以"毁书院并不能平息士大夫对朝政的不满，明朝的腐败主要是宦官、寺院擅权所造成的"为论点，写了一篇洋洋洒洒的文章。但在他自己看来，总觉有些文不对题，因此对这次考试没抱太多希望。

出乎意料，徐特立的答卷被考官看中，在3000多名考生中，考了个第19名，取得了复试资格。但复试要交1元的试卷费，徐特立又作难了：盘缠已经花光，哪里有钱交这试卷费呢？正在他发愁时，那位吴公子前来道喜了，得知情况后要解囊相助。但徐特立十分厌恶这等势利小人，不肯接受他的帮助。他想：受恩多则立朝难，受私恩就不能秉公理。如果考中，以后他肯定会拉拢我，要我为他办事，我决不能与这等人为伍。徐特立断然决定放弃复试，卷起行李回家，写诗一首，抒发胸中的志向：

> 丈夫落魄纵无聊，壮志依然抑九霄。
> 非同泽柳新稊弱，偶受春风即折腰。

不安分的学员

1906年,徐特立接受周南女校校长朱剑凡的聘请,来到长沙城里教书,一教就是四五年。由于他知识渊博、讲课生动,深得学生的欢迎和喜爱,他成了各校争相延聘的名教员,但他并不满足于这样的成绩,常常潜心研究怎样提高教学质量。为此,他走访了长沙、浏阳等县的许多学校,发现当时作为基础教育的小学教育并没有办好,在课程、教材、教法等各方面存在许多缺点。加之当时对小学教育有研究的人并不多,徐特立深感长此以往,小学教育将改进无望,觉得自己应该担起这个责任。于是,他决定去外面考察、学习中小学教育的先进经验和做法,以便改善和提高湖南的基础教育。朱剑凡支持他的这一想法,同意他辞去周南女校的教学工作,并出资相助,促其成行。

1910年春节过后,徐特立乘船离开长沙,沿江直下洞庭。这是他年满33岁后的第一次出省。船在岳州城边停泊了三天。他登上岳阳楼,饱览了巴陵胜状,观赏了岳阳楼的碑题石刻。他反复吟诵范仲淹"先天下之忧而忧,后天下之乐而乐"的名句,决心要使自己的一生,在平凡的教育岗位上做出不平凡的贡献来。

船抵汉口后,徐特立改乘轮船到上海,参加了江苏教育总会在上海举办的"单级教授练习所"的学习。入学那天,学习所的杨保恒、俞子夷两位老师,见到这位年龄比自己还大的学生,不禁感到惊讶,一问才知道他是湖南有名的中学教员,自费来上海专门考察小学教育,不禁对他深表敬佩。徐特立

▶ 杨保恒
(1873—1916)。

▶ 俞子夷
(1886—1970)。

要求杨、俞两位老师把他作为普通学生严格对待，并请求给他一些自由支配的时间，以便到上海各处的小学访问调查。两位老师热情地支持他，满足了他的要求，为他的走访提供了许多方便。

在考察过程中，徐特立十分注意学习这些学校的办学方法和特色。比如，在走访城东女校时，他对杨伯明先生因陋就简的办学精神极为赞赏。杨先生把堂屋当课堂、茶几做讲台，在堂前照壁贴上许多新闻资料让学生阅读；利用木笼放置学生不能带进教室的东西。杨先生本人既当校长，又当教员，除教国文和缝纫技术外，还要编辑杂志，一身数任。徐特立认为这种勤勉、艰苦的办学精神，是值得学习和发扬的。另有一处是郊区的万竹小学。他高度赞赏这所小学的教师和学生家长的亲密关系：教师来到学生的家里，坐在矮凳上聊天，随便尝尝门外晒的腌菜，关系十分融洽。他认为这是密切学校与家庭联系的重要方面。

在上海的4个多月里，他几乎每天都从事这样的考察，放弃了训练班的一些课程，以致后来考试没有及格。他自我总结说："因为我不大安分，不好好看心理学和伦理学等方面的书。我好参观在上海的各种教育活动。无论哪里开运动会、展览会，我都必到，每天五六小时的课，我至多上四小时就跑了，去进行我的参观考察工作，所以考书本知识不及格。"实际上，他的考察所得，是在课堂上听教育学、心理学所学不到的。"不大安分"，恐怕正是他以后在教育方面勇于改革、标新立异，能有所建树的一个重要原因。

考察日本的小学教育

在上海的训练班里，徐特立很钦佩年龄比自己小的俞子夷先生。俞先生是一位留日学生，曾多次向他介绍日本教育的情况，鼓励他到日本去考察。去日本学习，一直是徐特立多年的愿望，结束上海教育的考察后，1910年7月他再次起航，乘船东渡到达日本东京。

▶ 东京实践女校校长、著名女教育家下田歌子。

在参观日本学校之前，徐特立阅读了一些介绍日本教育的书籍，如《小学校事汇》《三千个优良小学校》等，根据这些书籍提供的情况和线索，来实地考察一些学校。在考察这些学校的过程中，令他感受最深的是，日本学校十分注意人力、财力、物力的节省和工作效率的提高。他访问了实践女校。这所学校行政人员只有校长下田歌子一人，其余都是教员。校内的日常事务，全部由学生自理。学校的房屋设备，都能充分发挥效用，如缝纫教室，只要把工作台搬走，便成了室内操场；课程的设置，也注意符合实际的需要；整个学校环境整洁清雅，井然有序。徐特立十分赞赏这位精明能干的女校长，心想她的办学经验值得好好推广。另外，日本某些学校根据学生的实际情况来安排授课时间，也给他留下了深刻的印象，如东京某小学，学生多是工厂学徒工，上班时间不一。为了适合他们的情况，学校在不同时间段开设多个班级、课程供他们选择，办学形式灵活多样。学校教员不足，学生也可以当助教。这些好的经验，不仅丰富了他的考察内容，也为他以后从事教育改革提供了借鉴。

在日本呆了两个多月后，徐特立怀着不虚此行的心情返航。在船上，他紧抓着自己的行李箱，生怕有半点闪失，因为里面装着的教育考察笔记，可是他最重要的宝贝呀。

"留法老学生"

1919年下半年的一天。随着一声汽笛的长鸣，一艘从中国开来的轮船，停靠在了法国马赛码头，从船上走下来一批穿着朴素、黄色皮肤的青年人。他们是远离祖国、到法国勤工俭学的中国留学生,徐特立就是其中的一员。

这年,徐特立已经43岁,教了20多年书,已经拥有了声望和成就,但他为了追求新知,一心来法国勤工俭学。有朋友劝他:"你这么大年纪了,还学什么?何必非跑到法国去,又当学徒,又当学生呢?"徐特立回答说:"你们都说年纪大的人不用再求学,这不对。要知道,虽然年纪大的人多数在社会上有些权柄,但倘若都不求学,不增进新的学识,那么,社会就会受害不少……"

◀ 留法时期的徐特立。

有亲友不解地问:"你现在不是已经很有学识了吗?"徐特立摇了摇头,笑笑说:"我现有的学识还大不够用。今年我43岁,不觉就要到44、45,一混60岁就来了,到了60岁,还同43岁时一样的学识,这17年,岂不冤枉过日子了吗?到了60岁才后悔,那就迟了,何不就从今日学起呢?"

亲戚朋友们的劝阻,没有动摇徐特立的决心。他变卖书籍,东拼西凑,筹集了一笔旅费,告别妻儿,乘上了开往法国的轮船。

到法国后,管理勤工俭学的人看徐特立年岁大,劝他住在校外,单独请人教,比在学校里自由些。徐特立拒绝说:"我到法国来,本来是想了解一些法国学校的规则,以便回国采用,如果不在学校亲身体会,那怎么行呢?"

管理勤工俭学的人担心地说:"你的年纪太大,学校的规则太严,恐怕你受不了。"徐特立说:"正是因为我的年纪大,人家对我很尊敬,如有不好的习惯,人家都不肯当面说。住在学校内,一方面有先生的指导,另一方面也可得到同学们的帮助。"徐特立说服了那位同志,进入法国木兰公学补习法语,同时在法国圣侠门钢铁厂做钳工,还替勤工俭

▶ 徐特立（前排右四）在法国与勤工俭学留学生合影。

学的中国学生做饭。

徐特立记忆力差，嘴里还缺了两颗门牙，发音很吃力，学习法语困难重重，但他很有信心地说："今年学起，到50岁还有7年，一天学1个字，一年学365个字，七年可学2500多字，到了50岁时，岂不就是一个通法文的人吗？若一天学2个字，到了46岁半，就可以读通啦。"

木兰公学的学生大都是年轻小伙子，他们学得较快，徐特立就拜他们为师，虚心向他们请教。其中有一个湖南来的15岁的学生，叫熊信吾，是徐特立学生熊瑾玎的儿子，应该称呼徐特立为"太老师"，可徐特立却请熊信吾当自己的法语"小先生"。有人见了，对徐特立笑着说："向你学生的儿子求教，不是降了好几级？"徐特立回答说："不错，是降了好几级，但你要知道，没有学问，当了'太老师'已是可耻了，如今法文一字不识，还要自高自大、怕失掉资格就更加可耻。只要学生不嫌我老，肯帮助我来学法文，尽管降了好几级，我也要做一个进步的老人。"

徐特立刻苦谦虚的学习精神，感动了学校里的法国教师。他们十分赞赏这位发奋学习的"老学生"。经过艰难的努力，徐特立克服了一个又一个难关，终于能够读懂法文的科学书籍了。一年多后，他考进了巴黎大学，选学数学和物理等课程，真正成为了一名"老学生"。

在莫斯科中山大学学马列

1928年5月，党组织派徐特立到莫斯科中山大学学习马列主义思想。这所学校招收的都是中国学生，开设了初级班和中级班。大革命失败后，董必武、何叔衡、林伯渠、吴玉章等一些老同志，都曾在这里学习。学校尊重这些年高德劭的同志，专门为他们开设了一个特别班。徐特立就是在特别班里学习。

徐特立的勤勉好学，给人们留下了深刻的印象。为了深研马列主义的理论，他不顾年老，努力学习俄语，有着一种甘当小学生的学习精神。他的门牙缺了，读起俄文字母来，发音很难准确，记忆上也有困难，今天熟读了明天又忘了。他就给自己制定了每天早起大声朗读俄语的计划。于是，不管刮风下雨，在学校僻静的走廊上总有一个身影在一边走动，一边咿咿呀呀地大声读着，每一个字母、每一个单词，都是一读就是几十遍甚至百多遍，直至完全记住为止。由于勤奋苦学，不多时间，也就有了显著的成绩。在学校任教的一些老师，也深深感到徐特立并不因自己年龄大、学识广而轻慢他们，相反，总是那么认真听课，恳切求教，令人钦敬。

莫斯科的冬天格外寒冷，人们喜欢躲在屋子里，尤其是早晨，多不愿出门。徐特立却一大早就到户外

◀ 莫斯科中山大学旧貌。

跑步，中午到林荫道上锻炼身体。他还常邀请同学一起去锻炼，要为革命锻炼好身体。

"争取时间很要紧"

1940年12月，从八路军驻湘通讯处回到延安的徐特立，被任命为中国共产党创办的第一所理工科高等学校——延安自然科学院的院长。由于学院创建不久，各方面工作都还有待规范，办学条件也很艰苦，因此徐特立每天的工作安排得十分紧张。他一边要考虑学院的方方面面，包括办学方针、课程建设、教学计划、师资队伍建设等，一边还要挤出时间来学习矿物学、地质学，组织编写这方面的教材，每天都有做不完的事情，总感觉时间不够用。

那时候，徐特立住在杨家岭，开会、工作都要跑到山下去。从杨家岭到山下，原本有一条有台阶的老路，但要绕个大圈子，徐特立嫌它远，走起来太浪费时间，便从杂草、灌木丛中另外开辟了一条新路。这条新路顺着山坡直上直下，峰回路转，十分险峻，有的地方荆棘丛生。每次走完这条路，徐特立总得出一身汗，呼哧直喘气。跟随他的秘书是个年轻的小伙子，也累得满头大汗。他对徐特立说："您现在又不是长征，天上没敌人赶，地上没敌人追，何必这样急匆匆赶路？下回还是绕大路走吧。"徐特立打趣地说："一寸光阴一寸金哩，我选的这条路，虽然走起来吃力些，但是能节省不少时间，因为它的长度只有老路的三分之一。我们干革命的，争取时间很要紧。我挤出的这些时间，可以多做不少事，多读不少书。"每天，他坚持走这条路。渐渐地，越来越多的人也跟着走这条小路了。

病房里的骷髅架

陕北交通闭塞，土壤贫瘠，物资奇缺，生活条件十分艰苦，但徐特立从无怨言，仍然事必躬亲，经常因工作繁忙，连吃饭也顾不上。有时过了吃饭时间，他也不愿再去麻烦帮厨师傅，就自己去厨房用开水泡着剩饭剩菜吃一点。由于工作太累，加之饮食不规律，徐特立得了比较严重的胃病，不得已只好在中央医院住院，进行治疗。医生嘱咐："这可不能掉以轻心，要好好休息，不能操劳。"但徐特立哪里闲得下来，在医院里仍然不放松学习和工作。

有一天，同志们去探望徐特立，推开病房门一看，被床头摆放的骷髅头吓得不轻，床旁还吊着人体骨骼。大家吃惊地问道："徐老，您这是在干吗呀？""没什么，躺久了不舒服，我就是利用医院现成的设备，抓紧时间研究点新学问呀！"就这样，徐特立把病房变成了教室。

结果，徐特立住了20多天院，又学会了一门新的知识——生理解剖学。

"这些书将来用处大着呢"

1946年底，国民党军队大举进攻延安。根据中央的安排，徐特立带领中央宣传部教育研究室的部分同志撤离延安。这时，他即将迎来自己的70大寿，迈入古稀之年。

离开延安的时候，考虑到路途遥远，组织上专门拨给他一个用三头骡子拉的"轿窝子"，这样他可以少走些路。徐特立不肯接受，说道："组织关心我，但我现在还能走路，不用给我特殊照顾。"但怎么也推脱不掉。他想了一下，说："要么，就这样吧，我就留下一头牲口，驮运我的书吧！"

书是徐特立的宝贝，他有好几大箱书，光有一头牲口还是驮不走。

他左思右想，终于想出来一个主意：每本书的边上都有空白，把它切去，书的体积小了、份量轻了，不就可以多运走一些书了吗？

主意拿定以后，徐特立卷起衣袖，拿菜刀切，用剪子剪，手都磨出了泡。有人劝他别干了，他说："这些书将来用处大着呢，我多切掉一点边，就能多带走几本！"

就这样，徐特立用牲口驮着书，自己步行，跟着队伍辗转跋涉，走向新的征程。

走到哪儿学到哪儿

撤离延安以后，在动荡不定的行军途中，只要队伍停下来休息，徐特立就拿出书来看，有时候还就地采集和研究各种矿石。有些同志见他翻山越岭的时候，老爱捡些石头来左看右看，敲敲打打，不明白他在做什么。徐特立告诉他们说："这些都是矿石。我们现在趁早研究研究它，将来革命胜利了，要生产，要建设，便都用得上了。"

徐特立就这样走到哪儿学到哪儿。他的警卫员知道这些石头大有用处，也来热心帮助他，边搜集边学习，也学会了辨认好几种矿石。有一次，一个同志问徐特立的警卫员，他手里拿的发亮的石头是什么？警卫员回答说："这叫石英石。"那个同志惊讶地说："你这小鬼真不简单，还懂得不少呢！"警卫员说："我跟徐老行军半个多月了，还会连这都不知道吗？"

活到老，学到老

1949年10月，新中国成立。这年，徐特立已经72岁了。

想到国家面临经济、文化建设等方面的艰巨任务，而且这些任务对于刚刚诞生的新政权大多是全新的任务，徐特立清醒地认识到："过去懂得的有些东西，现在用处不大了，参加新的斗争，就要有新的知识。只有不断学习新的东西，跟上时代步伐，才能永不衰老。要是不学习，思想一停止，人就真的衰老啦！"为了勉励自己，他制定了一个20年学习和工作计划，决心活到老、学到老，继续为新中国的各项事业贡献自己的一份心力。

◀ 徐特立在查阅资料。

徐特立继续担任中宣部副部长，同时兼任中宣部教育研究室、党史研究室主任等职，还被中国历史学会选为名誉主席。他和历史学家范文澜一道，领导一批史学工作者和中宣部、中央党校的干部，从事中国通史、中国革命史和党史及其资料的编纂工作。尽管学识功底深厚，但他总是和从前一样虚怀若谷，对任何事物都有一种从头学起的精神。他的办公桌上，摆满了各式书目。即使写篇短文或草拟一段讲稿，都要学习和参考许多种书刊，反复推敲比较，力求把问题说明白、说透彻，于人与事有所裨益。

徐特立有一个习惯，如果有个问题白天没有完全弄明白，晚上睡醒以后，还要继续思考，有时还半夜起床把它写下来。常常发生这样的事情：晚上，秘书徐乾替他把桌上的物品收拾得干净整齐，可第二天清晨，徐乾看到桌上又有了许多新的纸条，上面密密麻麻写了字。徐乾奇怪地问："徐老，这些都是您写的？"徐特立说："是呀，有些内容我半夜想起来了，怕第二天忘记，就起床把它记了下来。"

徐特立就以这种不懈进取的精神，克服种种困难，永不满足地学习，真正做到了"活到老，学到老"。

▼ 在生命的最后日子里，徐特立仍坚持学习。

他从旧货铺、废品店买来破铜烂铁玻璃瓶，高兴地对化学教员说："我今天买了一筐化学课上能用的便宜货！"

第二章

舍家办学，教育救国

"开创农村新式教学的先声"

1905年参加岳州会试后,徐特立的才学和骨气得到人们的敬佩,一些学校纷纷聘请他,许多学生也慕名而来向他求教。可是,徐特立并不满足于在偏僻的乡下教书度日,而是想到更广阔的天地去施展自己的才华,去探索救国救民的道路。不久,他以优异成绩考入了设在长沙城望麓园的宁乡速成师范。这是一所刚创办起来的新式学校。校长周震鳞是同盟会会员,他经常向学生宣传民族革命的道理,校内革命气氛浓厚。徐特立在这里读了4个月的书,学习了许多新的科学知识和先进思想。在结业典礼大会上,周震鳞校长慷慨激昂地向大家号召:"我们办这个学校,不光是为培养你们当一个好教员,更重要的是希望你们创造有利于国家民族的事业。"

周校长的一番话使徐特立非常激动,他和姜济寰、何雨农等同学一起商量,决定把新式学校办到农村去,让更多的人能读书认字,懂得救

▶ 梨江高小旧貌。

国救民的道理。

1905年夏,刚从宁乡速成师范学成结业的徐特立与姜济寰、何雨农等一起,在离长沙城15公里的椰梨镇,办起了一所新式小学——梨江高等小学堂,"开创农村新式教学的先声"。

椰梨镇坐落在长沙城东的浏阳河畔,是个店铺林立、买卖兴隆的大镇。可这里的文化教育却很落后,许多穷人家的孩子没钱上学。镇上新办了一所高等小学堂的消息不胫而走,很快在镇子和附近的乡村传开。

"听说学校收费很便宜,这下咱穷苦人的孩子可以上学啦。"

"嘿,听说还招收女孩子入学呢!"

"听说学校学的是新知识呢!"

……

是的,这所学校真是新式学堂。

每天奔波一百里

梨江高等小学堂开学后,徐特立负责教课,除了语文、数学、历史和地理等课程外,还主动做许多杂事,一天忙到晚,却不领一文薪俸。他一心扑在教育事业上,从不为私事影响教学。他家离学校有50里路,为了办学,他根本顾不上回家。

这年中秋节,徐特立从学校回到家里,正赶上妻子生了第三个孩子,3岁的女儿又得了痢疾,拉了几天肚子。妻子、孩子都需要人照顾,家里实在离不开他,可徐特立不愿因私事请假缺课,耽误学生的学业。怎么办呢?他一边收拾屋子、照料妻子和孩子,一边琢磨,终于想出了主意。回到学校,他做了这样的安排:把每天要上的课都排在上午,讲完课后赶紧回家,到家后煮饭、煎药,照顾妻子和孩子,第二天一大早再赶回学校。

有一天清晨,学生都进了教室。上课时间到了,还没见徐特立来校,姜济寰心中非常纳闷:徐特立从来不迟到、不早退,今天怎么还没来?临时找谁代课呢?他正在着急,只见徐特立大汗淋漓地跑进了校门,来不及说什么,走进教室就上课了。

后来,姜济寰、何雨农听说徐特立家里的事情后,知道他每天需要走几十里路赶来上课,十分感动,便要他回家照顾几天,可是徐特立说什么也不肯。就这样,徐特立为了家、校两不误,每天来回要走百把里路,一天休息不了三四个小时。一天两天过去了,八天十天过去了,过度的劳累使他迅速消瘦下来,但在近半个月的时间里,不论刮风下雨,他坚持天天如此,始终没有耽误过学生一节课。

白手起家办长师

1912年,中华民国建立,姜济寰出任长沙县首任知事。他励精图治,一心大力发展长沙县的教育,计划在长沙县办一千所国民小学。为解决师资问题,他邀请徐特立主办一所师范学校,徐特立一口应允。

开办学校需要经费,徐特立把目光投向了湘岸榷运局寄存在善化学宫内的一批硝磺上。当时徐特立正担任长沙县第一高等小学堂的校长,这所学校是由善化学宫改建的。徐特立找到榷运局的局长,征得他的同意后,将这批硝磺变卖,解决了部分经费问题。

▼ 善化学宫旧貌。

学校开办之初没有房子,徐特立就将善化学宫的一些破烂房间腾出来,连同过道走廊,加以修缮,改为教室,房子问题也算解决了。

1912年3月,长沙师范正式开学,招收了6个班,其中,学习五年毕业的本科两个班,学习一年毕业的一部讲习科两个班，学习半年毕业的二部讲习科两个班，共300多名学生。这所后来声誉远播、人才辈出的师范学校，就在这样艰苦的条件下创办起来了。

学校里没有化学实验设备，上化学课只能凭教员讲，学生听不明白，徐特立很着急。一天，他提着一筐从旧货铺、废品店买来的破铜烂铁、玻璃瓶，高兴地对化学教员说："我今天买了一筐化学课上能用的便宜货！"在他的指导下，一个虽然简陋但是比较实用的化学实验室终于办起来了。有人问他花了多少钱，他笑笑说："很便宜，我用的是穷办法。"

为了给长沙师范找一个永久性的校址，徐特立踏遍长沙城，最终选中了城北荷花池的泐谭寺。泐谭寺是一座古寺，经过战火的洗礼后早已荒芜破败。徐特立决意后，就向长沙县知事姜济寰提出申请，并得到了他的大力支持，同意将此地拨给长沙师范。

随着学校规模不断扩大，经费的筹措却越来越困难。为了不让学生失学，徐特立又忍痛把已具规模的全部校舍，租给湖南省立第一中学，以每月几百元的租金收入，支付学校的开支，而自己的学校则迁到简陋的城隍庙里，继续维持上课。

就这样，在徐特立的苦心经营以及他的精神的激励下，长沙师范历经百年风雨，渡过一个又一个难关，至今弦歌不绝。

校长的薪水哪里去了

万事开头难。徐特立白手起家创办了长沙师范学校并担任校长，为了让家庭贫困的学生安心学习，他把自己的大部分工资拿去周济学生，一连好几个月没往家里寄钱。

这几天，熊立诚犯难了。儿子笃本发着高烧，在床上躺了几天，眼窝都凹下去了。她既要砍柴担水、烧茶做饭，还要请医生、煎药、照看病人。给儿子看病抓药，把钱花了个光，眼看家里没米下锅，迫不得已,她便把孩子交给邻居照看,自己进城去找丈夫。

熊立诚天不亮就开始赶路,紧走慢走,到了城里,已是下午。她沿街四处打听,终于找到了丈夫新办的长沙师范学校。

学校的工友老王,看是徐师母来了,便张罗着要替她去找校长。熊立诚忙说:"你很忙,还是让我自己去找吧。"正在这时,一些学生跑来向老王要扫把,说之前看见徐校长在扫后院。但马上又有个学生说:"我们班上一个同学脚烂了,躺在床上走不得路,我看见徐校长提个桶给他打洗脚水去了。"学生们拥着徐师母到了宿舍。宿舍里只有那个烂了脚的学生在烫脚,却不见了徐校长。没办法,工友只好安顿熊立诚在徐特立房里歇息,学生们分头去找徐校长。熊立诚在房里正着急,眼见丈夫急匆匆地进来了,劈头就问:"老头子,你几个月不回家,又不捎钱回来,要我们怎么过活!""唉呀!看样子家里出了人命喽!"徐特立故意逗熊立诚。"笃本生了病,请医生,抓药把钱花了个精光,现在家里都没米下锅了,你还笑得出?唉!也不晓得你当校长的薪水到哪里去了?"熊立诚埋怨着。

徐特立苦笑了一下说:"当校长不是做官发财。你不晓得如今要维持一个学校有多难,政府不肯拨款,办学经费入不敷出。我除了吃饭,把剩下的钱都贴补了生活困难的学生,哪里还有什么钱寄回家呢?""那笃本的病怎么办?没饭吃怎么办?"熊立诚犯愁了。徐特立想了想,说:"这样吧!笃本的病一定要尽快治好,我想办法去借点钱,明天早上你先带回去。米,我抽时间送回来,顺便看看笃本。"听徐特立这么一说,熊立诚也不再说什么了。

第二天清早,徐特立把妻子送出了城,自己又回学校去上课了。下午放学后,他到厨房借了几斗米,连夜送回了家。

五美乡下的"洋学堂"风波

1913年的一天夜里,一团熊熊燃起的大火打破了五美乡的宁静。乡里的一座小院突然起火,院中的几间房子加上里边的桌椅板凳,被火烧了个精光。第二天,正在长沙教书的徐特立匆忙赶了回来。

这座被烧毁的院子,正是徐特立在家乡办的五美初等小学堂。不久前,徐特立从长沙城回到五美乡,看到家乡方圆几十里,只有寥寥几所私塾,没有一所学校,教育十分落后,于是决心筹建一所新式学堂。他自掏腰包,买了些桌椅、教具,开办了这所小学校。学校实行新的教育制度,采用新式教材,摒弃了私塾教学中那套旧东西。这一来,引起了顽固势力的围攻:

"听说学堂里不读'四书五经',净教些'洋书'!"

"这是办的什么学,简直成了洋学堂!会把老祖宗的传统都丢掉。"

"唉!学堂还收女的呢!男女坐一个课桌,这成何体统!"

……

这天夜里,顽固分子煽动一些不明真相的人,捣毁了校园,放火烧掉了教室。徐特立赶回五美乡后,一方面找顽固分子理论,理直气壮地告诉他们,新式学堂是教孩子们学习真正有用的知识的;一方面找来学校的老师,鼓励他们,干什么事情都不是一帆风顺的,办学校也是这样,只要对乡亲们有利、对国家有益处,你们就要挺起腰杆办下去。

一个老师为难地说:"徐先生,办下去可以,只是现在学校被烧了,乡亲们也吓得不敢送孩子们上学了,怎么办呢?"

徐特立仔细想了想,说:"村

▼ 五美学校校舍(建国后拍摄)。

头的观音庙不是很好的地方吗?就把学校搬到那里上课吧!学生我们一起去动员。"

说干就干,徐特立亲自带领几个教师到学生家中去走访,向乡亲们宣传为什么要废私塾、办学校。不少人很快觉悟过来,又纷纷送子女到学校学习,学生由原来的30多人增加到70多人。

腾出住房办学校

那些顽固分子破坏失败以后,仍不甘心。第二年,村里发生瘟疫,死了些人,顽固分子趁机造谣:"庙内办学堂,观音断了香火,菩萨生气了,给我们村降灾。"那个时候,不少人不懂科学,以为真是菩萨降灾了,于是纠集人员到学校闹事,阻止上课,要求学校马上搬出观音庙。

为了解决校舍问题,徐特立征得妻子熊立诚同意,决定将学校搬到家里来。他将自家老屋改建的一栋较为宽敞的新瓦房腾出来,作为校舍,另外又筹钱增建了两间教室,家人则搬进新搭的两间茅屋里,让学校又一次渡过了难关。在徐特立的坚持下,这所乡村小学终于办下来了,由此还带动了整个五美乡,先后办起了50多所国民小学或教学点。

他还以长沙师范作基地,在短期内为这些学校培养了一批合格的教师。

徐特立为学校亲笔写下"勤、俭、公、实"四个大字,作为校训。在一次讲话中,他特意向师生们阐述了这四个字蕴含的意义。他说:"这'勤'字,就是勤劳、勤快。我们在学校里要勤读书,在家里要勤劳动,做一个勤快的好学生。这'俭'字,就是节俭、俭朴。我们不论在什么时候,

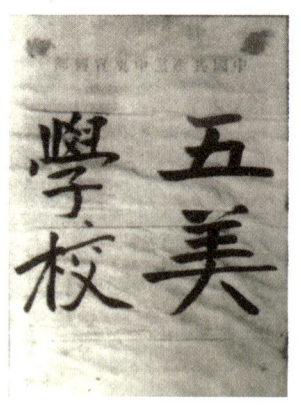

▶ 建国后徐特立为五美学校题写校名。

都要注意节约俭朴，不要铺张浪费，你们要从小养成这样的习惯。这'公'字就是公正，秉公无私，办事公道。一个人不管做什么事情，首先要考虑大家，不能只顾个人、自私自利。这'实'字，就是老实、诚实、真实。我们在读书劳动的时候，都要老老实实，勤勤恳恳，不弄虚作假，不说谎，不欺人，长大了不做伤天害理的事情。以上这些，你们都能做到了，那就是一个好学生。"

五美初小采取新式的教学方法，讲授实用的知识，深受大家欢迎，"洋学堂"名声大震，那些顽固分子再也不敢来破坏捣乱了。

"徐二镥锅"

徐特立在家乡有一个绰号——"徐二镥锅"。"镥锅"是湖南的方言，就是用烧熔的铁水补锅子。这个绰号的来历，还得从徐特立办学说起。

1924年暑假，一群投考湖南省立第一女子师范但没有被录取的女生，找到徐特立，表达她们迫切求学的愿望。

"不要着急，我们再来办一所学校吧。"徐特立听完她们的诉说，很是同情。他马上联系了教育界的一些同仁，商量办女校的事情，得到了大家的一致赞同。徐特立被推选为校长，着手筹办事宜。他向长沙师范借了几间空房子，又把附近一个菜园里的旧屋修缮粉刷一新，分别作为教室、办公室和学生宿舍。他在一扇狭窄的边门上贴一张白纸条，上写"长沙女子师范学校"几个字，这扇门就成了校门；在一间房门口放了一张课桌，摆上笔砚和报名簿，这里就成了报名处。而桌椅、教具等办公、教学用品，不是借来的，就是临时找来的旧东西。就这样，一所新的学校很快办起来了。有人开玩笑地说："徐校长又白手起家了。"

学校穷得雇不起校工，徐特立又当校长，又当教员，还当工人，白天教书、打铃、扫地，做各种杂事，课后辅导学生学习，晚上在煤油灯下批改学生作业，忙得一点空闲都没有，但整天都乐呵呵的。在学校里，遇到别的教员缺课的时候，徐特立总是赶去代课，他不但能教语文、历史、地理，还能教数学、物理、化学。大家不但敬重他爱护学生、对工作认真负责，还佩服他学识渊博、讲课生动。当时，长沙一家报纸登载过这么一条消息：某校校长，年老博学，无论什么教员缺课，他都去代课。他什么课都能教，只有音乐不行，因为牙齿缺了，唱起歌来，关不住风。报纸说的这个校长，就是徐特立。

为了节省开支，徐特立十分珍惜学校的财物，哪怕是一张纸、一截粉笔头，也决不随意浪费。他每天都要巡视全校几遍，看到桌椅摆放不好，花木、教具保护不周的，必定亲自去收拾好。刮风下雨时，不论白天黑夜，他必定带领教员，嘱咐学生，关好门窗。学校购置的图书和报纸杂志，他指定专人负责，按月装订，编好目录，分别收藏。有时，教师们用过的残余粉笔头掉在地上，徐特立也随时捡起，装在衣袋里，上课的时候拿出来再用。有人觉得徐特立太过吝惜。徐特立对他们说："粉笔头仍可写字，丢了，岂不可惜？积少成多，集小成大，可以节省许多办公费用。你们将来当了教员，必须随时随地注意勤俭节约，要培养少年儿童节省的习惯。"

就这样，在湖南长沙，徐特立创办了不少学校，每办一所学校都会遇到许多困难和阻力，但是，他从不畏惧，从不泄气，而是想方设法，因陋就简，艰苦经营，把一所所学校办了起来。

毛泽东后来曾说，徐先生常常把方便让给别人，把困难担在自己肩上，惯于摆烂摊子，顶烂斗笠；在没有一间房子、没有一个钱的情况下，居然创办一所规模不小的师范学校，这真是"鲁锅"精神。

让穷苦人读书认字

辛亥革命后,徐特立曾被聘请到湖南省教育司当科长。他看到许多劳动人民的儿女没有求学的机会,极力主张发展平民教育,开办一些半日制学校或夜校。教育司里一些旧思想严重的人不同意他的主张,说:"这些野孩子像田里的狗尾巴草,不堪教育,还给他们办什么学校?"徐特立听了十分气愤,便把科长的委任状退了回去,决绝地离开了教育司。

为了实行自己平民教育的主张,徐特立约了一些志同道合的朋友,办了一所平民夜校,以便让劳苦大众和他们的子女也有读书认字的机会。他白天在学校里教课,晚上和几位教师轮流到夜校来上课。夜校设在长沙北门外李大中丞祠堂,因为这附近有好几家工厂,便于工人学习。每到天黑以后,学生便从各处匆匆奔向这里。他们中有拉车的,有挑担的、抬轿的,还有商店里的学徒,都是一些当时被人瞧不起的"粗人"。但徐特立非常喜欢这些"粗人",他也深受他们爱戴和尊敬。夜校开了好几门功课,有国文、算术和地理,还宣讲时事,让学生了解国家大事。

夜校刚办起来的时候,来这学习的人还不是很多,但学校教师热情的态度和进步的教学方法及内容,很快赢得了大家的赞同和欢迎,要求入学的人越来越多,后来逐渐扩大到200多人。在他们的影响下,湖南城乡很多学校也先后办起了夜校和半日制补习学校,兴办平民教育也渐渐成了风气。

稻田师范树新风

自1925年春季开始至1927年,徐特立担任湖南省立第一女子师范(习称"稻田师范")的校长。在这里,他将西方学校的一些管理制度融

▶ 稻田师范旧照。

入教学管理中，大胆进行改革，为创建学校新风开辟了一条道路。他任校长后，第一件事就是宣布开放校禁：过去学生不许随意走出校门，现在可以在课余时间自由出入；过去不许学生过问政治，现在可以参加社会活动。甚至，他还带学生去周边郊游，破除学校对学生的禁锢。

同时，徐特立还坚决反对在学校搞派别、拉小圈子的不正之风。对那些有真才实学的教师，他总是以礼相待；对那些妄图以派系来控制学校的做法，则进行严厉批评："学校里搞小圈子，把政治上结党营私的作风发展到教育园地里来，是极其可耻的。"并明确表示自己决不当"傀儡校长"。他亲自去找教育界作风正派的老同事，请他们介绍一些没有染上派系色彩的优秀教师来校任教。他爱护教师，坚决同那些仇视进步教师的势力作斗争。有一次，一些学生因受派系势力的唆使，出面闹事，要求学校解聘一位物理教师。他了解情况后，对闹事学生说明真相，晓以利害，指出那位物理教师是难得的好教师，不能解聘，坚决制止了这起事件。不久，那些派系活动的煽动者又向一些进步教师投寄匿名信，威逼他们离校。这些行为，也遭到徐特立的正面回击，从而发挥了进步教师在学校中的骨干作用，使学校越办越好。

冒风顶雪聘教员

为了使学生学到真本领，徐特立总是想方设法请来各种有经验的教师执教。作为校长的他，平易近人，从不高高在上、对教员颐指气使，所以哪怕工资低一点，许多教师也十分愿意到他主持的学校去教书。

一个冬天的早晨，寒风瑟瑟，天空飘着大雪，徐特立穿着木屐，撑着雨伞，冒着风雪走了好几里地，去聘请一位姓鲁的地理教员。他来到鲁先生的家，敲了敲门。开门的是鲁先生的妻子，她问徐特立："从哪里来？"

"省立第一女师。"

"有什么事？"

"看鲁先生。"

"这么早，鲁先生还没有起床呢，你坐这儿等等吧！"她说完话，就进厨房准备早餐去了。

徐特立独自坐在板凳上等了半个钟头，还没见着鲁先生，只好寻到厨房去问："鲁先生起来了吗？"

"今天是大雪天，鲁先生哪能起得这么早，你要是不耐烦等，就先回去，改天再来吧！"原来她以为徐特立是女师的工友，就这样不客气地回答。

"没事，没事，我再等等。"徐特立没有计较她的态度，从厨房退出来，继续等着。又等了大半个钟头，鲁先生起来吃饭，才知道徐校长坐等了一个多钟头。鲁先生被徐特立耐心诚恳的态度深深打动了，尽管他已在别的学校里担任了课程教师，仍热情地接受了徐特立的聘请。

湖南教育界的"长沙王"

为了开发民智，实现教育救国的愿望，徐特立筚路蓝缕，辛勤努力。他60岁的时候回忆："我的职业和事业，一生都是教书。从蒙馆、初小、高小、中等师范，一直到高等师范，我都任过教员。在高等师范当教员时也没有脱离小学校职务，因为我爱教小学生。"

早年在长沙，徐特立曾办过两个高级小学和一个初级小学，其中有一个高级小学办了13年；办了一个200人的初级女子师范学校，但遭遇大革命失败，只办了3年就停办了；创办了一个男子师范，有400名学生，因没有能力支持下去，交给长沙县办。徐特立自嘲道："我自己没有财产，也没有办公赚过钱，有什么能力办学校呢？我的办法就是：1.每日多上课两小时，一个月多得60元，分给两个高小用。家留在乡下，节省日用，谢绝一切应酬，绝对不请朋友吃酒肉和茶点。2.小学不收费用，师范收费减少到一般私立学校之下。改良教法，自己做刻苦的模范，这样来发动教员和学生爱校的情绪，增加他们的积极性，赢得人力物力上的一切帮助。"

一分耕耘、一分收获，在徐特立的苦心经营下，长沙县的教育事业不断发展。在民国八年以前，长沙共有800所小学，很多教员都是他培养出来的。由于徐特立功名卓著，为当时的湖南教育做出了杰出贡献，被誉为湖南教育界的"长沙王"。

他忙去提来热水,帮助学生将脚洗涤干净,细心敷上药膏并叮嘱他养伤。

第三章

爱生如子,培育英才

悉心培养"现代的关汉卿"

徐特立对学生关怀备至，倾注了自己的全部心血。他对家庭贫困而有志向学的青年，总是极力给予支持和照顾，田汉就是其中有代表性的一位。

田汉是我国著名戏剧家、诗人、国歌歌词作者，被称为"现代的关汉卿"。他就读长沙师范时，曾得到徐特立的谆谆教诲和无微不至的关爱。

1912年，14岁的田汉考入长沙师范本科第一班。田汉自幼丧父，家境极为困难。为了供他读书，母亲也从乡下来到城里，起先在北门外摆了个小茶摊，后来在彭家井替人洗衣，赚取零用。夏天的长沙蚊虫特别多，田汉因家庭经济拮据，没钱购买蚊帐，晚上根本休息不好。徐特立检查宿舍时，发现田汉把自己严严实实地捂在被子里，捂出了一身痱子，第二天马上给他买了一顶蚊帐，对他说："你有困难，要对我说呀！这样子，晚上休息不好，白天怎么能好好读书呢？"

田汉特别喜爱读书，可是没钱买书，只好假日里到长沙图书馆去看书。进图书馆须门票钱一个铜板。为了省钱，田汉常常早餐只吃一个烧饼，留一个铜板买门票，常常一看书就是一整天，连中餐都不舍得出门吃。

▶ 青年田汉。

徐特立看到田汉爱读书而无钱买书，就把自己的购书折子给田汉，让他去选购自己喜爱的书籍，购书款就记到折子上，年底由徐特立去结账。

田汉爱好文学，喜欢写一些打油诗和剧本，徐特立支持他办起了"窗户报"。当欧阳予倩和春柳社话剧团的部分成员，到长沙文庙排演《热血》《不如归》《猛回头》等新剧时，徐特立便带着田汉和一些爱好文学的同学去观看,并鼓励他们大胆写作和排练戏剧。

在徐特立的支持下,田汉在学校恣意施展自己的文学才华,于1913年写成戏剧文学处女作《新教子》,发表在《长沙日报》上。1914年,他与黄芝冈等同学一起编《青年》杂志,并在上面发表了两个剧本。1915年,他仿照清代孔尚任的《桃花扇》,构思上模仿梁启超的《新罗马传奇》,写作了戏曲剧本《新桃花扇》,连载于上海《时报》副刊。田汉后来成为我国著名的戏剧家和文学家,与徐特立的支持和帮助是分不开的。

田汉对徐特立的教导之恩铭记在心,终身不忘。1947年徐特立70大寿时,田汉特意从上海寄来一首长诗,热情歌颂老师在教育方面的光辉业绩,其中有两句是:"学生遍天下,春风无不被。……海上举金尊,共为老人醉。"

窗户报

徐特立在长沙师范担任校长时,主张教育民主,对学生关怀备至,也很注意因势利导,调动学生的积极性。

当时14岁的田汉和黄芝冈、曹伯韩、周竹安、张怀等几个喜欢文学的同学,经常作一些打油诗,并且把它们用稿纸誊写出来,贴在自修室的窗户玻璃上。

有一次,他们写了几首藏头诗,把校长徐特立、教师首元龙和黄竹村的姓名嵌了进去。一首说:"特立狂涛骇浪中,宝刀血溅首元龙。"另一首写道:"黄竹村中鸡犬喧。"两位老师看后,非常生气,认为这是"目无尊长,有辱斯文",要求校长严斥学生。

◀ 长沙办学时的徐特立(画像)。

徐特立安慰两位老师后，找来了田汉等人。田汉说："我们对徐校长、黄先生和首先生毫无恶意，是一时兴起，开开玩笑，逗大家快乐。"徐特立首先批评了他们这种做法对老师的不尊敬，又觉得诗句中显露出孩子们的才智，便和气地告诉他们：喜欢写作是一件好事，只是不要把时间、心思花在游戏笔墨中，要把聪明才智、写作技能，用到正道上去，最好写些有意义的文篇，锻炼自己的才干。

徐特立的谈话鼓励了学生办"窗户报"的积极性。一时像雨后的春笋，几乎每个自修室的玻璃窗上都贴出了窗户报。他们还给自己的窗户报命名，如《晨钟报》《晚钟报》等。田汉则取晋朝刘琨"吾枕戈待旦，志枭逆虏，常恐祖生先吾著鞭"之意，办起了《祖鞭报》。这些窗户报上的文章和诗歌，多是以痛快淋漓的笔调抒发忧国忧民的思想，后来也出现了思想较为守旧的《闇谭报》，田汉等人便联合其他各报与之论争，气氛十分活跃。

徐特立是窗户报最热心的读者，常常认真阅读，有时还把其中一些写得好的文章转载到自己办的《教育周刊》上，这对学生们的激励非常大，大家写作的劲头更足了。一时间，窗户报里，各种文体纷出，读书心得、时事评论、诗歌、小说、杂文等，百花齐放，满园春色，就连曾感到受"侮辱"的首元龙、黄竹村两位先生，态度也大为转变，高兴地点头称赞。

校长与退伍兵

徐特立创办长沙师范并担任校长，苦心经营这所学校，一心为长沙的基础教育培养更多优秀师资。

有一天，徐特立正在办公室忙事，一位退伍兵找来了，他就是廖奕。廖奕原在城里做苦力谋生，辛亥革命后参加新军，只认识二三百字。1913年退伍后，他深感没有知识的困窘，非常想到徐特立办的长沙师范学习，于是找上门来，表达了对学习知识的热切渴望。

徐特立被他的精神感动了，为他安排了分班考试。可是成绩出来后，徐特立发现廖奕的基础知识太差，底子太薄，插班到任何一个班里都会很吃力。

廖奕面对自己的成绩，却坚定地说："徐先生，我愿意努力，我有志读书，请你一定要收下我。"

"就冲你'有志读书'这四个字，我破格录取你了。"徐特立深为感动，说："只是你一定要刻苦。"

"刻苦我一定做得到，可是我不知如何努力。"廖奕焦急地说，"我不知道怎样学习才能赶上其他同学，还希望先生多加指点。"

徐特立说："你放心，只要你有志读书，我每天晚上都可以为你辅导。"

"真的？"廖奕难以置信地问。

徐特立点了点头。

在徐特立的关心、帮助和鼓励下，廖奕刻苦学习，进步很快，后来还随徐特立到法国勤工俭学。回国后，在长沙办起了平民工艺厂。他一直念念不忘徐特立老校长对他的培育之恩："当初如果没有徐老对我的谆谆教导和大力支持，恐怕我早就离开了学堂，凭着一身力气，不知道在哪里混日子。"

收了个铁匠学生

铁匠黎升洲，文化程度比廖奕还低，但也一直想进学校学习。这一天，他身背打铁工具，来到长沙师范，请求入学读书。

看到黎升洲的这身装扮，徐特立问："你是来上学的吗？"

黎升洲说："当然是！都说这里的徐特立先生从来不嫌贫爱富，从来不会嫌弃学生的出身。怎么，我是个打铁匠，就上不得学吗？"

徐特立笑了笑，说："当然能上学，只是你得先参加一个入学考试，考考你的学问，我们才好把你安排到班里去。"

黎升洲放下肩上扛着的工具，规规矩矩坐到一张桌子前参加考试，态度非常认真，一丝不苟地作答。

改试卷时，徐特立发现，黎升洲虽然上过几年学，但是很明显知识早已经忘了，试卷上很少有答对的题目，不过他字写得非常认真，卷面十分整洁。

徐特立叫来黎升洲，对他说："这是你的答卷，只是结果不尽如人意……"

"我是有基础的，"黎升洲慌了手脚，以为徐特立不肯收他，忙说："只是这些年复习得少，都忘了。先生你给我一段时间，我肯定都能答得出来。"

徐特立微笑着劝导："别急别急，这些我都晓得，不过这学期你已经赶不上了，这样吧，这段时间你先在家复习复习，下个学期你直接报到就行了。"

"可是这段时间我要是回家，肯定无法复习，能不能给我个宿舍，我就做您的学生，住在这儿复习？"黎升洲急白了脸。

可学校里每个房间都是满满的，已经住不下人了。徐特立想了想，说："这样吧，我认识军械机修厂的人，你白天去那做事，赚点生活费，晚上你来我这，我帮你补习文化。"

不仅有工作，还能学文化，黎升洲对徐特立感激不尽。

经过半年的进修后，黎升洲终于补上了课程，在第二个学期开始时，顺利地进入长沙师范学习。

后来，黎升洲成了湖南有名的生物学教员，解放后还被评选为湖南省优秀教师。

给学生打洗脚水

担任长沙师范校长时，徐特立对学生关怀备至，从不摆校长的架子。他经常与学生同桌吃饭，以便随时了解伙食情况，及时加以改进；有段时间甚至与学生同寝室睡觉，以便督促学生按时休息。

有一次，徐特立去查看学生寝室时，发现有个学生躺在床上呻吟。一问，原来是脚上长了疮，痛得厉害。他忙去提来热水，帮助学生将脚洗干净，细心敷上药膏，叮嘱他："你这几天行动不方便，好生休息，暂时不要去上课了！"

这事不知怎么传了出去，当时教育界有人对此大加讥讽，认为徐特立身为公立学校的校长，竟然做这种下等人才干的事情。徐特立听了，不以为意，笑笑说："校长教员关心爱护学生，是应尽的责任。我还只做了一点好事，就被人家把好处夸大了。"他认为他所做的这种"怪事"，正是教育界的人应该做而很少做或没有做的事情。

"徐家外婆"

1925年1月，徐特立被任命为湖南省立第一女子师范学校的校长。他到任后，大刀阔斧地进行教学整顿，选用了一批德才兼备、思想进步的优秀教师，取消了女生不得随便出入校门、不得过问政治、不能公开参加社会活动等诸多校禁，解除了强加在女生身上的诸多封建桎梏。

这年秋天，有位名叫许德耀的女子，从湘潭乡下来到湖南省立第一女子师范学校求学。她找到徐校长，泪流满面地介绍家里的情况并表达了入学的强烈愿望。她告诉徐校长，自己的爱人在湖南大学读书，支持她冲破家庭的束缚来长沙学习。徐特立很同情她，同意她入学。许德耀喜出望外，进校后学习非常刻苦，事事不落同学之后。

不幸的是，许德耀很快发现自己怀孕了，可又实在不愿丢掉好不容易得来的学习机会,只好隐瞒下来。但婴儿总是要出生的,一天夜里,分娩来临,这时正值隆冬,来不及送回家,也来不及送医院。徐特立知道这事情后,毫不犹豫地决定让她在校内分娩。婴儿顺利降生了。

第二天,徐特立召开全校师生员工大会,说明了许德耀的这一情况,请大家理解包容,不要受来自社会的偏见和压力影响。女生当然更理解妇女的难处,对徐校长的决定和立场,打心眼里拥护,纷纷围着徐校长道喜,并亲昵地称徐校长为"外婆"。"徐家外婆"的称号很快在校内传开了。

这事很快传了出去,在教育界引起了一些非议,有人还造谣中伤,恶意诽谤第一女师的校风。徐特立顶住压力,坚持让许德耀学成毕业。

1956年徐特立回到湖南时,第一女师的一些老学生去看望他,并告诉他许耀德在湘潭当老师,30年前生的那个孩子如今已是国家干部了。徐老欣慰地笑了。

和蔼的外婆校长

"徐家外婆"称号的得来,可不仅仅因为学生许德耀的事,更因为徐特立爱生如子,对待每一个学生都给予外婆般的温暖与关怀。

在湖南省立第一女子师范,冬天一来,徐校长每天都要嘱咐学生们多穿衣服,不要受寒,教室里很早就生起炭火;夏天了,又替学生们将窗户打开,使空气流通。晚上下了自修后,徐校长要求学生爱护身体,按时休息,不准再看书,还经常在女训育员陪同下,巡查每一间寝室是否还有人讲话或做别的事,一旦遇到没按时就寝的学生,他总要问:"为什么还不睡?宁可早点起,不要耽误了睡眠。"徐校长还经常与学生们一起吃饭,以考察伙食的好坏。正因为徐校长对学生无微不至的关爱和体贴,学生们感受到徐校长和蔼慈祥,就和自己的外婆一样,因此"徐家外婆""外婆"的名号在全校传开了。著名作家谢冰莹当时正在学

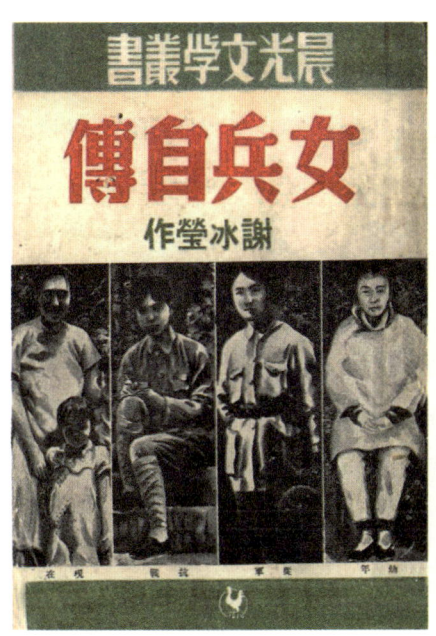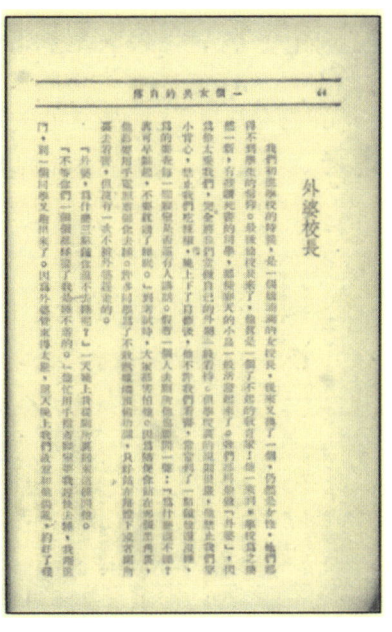

◀ 谢冰莹的《女兵自传》及其中的"外婆校长"一章。

校求学,她后来回忆道:"他真是一个了不起的教育家!他一来到,学校便焕然一新;有些读死书的同学,都像春天的小鸟一般活泼起来了。我们都叫他'外婆'。"

当年,在徐校长的支持和湖南省立第一女子师范民主而自由的学习氛围下,谢冰莹阅读了大量进步的文学作品,如郭沫若、郁达夫、成仿吾的诗作和散文,莫泊桑、左拉、托尔斯泰、陀斯妥耶夫斯基、爱罗先珂等人的小说……思想逐渐成熟,开始形成自己明确的世界观。1926年冬,她毅然报考了武汉中央军事政治学校,成了当时极少见的一名女兵。后来,谢冰莹成为著名作家,出版了包括《女兵自传》《从军日记》等在内的多达2000多万字的作品。

温柔敦厚兴诗教

徐特立在担任湖南省立第一女子师范校长期间，实施了温柔敦厚的诗教。他在学生经常通过的走廊上挂上一块大黑板，发现学生的优点或缺点，就写成明白浅显的诗歌进行表扬和批评，对学生进行思想道德教育。这些诗歌，后来被称为"校中百咏"，生动地反映了徐特立对年轻一代的真诚爱护和真切关怀。

一天，个别学生嫌食堂饭菜不好，晚饭后借故到厨房里打碎不少碗。对这种损坏公物的行为，徐特立在对当事人进行批评教育后，第二天一清早写了这样一首黑板诗，借以教育全体学生：

我愿诸生青出蓝，人财物力莫摧残。
昨宵到底缘何事，打破厨房碗一篮。

在办学中，徐特立处处节俭。他看到地上的粉笔头总是把它捡起来，留着自己上课时用，有些学生对他这样做很不理解，他向学生讲述了古人珍惜木屑的故事及其意义，并写了黑板诗，教育她们养成勤俭的习惯：

半截粉条犹爱惜，公家物件总宜珍。
诸生不解余衷曲，反谓余为算细人。

每天学生就寝后，徐特立都要和训育员一道去巡视寝室。一次，他发现有学生不按时就寝，还在聊天，有一个学生还借着厕所的灯光编毛衣，就教育她们要按时休息。这些学生觉得自己违反了作息制度，心想明天要受到责骂和处罚了。第二天，徐特立却没有这样做，只是在黑板上写了这样两首诗：

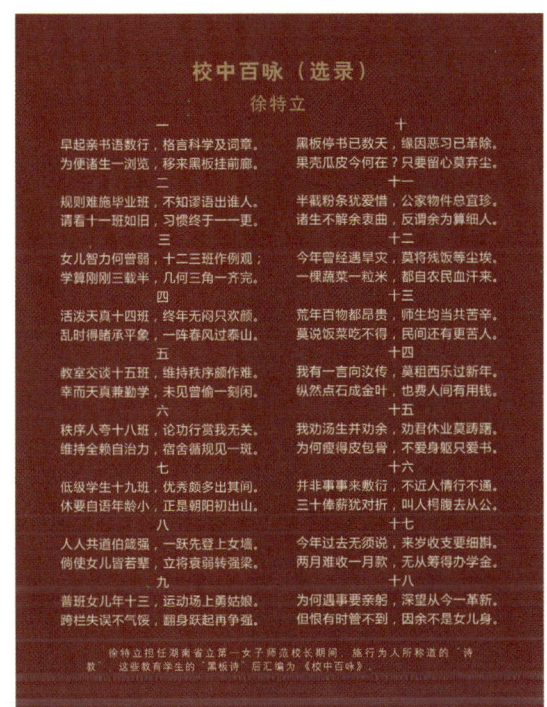

◀《校中百咏》选篇。

昨夜已经三更天，厕所偷光把衣编。
爱人要紧我同意，不爱自己我着急。
东边奔跑到西边，不仅打衣还聊天。
莫说交谈声细细，夜深亦复扰人眠。

读了诗后，学生们很受感动，按时就寝的自觉性得到提高，从此再也没有出现类似的现象了。

姓汤和姓余的两个学生，平时不注意爱护身体，只是埋头读书，结果严重影响了身体健康。徐特立特地就此事在黑板上写诗，教育全体学生平时要注意锻炼身体，做到身体好、学习好：

> 我劝汤生并劝余,劝君休业莫踌躇。
> 为何瘦得皮包骨,不爱身躯只爱书。

有学生吃过橘子、花生等零食后,将橘子皮、花生壳丢得满地都是。徐特立提出严肃批评:

> 花生橘子弃残余,铺满阶前弗扫除。
> 学生本是人中秀,习染还同未读书。

由于徐特立太爱学生了,学生们都亲切地称他为"徐外婆"。为此,徐特立自己也写了一首有趣的诗:

> 深恐同学失眠多,更深寒夜自巡逻。
> 身品不是女儿像,却听声声唤"外婆"。

教育部长扫盲

1930年底,徐特立从苏联回国,来到江西中央苏区革命根据地。

当时,中央苏区的广大地区地处偏僻,文化落后,大约百分之九十的人是一字不识的文盲。建立革命政权后,贫苦百姓当家做主,迫切要求读书学习文化。徐特立到达中央苏区后,被任命为中华苏维埃教育人民委员部副部长、代部长。他决心改变苏区文盲遍地的状况。

在炮火连天的战争年代,要建立和发展教育事业,困难非常多。那时书籍很少,连找一张报纸都不容易。有时候红军部队攻打下一座县城,才能获得一些报纸。写字用的纸张也非常缺乏,谁要是能找到手掌心那么大一张纸,都特别宝贵。就在这种极其艰难的条件下,徐特立苦心筹划,开设了识字班、训练班。没有教师,他坚持能者为师,提出了"老公教老婆,儿子教父亲,秘书教主席,马夫教马夫,伙夫教伙夫,识字多的教识字少的,先识字的教后识字的"这样一种非常有效的扫盲方针,开展起轰轰烈烈的群众性识字运动。

每到夜晚,在昏暗的油灯下,大伯大婶们吃力而又认真地认着生字。徐特立经常到各个识字班去,一个一个地教学

◀ 1932年春,徐特立在江西瑞金洋溪借用刘氏宗祠创办列宁师范并任校长,以培养扫盲需要的师资。图为刘氏宗祠旧址。

生认字,一句一句地教大家读课文,发现有好的经验就推广开来。在徐特立的积极倡导下,群众创造了许多识字的好方法:用沙盘当纸,用树枝做笔,练习写字;在井台上挂识字牌,在村口设立识字岗,督促大家学习,等等。

徐特立还亲自编写教材、做教具,办起了小学校。娃娃们高高兴兴背着书包,跨进教室,打开油印课本,高声朗读:

太阳光光,照遍全场,
儿童团员,都进学堂。
读书识字,消灭文盲。

此外,徐特立还创办师范学校和农业学校,又抽时间写剧本、当导演,培养了一批做文艺宣传工作的人才。

当时打仗是头等大事,为了抽出更多的人力到前方参加战斗,后方机关的人留得极少。有段时间,教育部只剩下两个人,一个是部长徐

特立，另一个是一位14岁的小勤务员。学校的工作人员也减少到最低限度，徐特立除了教课，还自己扫地、摇铃、种菜、做饭，每天忙碌不停。

国民党军队包围了中央苏区，封锁得很厉害，食盐、必需的日用品运不进来，大家的生活十分艰苦，学校里常常几个月都尝不到一点盐味。一次，瞿秋白好不容易弄到一点盐，特地约徐特立到他那里去吃了一顿有盐的饭，算是很丰盛的招待了。

就是在这样艰苦的环境中，徐特立愉快而积极地工作着，使中央苏区的文化教育事业迅速发展起来。

"不聚财"的教育部长

1935年，红军胜利到达陕北后，徐特立担任中华苏维埃共和国西北办事处教育部部长，全面领导陕北边区的教育工作。尽管是教育部长，徐特立却从来不曾离开教育一线，亲自参与创办、管理学校，担任教学任务，关怀、救助贫困学生，留下了许多脍炙人口的故事。

有一个名叫晏景山的青年，一心要来陕甘宁边区学习，但路途艰险，途中必须经过国民党军队的封锁线。晏景山随身携带的行李丢弃了许多，被子也在途中弄丢了。到鲁迅师范入学时，晏景山没有被子盖，只能和别人共铺，或者把自己的衣服盖在身上。

▶ 担任中华苏维埃共和国西北办事处教育部部长时的徐特立。

眼见天气越来越冷了,晏景山内心焦急。他把所有的劲头都用在学习上,每天天未明,就起床读书。

徐特立每天照例早起巡视学校,发现总有一名学生在自习室的石板凳上孜孜不倦地学习。他很好奇,于是向别的同学询问,才得知晏景山的情况,夸赞说:"这是个好娃娃,我的被子给他盖吧!"徐老把自己的被子抱来,送到晏景山的手里,对他说:"景山,天气凉了,你要注意身体,不要冻出病来!身体是革命的本钱呀!"晏景山十分感动,表示自己会更加努力地学习,报答徐老的恩情。徐老的被子给了晏景山,每天晚上就拿着周恩来送给他的雨衣当被子盖。

还有一个叫罗锦华的同学,是陕西黄陵县人,在当地的一所中学读书,也一心想去延安。一天晚上,为了防止脚步声被人听到,他脱掉了鞋子从学校偷偷跑出来,赤着脚走到了鲁迅师范。徐老看到后,想都没想,马上把自己的鞋子脱下来给罗锦华。罗同学觉得很过意不去,说:"徐老,我哪能要您的鞋子呢?何况,您的鞋子给了我,您穿什么呢?"徐老摆摆手,坚定地说:"锦华同学,你一定要把鞋穿上。我宿舍还有鞋,等会儿我回去就换上。"罗锦华心怀感激地穿上了鞋子。而徐老把鞋送出去后,好一段时间穿着麻鞋。后来蔡畅看到了这一情况,反映给李富春,李富春就把自己的一双鞋送给了徐老,又经林伯渠主席批了条子,为徐老解决了被子的问题。

徐老为人慷慨,满怀热诚,爱生如子,关心他人胜过关心自己。当时人们称赞徐老说:"徐老不聚财,不是没被子,就是没有鞋。"

培植自然科学的幼苗

1940年8月,徐特立回到延安,年底被任命为中国共产党创办的第一所理工科高等院校——延安自然科学院(今北京理工大学前身)的院长。

当时，有的同志对办自然科学院存有异议，说延安人力、物力基础都很差，发展自然科学的条件还不具备，但徐特立办学的态度非常坚决。他说："干革命不能只顾眼前，不顾将来。培育科学人才，要十年、几十年才能看出效果来。古人所说的'十年树木，百年树人'，就是这个意思。如果我们现在不抓紧，将来用什么？光坐等条件具备，不去创造条件，科技人才难道会从天上掉下来吗？"徐特立认为，虽然现在处在国力艰难之时，但决不能忽视对科学技术人才的培养，让我们国家科技落后、国弱民穷的惨痛历史继续下去。他在报刊上写了许多文章，宣传发展科学技术的重要性。他说："我国近代科学技术落后，吃了不少苦头！前车之覆，后车之鉴。我们今日之延安怎么能够忽视这么一件大事呢？"

当时，陕北是个偏僻狭小的地方，交通闭塞，文化落后。特别是在日本帝国主义侵略、国民党封锁的大背景下，科技人才很难来到这里，既没有科学仪器设备，也没有必要的图书资料，甚至连普通的校舍、黑板、纸、笔都很缺乏。但是，徐特立没有被困难压倒，他带领师生们自己动手挖窑洞、建校舍，自己制造教具、实验仪器，自己编写教

▶ 1940年12月，徐特立被任命为延安自然科学院院长。图为延安自然科学院旧照。

材……他们用辛勤的汗水，把自然科学这棵幼苗在瘠土荒山上培植起来，并让它茁壮成长。

这所有几百人规模的学校，座落在几个山坡上，每个山头又有好几层窑洞，学生们分散在不很明亮的窑洞里上课，如果开大会或上大课，就在窑洞外面的空坪上。徐特立对学校的教学方针、课程安排、思想工作以及后勤供应，一件件、一桩桩，都亲自过问，每天上上下下要爬好几个山头。下雨天，山陡路滑，他就赤着脚，拄着棍；上大课的时候，他在土坪上讲课，无论酷暑严冬，总是不戴帽子，一讲就是几个小时。他是院长，按规定可以单独住一孔窑洞，可他一定要叫上另外两个老师和他一起住，晚上共用一盏小油灯。他说："大家住的都很挤，为什么我要一个人住呢？"

自然科学院的师生大部分是来自祖国各地的知识青年，一开始对这样的艰苦生活不习惯，但在徐特立言传身教下慢慢都适应了。同学们用砖头当凳子，膝盖当书桌，树枝当笔，大地当纸，投入了紧张的学习。条件虽然艰苦，但人人都精神愉快，苦中作乐。每到课余时间，窑洞内外，就响起了愉快的歌声：

> 我们的生活艰苦而又紧张，
> 我们的革命热情却日益高涨。
> 谁说我们没有课堂？
> 我们有着世界上最好的课堂。
> 蓝天是我们的屋顶，
> 高山是我们的围墙。
> 谁说我们没有教具？
> 自制的教具更加漂亮。
> 谁说"土包子"不能办大学堂？
> 我们的信心比泰山还稳固，
> 我们的意志比钢铁更坚强，

> 为了祖国的新生，
> 为了民族的解放，
> 任何困难也不能把我们阻挡……

在战火中诞生的延安自然科学院在徐特立的领导下，培养了一批又一批的科技人才，为建国后的科技发展作出了巨大贡献。

"要做园丁，不要做樵夫"

徐特立从18岁开始担任乡村蒙馆塾师，直至91岁高龄辞世，一生都从事着他深爱的教育事业。他认为，教师是真理的传播者，是灵魂的工程师，并一再强调教师"要做园丁，不要做樵夫"。教师要谨慎、严肃、认真地对待自己的工作，要培育好幼苗和花朵。当学生触犯纪律或犯错时，不能轻易地采取处分、开除学籍的方式，而是要从爱护的角度出发，细致耐心地做工作。对于惩戒学生的方式，徐特立非常反对体罚或变相体罚，认为"体罚是野蛮的事情"。

在全国解放后的最初几年中，小学教育有很大的进步，但学校中的体罚现象依然存在。1952年冬天，徐特立在一次听取教育工作汇报时，听与会者谈到各地小学体罚现象，说有位老师拉伤了学生的手腕，有位老师甚至逼着学生去舔自己吐在地上的痰。徐特立怒不可遏，气愤地说："这些人不配做教师！不但不爱护儿童，反而虐待儿童，摧残儿童！这种违法行为，应该处分！教育行政部门和学校领导，没有教育好老师，不去消灭学校里的体罚现象，也是不负责任的表现！"徐特立越说越愤怒，在座的人都为之动容。大家都知道，徐老平时很少发脾气，对人总是和颜悦色的，都说从来没见过徐老发这么大的火。大家都深为徐老对学生的爱而感动，一致希望教师们改变体罚、侮辱学生的不好的教育方法，改用新的教育方法去培育下一代。

"永远的老师"

1937年1月,党中央在延安为徐特立六十寿辰举行庆祝大会。毛泽东到会讲话,说:"我在湖南第一师范求学时,最佩服的有两位老师,一位是杨怀中先生,一位是徐老。"

1913年春,毛泽东考入湖南省立第四师范。第二年春,该校合并于湖南第一师范,毛泽东被编入第八班。在这里,他认识了许多德才兼备的好老师,其中一位就是徐特立。对于徐特立,不少同学早就有所耳闻,都知道这位徐先生是个了不起的人物:他是长沙师范学校的校长,又曾担任过湖南省临时议会副议长、省教育司的科长,在社会上颇有名气;他只读过6年私塾,靠自学而精通古文、历史、地理和数学等多科知识;他18岁开始当塾师,以后又亲手创办了多所新式学校,门生遍长沙……能遇到徐特立这样有名的老师,同学们都引以为荣。毛泽东也是如此。

◀ 任教湖南省立第一师范时的徐特立。

湖南省立第四师范是春季开学,第一师范却是秋季始业。当时的学制,师范预科1年,本科4年,因此,毛泽东多读了半年书,直到1918年暑期才毕业,共读了5年半。徐特立从1913年春至1919年夏在第一师范教书,共教了20个班、762名学生的教育学、修身科和各科教授法,并兼实习主任。在湖南省立第一师范,毛泽东与徐特立有四年半交往甚密的师生关系。

有一天,下课后,毛泽东走到正在教师休息室里看书的徐老师身边问道:"徐先生,您读书的经验,可以谈一些出来,让我们效仿吗?"徐特立打量着这位大名鼎鼎的毛润之同学,回答说:"润之,我认为读书要守一个'少'字诀,不怕书看得少,但必须要看通、看透。要提高自己的分辨能力,认识书籍的价值,要用一个本子摘录书中精彩的地方。总之,我是坚持不动笔墨不看书的。这样读书,也许进度会慢一点,但读一句算一句,读一本算一本,不但能记得牢固,而且懂得透

▶ 1937年1月毛泽东祝徐特立六十大寿的贺信。

彻。"毛泽东认真聆听和学习徐先生"不动笔墨不读书"的方法，并且终身实践。徐特立高尚的品德、渊博的学识以及严谨的治学态度和良好的学习方法，对求知若渴的毛泽东产生了深刻的影响，成为毛泽东在湖南第一师范求学时关系最为密切的老师之一。

1937年1月30日，毛泽东于百忙之中抽出时间，给老师写了一封情真意切的祝寿信，并当晚派人送到了徐特立手中。信的第一句是"徐老同志：你是我二十年前的先生，你现在仍然是我的先生，你将来必定还是我的先生"，表达了自己对恩师的崇敬之情。

徐特立约集一些学校的进步教员,到处宣传讲演,
号召大家支持革命,响应武昌起义。

第四章

"读书不忘救国"

断指写血书

徐特立是一位教育家，但他从不局限于学校、教育这个小圈子，而总是密切地关注着国家、民族的前途与命运。他曾明确向学生提出"读书不忘救国"，并忠实地践行着"教书不忘救国、兴教育以救国"的宗旨。

辛亥革命前，由于清政府的腐败无能，帝国主义列强对中国的欺压凌辱，一天比一天凶狠。一些外国传教士纷纷进入中国内地，享受特权，欺压百姓，引起各地人民的痛恨和反抗，不断发生所谓"教案"。江西南昌教案，就是因为一个地方主要官员坚持外国传教士必须受中国法律约束，竟被洋人杀害。

面对祖国遭受的种种屈辱，徐特立悲愤至极。1909 年 12 月的一天，在长沙修业学校教书的徐特立，召集学生和教职员们在大操坪里讲演时事。他援引最近各地发生的"教案"为例，历数帝国主义侵略中国的暴行，以及清政府对内镇压人民、对外丧权辱国的行径，越讲越激动，声泪俱下。忽然，他奔下讲台，跑进厨房取了一把菜刀回来，大声喊：

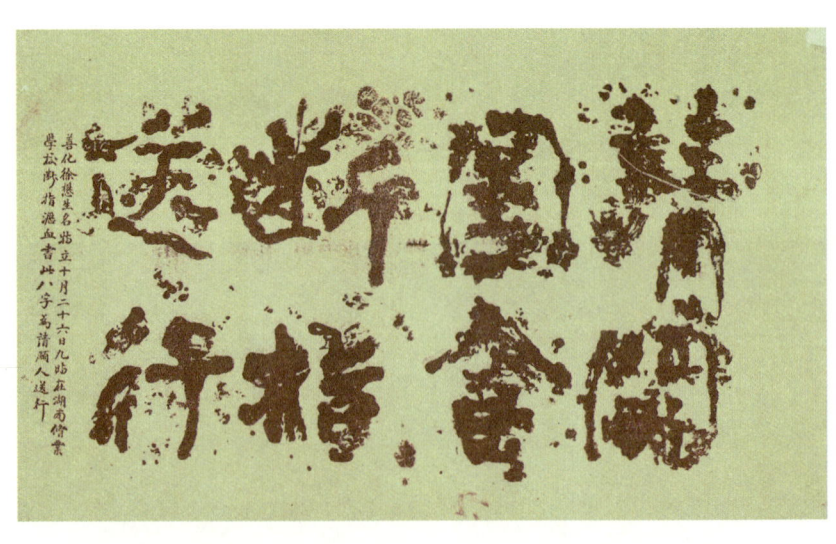

▶ 国家博物馆收藏的徐特立血书。

"我徐特立愿与诸位同胞奋勇杀敌，誓不回头！"说完，拿起菜刀砍断了自己左手小指的一截，用鲜血写下了"驱除鞑虏，恢复中华"八个大字！目睹徐特立的爱国壮举，全场沸腾起来，"打倒列强""恢复中华"的口号声响成一片。

修业学校的校长眼见全校群情激愤，担心出事，忙用徐特立断指的血，在另一张白纸上写了"请开国会，断指送行"八个字，送给当时赴北京请求清政府立宪的代表。

几天后，各地报纸都以醒目的标题登载了徐特立断指血书的新闻。徐特立的爱国行动很快传遍长沙城，也影响到整个湖南，使更多的人觉醒起来，投入反帝斗争。

年轻的毛泽东听说这事后，非常敬佩，在延安时回忆此事，以饱含敬意的口吻说："……经过打听，才知道这位中年人叫徐特立，于是对徐特立尊敬起来，对革命第一次有了感性认识。他后来是我上湖南第一师范时的先生，他还是我革命的老师哩！"

辛亥革命一斗士

1911年10月中旬，长沙城里气氛分外紧张，清政府安排军队在大街小巷巡逻，到处张贴着追捕革命党人的布告，抚署大堂上也架设起机关炮。原来，10月10日武昌新军中的革命党人起义，占领武汉三镇，成立了湖北军政府，宣告独立了。湖南巡抚余诚格害怕湖南新军中的革命党人响应，便严加设防，大肆搜捕革命党人，一时间闹得店铺关门，家家闭户，市民们不敢外出。

一天晚上，长沙县教育会馆中，一群人围着一盏煤油灯，低声争论着。原来，这是长沙县各学校校长的秘密集会，他们正商量响应武昌起义的事。

在激烈的辩论中，两种意见相持不下：一部分人主张湖南教育界立刻发动起来，响应武昌起义，参与革命；另一部分人认为此时革命形势并不明朗，还是采取观望态度为好。

这时，实业学校的周校长压低嗓门开了腔："刚才诸位发表了许多高见，对于武昌方面理应快速支援，只是我们手里没有武器，赤手空拳，怎么能够响应武昌起义呢？我的意见是先等待几天，看看形势的变化，等到各地都起来响应的时候，我们再行动也不迟。"

他刚说完，便有好几个人附和。"周校长说得对，我们还是看看再行动吧！""是呀，急急忙忙要坏事的！"

"不对！"一个身着蓝布长衫的中年男子挺身站起来。大家一看，原来是周南女校校长徐特立。早在两年前，徐特立的"断指血书"义举，早已使他声名鹊起，大家都静待他的发言。

徐特立坚定地说："诸位校长和同仁们，革命是一件危险的事情，难免有流血牺牲。现在形势万分危急，如果我们不响应起义，那么武昌的革命行动就有可能失败，革命党兄弟会被清廷赶尽杀绝，到时候想要起义，恐怕连人都凑不齐了！"他紧接着说："照如今的形势，我们应立即响应武昌起义。怕死的不要动，不怕死的一起来。趁着当局的惊魂未定，赶快组织进步学生到城外新军兵营中宣传鼓动，争取在近日起义。"

徐特立宏亮的声音、坚定的神情和无所畏惧的气概，深深感染了到会的人，会场顿时活跃起来，大家都表示拥护徐特立的主张，决定积极行动起来，响应武昌起义。会后，徐特立约集一些学校的进步教员如何雨农、凌振嘉、刘鸣翳、李洞天等，力排险阻，到处宣传演讲，号召大家支持革命。

10月22日，长沙起义成功，新的都督政府成立，焦达峰、陈作新被推举为湖南正副都督。起义军民人人笑逐颜开，奔走相告。徐特立在拥挤的人群中，到处奔忙着。他把抬轿的、拉车的和搬运苦力的人召集在一起，给大家讲述通俗的革命道理，还跑到城外买牛，慰劳起义的军队，并为他们传递消息。

不作议长，仍当教员

长沙起义后，由于徐特立对武昌起义的积极响应和实际行动，他被选为湖南省临时议会副议长。

新政府成立后，徐特立满腔热情，认为封建帝制被推翻了，民主政府建立起来了，这下中国有希望了。可是，湖南的革命形势急转直下，1911年10月31日，革命党领袖焦达峰、陈作新被叛乱的士兵杀害。立宪派首领谭延闿被推举为都督，不仅不处置杀害焦、陈二人的凶手，而且还提出"维持治安，保全秩序"的施政方针。这使得徐特立对资产阶级民主革命的信心开始动摇。

不久，徐特立在省议会提出县知事民选的提案，引起了议会内部激烈的争议。最后，提案虽然通过了，却被议长无理搁置，不交都督府执行。这对徐特立是一个极大的打击。徐特立还看到从议长到议员，绝大多数人关心的不是国计民生的大事，而是汲汲于升官发财、争权夺利。一个民意机关，竟被贪污腐坏的风气所充塞、笼罩。徐特立对省议会异常失望，愤而辞去副议长之职。

随后，他接受湖南教育司司长陈润霖之邀，到省教育司当科长。他主张大力发展普通教育，让那些贫苦大众的子女都能读书，但也根本得不到上司的支持。这使徐特立大失所望，他想到辛亥革命以来自己一直努力奋斗，现在一切希望似乎都已破灭，政府总是坏的，革命党做了官就要叛变。他苦苦思索，觉得国家不能富强、人民没有觉悟，关键在于老百姓的文化太低。他想，要真正救国，就要用教育来改革人心，多办些学校以开启民智。于是，他辞去科长职务，回到教育界去当教员。

"驱张"急先锋

1918年3月，皖系军阀首领之一的张敬尧担任湖南省督军兼省长。张敬尧专横跋扈，贪婪成性，更伙同他的三个兄弟——张敬舜、张敬禹、张敬汤，在湖南恣意施行暴政，耀武扬威，他们的部下更是横行霸道，残害百姓，无恶不作，弄得全省百姓人人自危，怨声载道，以致民间当时流传出这样一句话："堂堂呼张，尧舜禹汤。一二三四，虎豹豺狼。张毒不除，湖南无望。"

8月，张敬尧大施淫威，强行封闭了湖南学生联合会和毛泽东主编的《湘江评论》，镇压长沙各界群众举行的焚烧日货的示威大会，还派兵强占学校，捣毁学校的教具，烧毁图书，并扣压学校的经费。这些暴行激怒了广大人民群众，毛泽东等人因势利导，积极联合省内外各界进步力量，发动了一场驱逐张敬尧的斗争。

这时，徐特立正在湖南第一师范当教员，并兼任湖南孤儿院院长。他对张敬尧兄弟的所作所为，早已恨之入骨，便积极投身于这场斗争。

这天，徐特立联合各校进步校长和教师集会，他慷慨激昂地鼓动大家说："诸位校长，诸位教师，我们不是要办学校吗？不是要发展湖南教育吗？可是，张氏兄弟派兵强占学校，扣发教育经费和教师们的薪水，破坏教育。不把这些凶残的野兽驱逐出去，不仅湖南教育无望，全省人民都有被他们吃掉的危险。"校长和老师们激愤起来，有的说："找张敬尧这小子算账去！"有的大叫："不干了！我这校长谁愿当谁当！"徐特立趁势号召大家："对！当校长的向张敬尧辞去校长职务，当教师的向张敬尧索薪去！"一场辞职索薪的活动就这样爆发了。

徐特立还通过教育会组织所属各校教职员，成立讲演团，统一训练后，派往各县乡镇进行爱国反帝宣传，抵制日货，惩罚奸商、洋奴等活动。他本人往返于城乡之间做演讲，向学生、教师和群众揭露张氏兄弟的罪行，号召大家起来驱逐张敬尧，结果被张敬尧诬以"通匪"，明令通缉，并声言要封闭他创办的五美学校。

面对张敬尧的暴行，徐特立决定赴欧勤工俭学。行前，他以湖南孤儿院院长的名义，给张敬尧写了一封信，历数张来湖南后的种种罪行。他在信中写道："自北兵南来，劫杀淫掠无所不至，老者弱者或流或亡，壮者少者生计陡绝，逼而为匪。然所谓匪者，实兵事制造成之，非吾湘固有之物也。时势稍静，官厅举议，清乡风起云涌，匪去而清乡队来。所谓局长坐办，莫非由无赖流氓，营缘贿得，差委既获，本利尤偿，于是大长其敲诈威胁……"最后，徐特立警告说，如不除张，他将"诉之中外舆论"。这封信于1919年11月20日在北京《晨报》上公开发表，推动了驱张运动的深入进行。

当张敬尧读到此信，暴跳如雷，而徐特立已如《晨报》特约通讯员在稿件中提到的那样：他现在已到法国巴黎去了！

1920年，随着人民反张声势的不断高涨，张氏兄弟这群豺狼虎豹终于被驱逐出了湖南。

投身农民运动

1924年1月，国民党第一次全国代表大会召开，提出"联俄、联共、扶助农工"的政策，国共实现第一次合作，这不仅促进了全国工人运动的高涨，也推动了农民运动的开展。此时，随着北伐战争的节节胜利，湖南的农民运动在毛泽东的亲自推动下，如暴风骤雨般蓬勃发展起来，"打倒土豪劣绅""一切权力归农会"等口号响彻广大农村。

1926年12月中旬，徐特立在长沙望麓园与回湘考察农民运动的毛泽东见面，毛泽东建议徐特立回乡下去看看。1927年春，徐特立回到五美老家，调查农民运动的开展情况。他发现虽然只有3个月没回，但农村已经产生了翻天覆地的变化：

农民协会改革了农村中的一切，恶霸没有了，流氓、烟、赌没有了，富欺贫困、男欺女、智欺愚的事情，也没有了；

农村中有了公是公非，一切诉讼由农民协会解决；不需要一分钱的诉讼费，广大农民的千万只眼睛看着，千万双手指着，公是公非，没有人敢颠倒；

从前被人瞧不起的贫苦农民、妇女、儿童都组织起来，昂首挺胸地当家做主了；

一切为非作恶的人，都不敢动，一切坏事没有人敢做……

徐特立几乎难以相信这是真的，他第一次看到了这样一个亘古未有的新气象。他逢人便讲：农民运动了不起；见人就说：农民协会真伟大。皇帝办不到的事情，老百姓办到了；"大人物"办不到的事情，"小人物"办到了。他开始真正认识到了民众的力量。

不久，徐特立读了毛泽东写的《湖南农民运动考察报告》，觉得深刻极了。多年来，他一直在寻找一条改造社会的道路。他支持过革新派，也参加过一些斗争，但都没有使社会面貌发生根本的变革。如今，农民运动一下就改变了社会的面貌，实现了他多年的愿望。徐特立决心投入到这轰轰烈烈的农民运动中去，拜工农为师，做他们的小学生。

这期间，他除了担任国民党长沙市党部工农部长外，还兼任湖南农民协会教育科长、湖南农村师范农运讲习所主任，同时还担任着长沙师范、湖南省立第一女子师范校长职务，忙得喘不过气来，但他仍以极大

▶ 湖南省农民协会遗址——长沙市局关祠。

的热情投身革命中去，常常身着短衫、脚穿草鞋去长沙县各乡镇了解农民运动，并进行深入的考察。他掌握了大量农民运动的材料，同时还为湖南各县基层的农民组织培训了大量骨干。他的长子徐笃本在父亲影响下，积极参加农民运动，曾担任醴陵县农民协会会长，不久加入共产党，后来在大革命失败时牺牲，年仅21岁。

"没有字的教科书"

一个天气非常阴沉的下午，正下着淅淅沥沥的小雨。徐特立撑着一把纸伞，踏着泥泞的小路，心情沉重地来到离长沙城十公里的乡下——黎托。他到这里来干什么呢？

事情还得从国共合作破裂、国民党右派发动清党运动说起。1927年4月，蒋介石在上海发动"四一二"政变，向共产党人举起了屠刀；5月，许克祥在长沙发动"马日事变"，疯狂地向革命者和工农大众猛扑过来。白色恐怖笼罩着上海、笼罩着长沙、笼罩着全国，反革命势力捣毁工会、农会、学生联合会等革命组织，释放在押的土豪劣绅，到处搜捕、屠杀共产党员、工农群众和进步人士。许多共产党员被迫转入地下，一些意志不坚定的人离开了党，革命陷入了低潮。

这时候，徐特立虽然还不是共产党员，但是，面对反动派背叛革命、野蛮屠杀的罪行，他感到无比的震惊和愤怒。在这以前，徐特立就对共产党很有好感，喜欢看共产党的书刊，喜欢与共产党员来往。在他创办的学校里，就聘请过陈章甫、罗学瓒、周以栗等许多共产党员做教员，他的学生也有不少人是共产党员。特别是在参加农民运动以后，他更加了解共产党，拥护共产党，经常做讲演赞扬共产党的主张，还掩护过党团组织的活动。

"马日事变"后，由于他在湖南教育界的声望较高，国民党右派不敢随便抓捕他，甚至试图拉拢他，但徐特立不为所动，秘密离开了长沙

▶ 徐特立的入党介绍人李维汉。

城。徐特立先在五美老家隐蔽了一段时间，因形势的严峻，便来到黎托，准备到自己的学生、女共产党员黎尚瑾家中躲避一阵。黎家是个大户，有旧屋百余间；黎尚瑾的父亲黎雪渠曾任教于徐特立创办的梨江高小，与徐特立关系很好，倾向革命并赞助过革命。因此，这里是一个理想的藏身之所。

在这里，徐特立意外地遇见了任教湖南第一师范时的学生罗迈（即李维汉）。罗迈曾是中共湖南省委的领导人，现已交卸职务，准备去武汉，由于铁路被反动分子封锁了，只能暂时在黎家隐蔽。危难时刻师生相逢，徐特立和罗迈都特别高兴。两人交换了对大革命的一些看法。罗迈还告诉徐特立，"马日事变"后，党组织非常担心他的安全，曾派人到处寻找他。

面对这位尊敬的老师，罗迈轻声问："老师，您愿意加入共产党吗？"

"什么？"徐特立一时以为自己听错了。

看到老师那惊奇的神情，罗迈又一字一句地说："组织上让我来征求您的意见，看您是否愿意入党？"

徐特立这时完全明白过来，十分激动地说："我是非常崇拜共产党的，共产党人积极，不争个人权力，完全为社会工作。但共产党员都是有为的年轻人，我年纪已这样老，共产党会不会收我这样的老朽呢？"

罗迈说："老师，革命是不分年龄大小的。但现在革命形势转入低潮，加入共产党不仅要吃苦，而且随时会有生命危险。"

徐特立坚定地回答道："革命，总免不了流血牺牲！我愿意跟着共产党干，只要党需要我，我什么都舍得出去！"

罗迈点点头，紧紧地握住徐特立的手，对他说："老师，省委早就注意和研究过您对革命和我党的态度，也十分了解您内心的要求，曾让薛世纶同志来联系您入党，没料想革命事业突然遭受这么重大的挫折。老师，既然您决心跟着党走，从此以后，我们就是并肩作战的同志了！我来作您的入党介绍人，您今后就是中国共产党的党员了！"

就这样，在革命最困难的时候，在白色恐怖笼罩下的长沙，年过半百的老教育家徐特立正式加入了中国共产党。他觉得自己"从此真正获得了新生"。

陆定一后来这样评价："人民教育家徐特立同志，就这样给全党同志上了第一课：困难时不要动摇，应当更坚定地奋斗，革命是一定会胜利的。徐老给我们的教科书，就是他的入党。这本没有字的教科书，比什么教科书都好，也比什么教科书都重要。"

南昌起义立奇功

徐特立入党后，经中共湖南省委和罗迈介绍，先到武汉，住在武昌农民运动讲习所，会见了毛泽东、方维夏、周以栗、张国基等人。孰料，武汉形势也风云急变，7月15日，汪精卫在武汉公开叛变革命，实行宁汉合流，革命形势更趋紧张。7月18日，中共中央在武汉召开会议，初步作出了在南昌举行武装起义的决定。徐特立与方维夏、张国基、易礼容一行4人化装成商人，先乘小火轮到九江，再乘火车赶到南昌。起义前，徐特立被安置在江西大旅社贺龙的总指挥部住宿。

这时的南昌，从外表看来十分平静，但是政治局势异常紧张：在敌方，江西省主席朱培德正与汪精卫、张发奎等在庐山召开反共会议，密谋策划镇压革命；在我方，遵照起义总指挥部的指示，参加起义的部队正在向南昌靠拢，各地革命人士和热血青年正在向南昌云集。南昌，像一座瞬间就要爆发的火山，一场你死我活的战斗即将来临，国共双方都在极力争取江西省政府的地方武装。

由于朱培德不在南昌，省主席暂由民政厅长姜济寰代理。因此，姜

▶ 姜济寰父子。

的态度和行动，对于这场斗争具有举足轻重的作用。而这位姜济寰，正是徐特立青年时代的同学和好友。他们曾一起在宁乡速成师范学习，曾一起创办梨江高小、长沙师范，彼此是十分熟悉的好友。

徐特立将他与姜济寰有着多年情谊的这一情况，告诉了中共前敌委员会书记周恩来。周恩来当即指示徐特立和林伯渠利用旧友关系，去做姜济寰的工作。

徐特立写了一封信，派人送到江西省政府。姜济寰收信后，马上派人来接徐特立到自己的公馆去住。徐特立欣然前往，住进了姜公馆，多次与姜彻夜长谈。

这天，姜的好友林伯渠以及姜的学生郭亮，也一起来拜访姜济寰。姜济寰对三位老朋友的到来，非常高兴。宾主依次坐下，一阵寒暄，大家好像又回到当年。徐特立抓住时机，一下子把谈话引入了正题。

"济寰，还记得当年我们在宁乡速成师范读书的日子吗？周震鳞校长为人正直，深明大义，他是同盟会的老会员。在毕业典礼大会上，他慷慨激昂地向我们说：'同学们，我们办这个学校，不光是为培养你们当一个好教员，更重要的是希望你们创造有利于国家民族的事业，救国救民于水火。'"

"记得！记得！那时候我们都还是热血青年哩。整天想的是干一番惊天动地的大事业。我们一起创办了梨江学校，就是要让更多的人读书识字，懂得救国救民的道理，实行教育救国。"姜济寰侃侃而谈。

"唉！快别提'教育救国'啦！"徐特立紧接过话茬，"我从事教育几十年，讲教育又讲历史，常借王莽、董卓来骂袁世凯，但是并没有办法改革现在的恶劣政府，找不出一条救国救民的光明之路。可是今年春，我回到老家，亲眼看到农民运动的力量，终于找到了真正的救国之路。"说到这里，徐特立笑了笑，从姜济寰表情上的变化，断定他已听明白自己的意思了，就没有再说下去。

"是啊！是啊！姜先生，我们二人也有同感。"林伯渠、郭亮一起心照不宣地打着圆场。

姜济寰沉思了一会，慢慢地说："诸位的意思我明白，咱们打开窗子说亮话，共产党领导的农民运动我也是目睹的。他们的做法深得民心，他们的政见我也很认同，只是目前政局对他们十分不利。"

"济寰兄，这话看怎么说。"徐特立哈哈大笑："蒋介石、汪精卫背叛孙中山先生的三大政策，背叛革命，疯狂屠杀共产党人和革命民众，他们把自己摆在与人民为敌的立场上，只能嚣张一时，绝不会长久。要知道共产党人是杀不尽的，如今湖南、湖北的农会、工人赤卫队又都重新组织起来了，革命烈火会越烧越旺！"

"道理是对的，共产党有民众，代表了民族的利益。不过这事是不是考虑考虑再说。"姜济寰仍然有些犹豫。

"还考虑什么？"徐特立焦急地站起来说，"济寰兄是不是怕担风险？是不是对高官厚禄还恋恋不舍？你过去可不是这个样子！在这国家、民族、革命的紧要关头，只有坚定不移地跟中国共产党走，才能救国家民族于水火之

▼ 国民党江西省政府西华厅。1927年8月1日上午，南昌起义革命委员会在这里成立，徐特立就任革命委员会委员和党务整顿委员会主任。

中！希望你挺身而出，做出榜样给后辈看看，千万不能倒退啊！"

姜济寰被徐特立的诚恳和激情打动了，他站起身来，在客厅里来回踱了几趟，突然转过身来，紧紧地握住徐特立的手，坚定地说："你的为人我还不知道吗？你说怎么干，就怎么干！我坚决跟共产党走，同你们共患难。"

在徐特立、林伯渠和郭亮的争取下，姜济寰参加了南昌起义。在姜济寰的带动下，国民党江西省政府4个厅长有3个参加了起义，这为起义的顺利进行以及起义后秩序的维护、粮食的筹备、部队的转移等，都创造了极为有利的条件。

"夜行军不算什么事"

1934年10月，由于第五次反围剿的失败，中央红军8万余人被迫进行战略大转移。部队从瑞金出发，带着大量的设备和辎重，还有大批民夫，在山中的羊肠小道上缓慢前行。有时一天只走了二三十里，甚至十几里，经常处于被动挨打的局面。

为了避开敌机的轰炸扫射，躲开敌人的跟踪追击，不让敌人侦察到红军的行动方向，部队经常晚上悄悄地行进。徐特立回忆："我们有几十个担架，有二三十匹马，有几十个药箱子，集中起来，目标很大，行动很慢，飞机来了，就没有办法。跑吧！担架笨重。隐蔽吧！浅草灌木，不能掩蔽。因此，夜行军就成了经常的行动。"

然而，夜行军是极其艰难和充满危险的。由于怕暴露目标，不许说话，不许点火，不许让东西碰出响声。一个跟着一个，前后距离稍一拉开，就会听到低声催促："快跟上。"遇到伸手不见五指的夜晚，就在手臂上缠上白布条，防止掉队。这些方法，可以防止被敌人发现，或者掉队，可一路上因自然环境形成的威胁如路滑、深坑、陡坡、悬崖、河流等，却很难避免，一不小心就可能出危险。可在徐特立眼中，这算得了什么呢?"夜行军不算什么事,天雨路滑黑暗,也是经常的,我们习惯了,可以抵抗一切。妇女儿童也有同样的抵抗力,并不奇怪,算不得什么事。"

征服三座大雪山

1935年6月,红军突破敌人设置的芦山、宝兴防线,随后翻越了长征路上第一座大雪山——夹金山。

夹金山,当地老百姓叫做神仙山,连鸟儿都飞不过去,只有神仙才能登越。还有不少神奇的传说:如果在山上张开嘴,山神会把你掐死;说话的声音大了,山神听到后会立马变天,不是下雨就是下冰雹;上了九坳十三坡,鬼儿子拖住脚,不能坐下,一坐下就永远起不来了。

13日,徐特立跟随部队来到了夹金山前。过雪山的前夜,部队在山下露营。这时,徐特立的伞坏了,也没有油布,没有饲养员和马。晚上,他找了个石板间的凹陷处,因为这样相对比较稳当。可是,睡在两块石板中间,冰冷得简直就好像睡在棺材中一样。上面盖上一幅蓝布,遇上下雨,蓝布便湿了,好在毯子和衣还是干的。

一大早,部队开始登山,从山下就可看到覆盖山顶的积雪,似乎并不远。开始,大家根本意识不到要爬这么高。到了雪界后,人已经是精疲力竭了,白茫茫的积雪刺得睁不开眼睛,又没有路,越往上爬,空气越稀薄,寒气袭人,严重缺氧,呼吸越发困难,嘴唇冻得乌青。半路上还下起雨雪,湿衣湿毯贴在身上,冰冷冷的。

徐特立拄着从苏区以来一直用作拐杖的红缨枪,一步一步向前移,途中还不断地招呼:"同志们,不要坐下,不能停下,坐下就起不来了。"好不容易终于冒着雨雪爬到了山顶,根本不能休息,必须马上下山。这时,雪倒是渐渐停了,往下走相对也没那么费力,但湿衣湿毯紧贴在身上,开始感觉凉得厉害。徐特立干脆加快步伐,时不时还跑上几步，这样身上倒还暖和一些，下山后衣服竟然被体温烘干了。当晚，他们露营在大雪山的山谷中。

翻过夹金山后，徐特立感到精神特别愉快，自认为抵抗力超过一般的同志，更加信心满满了。许多同志称赞徐特立，说他至少可以活到90岁。

24日，红军来到两河口与卓克基之间的另一座雪山前，这座叫做梦笔山的雪山高4100多米，上下山共90里，当地藏族老人说这座白皑皑的雪山是神妖，发起怒来比夹金山厉害多了，因为红军战士们都有了过雪山的经验，所以比较顺利地通过了。徐特立征服的第三座雪山叫做长板山，海拔4800多米，上下80里，有的地方非常陡峭，行走相当困难，上山时徐特立每走几十步就站着休息一会儿，节省体力；下山时就不停地快步前进，赶上队伍。原定走70里在马塘宿营，当徐特立赶到马塘时，队伍还在继续前进，只见桥上插着一面旗子写着："再前进30里，到康猫寺宿营。"政治科的同志都劝他："徐老，都傍晚了，你已走了70多里，从这里到康猫寺一路又没有人家，还是在马塘住下，明天再赶队伍吧！"可徐老呢？"我认为我应该做模范，不应该掉队，我一个人单独去赶队伍。"

"你们不要管我"

长征队伍中，徐特立是年龄最长者，又是德高望重的老教育家，因此，组织上和同志们对他非常尊重，一直对他多加关照。行军途中，每到一个宿营地，同志们一般总想着先安排他的餐宿。但徐特立为了减少同志们的负担，他总是把自己能做的事抢先做好，不让他人动手。每次行军快到宿营地时，他都沿途捡些干柴、拔些野菜，一到营地，就架起两块石头，拿出小脸盆，烧水洗脚，接着便煮点面糊野菜吃。然后，他笑眯眯地对大伙说："我饭也吃过了，脚也洗了，你们不要管我。"如果有同志给他安排了房子或睡觉的门板，他总是说："我已经找到了更好的地方。"他把房子和门板让给伤病员和其他同志，自己抱一小捆禾草或麦秆，挤在人家的门楼里或过道上，铺开禾草麦秆就睡。他的衣服破了，自己缝补；鞋子坏了，自己修钉；肚子饿了，啃野草树根；万一没处住宿，就坐在山坡野地里。

表演猴子捉虱子

尽管长征途中充满着千难万苦，徐特立却始终充满着积极的乐观主义精神。

1935年春节前，部队转战在云贵川一带。艰难的行军和恶劣的环境，使官兵疲惫不堪。在过年的前一天晚上，李伯钊等人筹划了一场联欢会。大家围坐在篝火旁欣赏节目，沉浸在难得的欢乐中。正当大家为李伯钊刚跳完的苏联水兵舞使劲鼓掌时，徐特立反穿羊皮袄，头戴破毡帽，慢慢悠悠走上场。他站在场上并不说话，而是表情认真地将双手伸进羊皮袄里，上一抓、下一挠、左一扭、右一拽，皱紧眉头，捉出个东西，放进嘴里，只听见"噼啪"一声，然后蹙着鼻子说："嗯，这个肥。"他反复做着类似的动作，将虱子在人身上上蹿下跳、令人奇痒难耐的神情表现得淋漓尽致，引得大家捧腹大笑。突然，他停下表演，非常认真地说："孙猴子是大无畏的，不怕天，不怕地，不怕妖魔鬼怪，我们要向他学习，战胜眼前的困难。"停了一下，他又说："猴子不讲卫生，身上长满了虱子，只好一个一个地抓住送进嘴里去吃掉。我们不要学习它，我们要讲究卫生，要洗脸、梳头、洗澡、换洗衣服，不要生虱子。虱子这家伙尽吸我们的血，还传染疾病，要坚决把虱子消灭掉。"

大家听了，才知道徐老的表演，不仅仅逗大家一乐，还在鼓舞士气、进行思想教育呢。

"岁岁不忘歼敌事,朝朝只见诲人忙"

艰苦的长征途中,作为老教育家的徐特立从来不曾忘记教书育人的职责。他抓住一切时机教红军战士学文化。

在行军途中,徐特立想出了许多办法教战士们识字。他在前面战士的斗笠上写几个字,就成为后面战士们的活动识字板,日子长了,战士们识的字也就多了。他叫先头部队把路边宣传鼓动标语上的字写大些,以便于战士们在行军途中辨识。

徐特立还教战士们学拼音。有些年轻女战士调皮地说:"这是外国字,我们不学!"他耐心地解释:"这是我们创造的拼音,是我们自己的,应该学习。将来我们的条件改善了,外国的语言文字也要学习嘛!"徐老鼓励女战士们不仅要做妇女革命的模范,而且要做文化的主人,这样才能在政治、经济、文化等方面,求得妇女的彻底解放。

当部队停下来休息和宿营时,徐特立要战士们以树枝作笔,以大地为纸,在地上写字。他风趣地说:"那是取之不尽,用之不竭的呀!"

▶ 长征路上,徐特立抓住一切机会教指战员们学习文化。图为红军指战员长征路上学文化的雕塑。

朱德和康克清后来写诗称赞徐老:"岁岁不忘歼敌事,朝朝只见诲人忙。"在这样一种艰难的环境下,作为教育家的徐特立,时刻不忘自己的职责,因为他对前途充满必胜的信心,坚信困难只是暂时的,革命成功后一定需要文化。

回湖南宣传抗日

"卖报!卖报!请看八路军代表徐特立先生赴长沙到任的新闻。"

报童阵阵响亮的叫卖声,打破了城市的沉默,过往行人都被这条重要新闻吸引住了,纷纷围拢过来。

"我来一份!"

"我也来一份!"

"给我一份!"

人们争先恐后地购买着。有的当即高兴地阅读起来:"湖南教育家徐特立离湘十余年,昨天下午二时又来长沙。徐鬓发皆白,着灰布短衣,精神奕奕,不减当年气概……"

这是怎么回事呢?原来1936年"西安事变"以后,蒋介石被迫接受了中国共产党"停止内战,一致抗日"的主张,实行了国共合作抗日。中国共产党为了更广泛地发动群众,加强抗日民族统一战线的工作,在重庆、西安、武汉、长沙、桂林等地,设立了八路军办事处或通讯处。这年年底,徐特立担任八路军(后改名

◀ 担任国民革命军第八路军高级参议、驻湘代表时的徐特立。

第十八集团军）高级参议、驻湘代表，回到湖南领导八路军驻湘通讯处工作。

这时，从国内形势看，我国最大的城市上海已经沦陷，国民政府所在地南京也十分危急。面对国破家亡的困境，湖南人民心急如焚，对打败日本侵略者，很多人信心不足。现在，一听说八路军派代表来了，便如迷雾中的航船看到了灯塔，顿时感到有了希望。特别又听说代表就是他们尊敬的老教育家徐特立先生，大家怎能不高兴呢？大家奔走相告，纷纷前往通讯处驻地——寿星街二号访问。他们中有工人、农民，也有教师、青年学生和记者；有长沙市区的，也有从湖南各县远道专程而来的，从清晨到深夜，络绎不绝，寿星街天天就像赶庙会一样热闹。

人们见到徐特立，就如见到尊敬的师长，是那样的信任，那样的亲切，向他请教各种问题。

"共产党与国民党是死对头，能合作抗日吗？"一个记者问。

"可以，共产党、国民党，都是中国人，都是炎黄子孙，只要不愿当亡国奴，就应当齐心合力，抵抗外来侵略。至于国共合作后，是否再次分裂，我认为历史的发展是不会循环的，而是不断前进的。人民是不会同意分裂的，谁要再搞分裂只能自取灭亡！"徐特立微笑着说。

"即便国共两党能够联合抗战，可是日本很强大，我们能打赢吗？"一个青年学生接着问。这可是大家最关心的问题。

"能！一定能打赢！"徐特立坚定地回答。他用毛泽东同志《论持久战》的理论，仔细地分析："我们说能打赢，并不是像有些人说的那样：日本没有煤、没有铁，抗战六个月，敌人就会自己完蛋，这是不符合事实的。我们说能打赢，是打持久战，慢慢地打，多打几年。我们国家人口多，可以慢慢把敌人的人力、物力消耗掉，把自己的力量发展起来，那时，不是它来战胜我们，而是我们要战胜它了！抗日抗战，是一场关系到国家民族生死存亡的斗争。只要举国上下紧密团结，组成坚强的抗日民族统一战线，将抗战坚持到底，胜利是完全有把握的。"

"共产党是真心抗日的吗？"又一个学生高声提出疑问。

◀ 寿星街二号八路军驻湘通讯处旧照。

徐特立回答："我们共产党是坚持抗日到底的,是真诚讲团结的,这一点是不容怀疑的。现大敌当前,'兄弟阋于墙,外御其侮',国共两党联合抗日,是大势所趋,人心所向。"徐特立还列举种种事实,说明八路军会越战越强。他满怀信心地说:"打游击是共产党红军的拿手戏,游击战几乎是百战百胜。有人问:共产党、八路军有没有武器,有没有兵工厂?我们回答:有!又问:在哪里?我们说:过去设在南京,现在设在东京。就是夺取敌人的武器武装自己,用游击战占领敌人的后方作为我们的根据地。"

徐特立越讲越激昂,边讲边打着手势,听的人都被他紧紧吸引住了。他真诚的态度,风趣、生动、雄辩有力的话语,解开了人们心头的疙瘩,点燃了人们心中的希望之火。

徐特立在长沙,经常深入学校、机关等去讲演,每次都有成百上千的听众。有一次,他在银宫电影院讲演抗日救国"十大纲领",一下子到了三四千人,把整个会场挤得水泄不通,门外站不下了,许多听众就爬到窗台上听。

为了扩大抗日的宣传,让更多的人了解中国共产党的正确主张,徐特立还把这些讲话稿登载在报刊上,并经常为长沙《抗战周刊》《救亡日报》等撰写文章。

由于徐特立和同志们的出色工作,湖南的抗日群众运动掀起了新的高潮,成立了妇救会、农抗会、工抗会、学抗会等许多抗日救亡的群众团体,成千上万的热血青年杀上了抗日前线,有些还奔赴延安,走上了革命的道路。

"抢去了不少说书人的买卖"

长沙城里有个火宫殿,历来是说书、卖艺、摆零食摊贩的场所。每天有许多码头工人、拖板车的苦力、拉黄包车的脚夫等当时社会底层的人们,聚集在这里娱乐、饮食,非常热闹。

一天早晨,徐特立来到这里,先是坐在那里静静地喝茶,看看人多起来时,借了一条宽板凳往上一站,就大声演讲起来。他从中国共产党的抗日主张,讲到抗日战争的光明前途;从抗日民族统一战线,讲到湖南一些顽固分子破坏抗战的罪行。他说:"现在有些人搜刮钱财,说要购买抗战用的飞机,建设防空设施,可是飞机和防空设施都在哪里了?我告诉大家,老百姓的钱被刮去修公馆去了。我们要向他们大声疾呼:赶快停止假抗日、大

▶ 为了宣传共产党的抗日主张,徐特立经常在长沙市民集中的火宫殿等地进行抗日演讲。图为火宫殿旧照。

发国难财的活动，把钱拿出来购买飞机大炮。"徐特立义正辞严，一口气讲了好几个钟头，把听说书的、看卖艺的、喝茶的、吃饭的，都吸引了过来，使喧闹的火宫殿变成了一个大会场。

当天，长沙有家报纸对徐特立的讲演作了十分形象的描述："不要小看了这个地方，老教育家徐特立先生还在这里讲过话呢！徐先生本来是深入民间的，以他那生动的民间语言，把国家大事说得很周详，抢去了不少说书人的买卖。听众越来越多，徐先生讲了又讲，到了午餐的时候，大家公请了徐先生一顿。这充分地表现了那一群的民众，并不是不关心国事的。"

"把国家的前途、民族的解放摆在第一位"

释放政治犯，是抗日战争时期国共两党合作协议的一个重要内容。徐特立主持八路军驻湘通讯处工作，多次向国民党当局交涉，要求释放被关押的政治犯。

一天，徐特立接到可靠消息：原中国工农红军抗日先遣军第二十师参谋长乔信明等30多位同志，从国民党江西监狱被解到长沙陆军监狱。他决定立即到监狱去探望他们。

徐特立来到长沙陆军监狱。监狱长知道徐特立在湖南人民群众中的威望很高，又是八路军驻湘通讯处的代表，估计不让他探望是不行的，于是为了表示对他的尊重，下令打开监狱大门。

徐特立不管国民党监狱的各种规矩，站在监狱的院子里高喊："政治犯集合！"乔信明等同志缓步走出牢房，他们做梦也想不到能在国民党的监狱院子里见到我党的高级领导人、毛泽东主席的老师徐特立。徐特立一个一个地与同志们握手，表示亲切慰问，难友们激动得流下了热泪。徐特立笑容满面地向难友们讲了话。他先讲了国共重新合作、一致抗日的形势，又讲到党的抗日方针和政策，最后满怀激情地对大家说：

▶ 经徐特立斡旋，张治中释放了关押在长沙陆军监狱的中国工农红军抗日先遣军二十师参谋长乔信明等30多位同志。图为当时的长沙陆军监狱。

"同志们，太阳快出来了，天就要亮了！不要着急，要好好的保重身体。你们要鼓起斗志，坚定信心，新的斗争在等待着你们。"

从监狱回到通讯处后，徐特立马上开列了乔信明等30多个同志的名单，要求国民党当局立即释放，可是国民党顽固派不但不予释放，还偷偷把他们押送到湖南桃源乡下的一个中学里，妄图杀害他们。

徐特立听到这一消息，满腔怒火，直接去找国民党湖南省政府主席张治中进行交涉。

"释放政治犯，这是国共合作谈判桌上签了字的，你们为什么背信弃义，拒不执行？"徐特立义正言辞地质问。

"徐先生，不必动气，不必动气，有话好说嘛！"张治中劝说。

"好说话，就应该赶快放人。"徐特立寸步不让。

"放人嘛，据我所知，狱中没有贵党同志，徐老先生所列名单不会是道听途说吧？"

"什么道听途说！他们是从江西监狱刚刚解到的，我早已去狱中探望过了，想不到张主席消息这样闭塞！"

张治中是国民党中比较开明的人士，在徐特立的坚决要求下，同意释放乔信明等狱中同志。由于徐特立的营救，先后有几批同志得以出狱，为党保存了许多重要的骨干力量。

就在徐特立为营救乔信明等同志而日夜奔忙时，他的小儿子徐厚本在从延安回长沙的途中染上了伤寒病，因病情严重被送往医院抢救，可徐特立顾不上去看一眼儿子。等乔信明等最终获释，他赶到医院时，见到的是一死一伤。儿子不治而亡，未能同父亲见上最后一面；儿媳刘萃英因伤心过度，从二楼楼梯一头栽下去，滚到一楼，不省人事。

刘萃英虽然得救了，但落下了十几年的头疼症。徐厚本是徐特立的小儿子，也是他当时唯一的儿子，他的大儿子徐笃本早在1927年大革命期间就为革命牺牲了。可以想象，年已六旬的徐特立心中是何等的伤痛！

后来，徐特立的孙女徐禹强问起此事时，徐特立沉痛地说："30多名同志是我们党多大的财富呀！在30∶1面前，我只能把国家的前途、民族的解放摆在第一位。当我赶到湘雅医院时，见到的是一死一伤的场面。你父亲已经去世，你母亲头上包着纱布，躺在病床上，我悲痛不已。"

熊立诚去世后,徐特立深感悲痛。
他将两人的合影装在随身口袋并经常拿出照片看。

第五章

家风家教,遗泽后人

与结发妻"童携到老"

徐特立的结发妻子名叫熊立诚，11岁就过门到徐家做童养媳，直到82岁去世。两人70年如一日，相敬相爱、相濡以沫、相互支持，始终坚守着忠贞不渝的爱情。1957年12月徐老太太过生日的时候，有人送了一幅横幅，上面写了四个大字——"童携到老"，看了的人都说写得太好了，是徐老夫妻两人的真实写照。

作为一位职业革命家、教育家，徐特立长期离家在外。因此，在家庭生活方面，他们一家过着并不平静的日子，而是饱经困难，饱尝别离之苦。

出于对人生理想信念的追求，徐特立早在1905年就离开家乡，外出办学和从事教育工作，在家时间少，在外时候多；1919年，为了学习新知识，他又远渡重洋赴法国勤工俭学，与妻子分别达5年之久；1927年，他加入中国共产党，投身革命，先后到江西参加南昌起义，到苏联学习马列主义，在中央苏区开展文化教育工作，后来又跟随中央红军长征到陕北，在陕甘宁革命根据地开展文化教育工作，10年间与妻子音讯断绝。抗战初期，徐特立回到湖南主持八路军驻湘通讯处工作，两

▶ 徐特立、熊立诚夫妇合影。

人终于有了短暂的一年多的团聚,但从1940年起又是两地分离。直到1949年全国解放后,两人才终于得以在北京团聚。

虽然相聚日短、分离日长,但徐特立与熊立诚始终心相通、情相系。

熊立诚11岁到徐家,从小帮助操持家务,后来支持徐特立破产读书,支持徐特立舍家办学,更支持徐特立走上革命道路。对于这样一位虽然没有文化却有见地、有胆识,不顾一切支持自己读书、办学、革命的妻子,徐特立充满感激、充满爱意。徐老的外孙女徐舟回忆道:外祖父常跟孙辈谈起外祖母的优秀品德,始终如一地关心爱护外祖母。在外的日子里,徐特立一直惦记着妻子、惦记着孩子。在繁忙的工作之余,他经常抽出时间给妻子和孩子写信。

1939年,徐特立写信给在家里的小女儿徐陌青,反复叮嘱她要孝顺母亲、关心照顾母亲。他在信中写道:"你的母亲年已七十,她不独维持了一家,并且办高级小学共十三年,培养了许多学生。她没有念过书,却替地方教育事业出了很多力。许多读书识字的女人不如她,我是很尊敬她的。你是她所生,应该特别孝敬她。家中许多困难你们夫妇如能帮助,请你尽可能帮助。如不能帮助,还是把田卖出一些。"话语不多,但纸短情长,从中可以看出徐特立对妻子、对家庭的深深牵挂。

由于长期孤身一人生活,不少好心的同志私下劝徐特立找个女朋友,但徐特立坚决不同意。他说:"我是一个有血、有肉、有情感的人。我爱自己的家庭,爱自己的妻室儿女。……我的妻子是童养媳,没有文化,从小与我患难与共。我一直在外从事教育和革命事业,她在家里抚养儿女,还兼劳动兼办学,她支持了我的事业,也成全了我的事业。我一生提倡妇女解放,我假如丢弃了她,岂不又增加了一个受苦难的妇女?"听者无不为之感动。

中华人民共和国成立后,徐特立马上把妻子接到北京。这时,两人都已是古稀之年,终于得以团聚。在朝夕相处的日子里,徐特立关心体贴夫人,经常对身边的工作人员说:"你们对我的生活不要特殊照顾,

▶ 1960年2月，熊立诚去世，徐特立伤心不已。

可一定要在生活上照顾好老太太。她是家庭妇女，没有文化，容易有自卑感，不要叫她有思想负担。"他每次到外地休养，总是带夫人一道去；吃饭时，把好一点的菜让她吃；自己穿着简单朴素，却不时给妻子买点好布料做新衣服；家里的钢丝床坏了几根弹簧，自己睡坏了的一边，好的一边让给妻子。

熊立诚去世后，徐特立深感悲痛，怀念不已。他将两人合影的照片，一直装在随身口袋里，走到哪里带到哪里，并经常拿出照片观看，以致照片中间有了深深的折痕。

"要先想为社会出力"

徐特立长期在外从事教育和革命工作，很多时候无暇顾及家庭，但作为教育家的职业意识，又使他非常注意对子孙后代的教育。他指出："作为革命的前辈、作为父母、作为家长，时刻都不应忘记教育子女的责任。因为在我们这个社会里，子女不仅是自己家庭的成员，自己的后代，而且也是社会的成员，是整个革命的后代。他们的好坏，不仅关系着自己的家庭，而且关系着社会。"因此，"要想使我们的后代都能成为革命的红色接班人，并且希望他们能够'后来居上'，这就应该从思想、学习、生活等各个方面来关心和帮助他们。生活上关心他们，使他们能吃得饱、穿得暖，精力充沛地去学习和劳动，自然是重要的、必需的。但是更重要的是要关心他们的思想状况和政治生活。"

徐特立与妻子熊立诚一共生育过8个孩子，但长大成人的只有4个：大女儿徐守珍、大儿子徐笃本、小女儿徐陌青、小儿子徐厚本。徐特立对子女严格要求，谆谆教诲。他经常讲，青年人一定要多替别人着想，要为社会多做些工作，而不要过多地想自己、想家庭。

徐笃本是徐特立的大儿子，出生于1906年。当时的徐特立，正在一心一意地实践着自己教育救国的理想，离开五美老家，在长沙城里的周氏女塾（后改名周南女子中学）、修业学校等学校任教。后来，徐笃本到长沙的一所中学读书，有人给他介绍女朋友，他自己也打算接受。但徐特立知道后，语重心长地对儿子说："你还年轻，应该为革命刻苦学习，在事业上打好基础，做一个有益于社会的人；要先想为社会出力，不能先安排自己的小家庭，如果大家都只顾一己之私，社会怎能前进呢？"

听了父亲的话后，徐笃本打消了恋爱、成家的念头，将心思全部投入学习和工作之中。他刻苦学习，认真做事，关心社会问题和老百姓的疾苦，中学时就秘密入党，成为我党的早期党员。第一次大革命时期，年仅19岁的徐笃本积极参加农民运动，担任湖南醴陵农民协会主席，把那里的农民运动搞得蓬蓬勃勃，如火如荼。这时，当父亲徐特立再问到他的婚姻问题时，他回答说："现在没有时间谈这个了，斗争那么激烈，革命的事还忙不过来呢。"就这样，徐笃本把全部精力都扑在革命事业上。

大量繁重艰苦的革命工作使徐笃本积劳成疾，1927年病逝于长沙仁术医院。他去世后，组织为他开了隆重的追悼会，将他的灵柩运回老家安葬，当时很多人还为他的灵柩送行。

徐笃本去世时，年仅21岁，还没来得及成家。

让子女到应该去的地方去

徐厚本是徐特立的小儿子,出生于1917年,两岁多时,父亲徐特立就远赴欧洲勤工俭学,一别5年,直到1924年7月才回国。回到国内后,徐特立继续实践自己的教育救国梦想,马上投入到办学之中,先是创办了长沙女子师范,后来又担任长沙师范、湖南省立第一女子师范学校校长。在繁忙的工作中,徐特立难得与家人团聚一次,但这种生活很快就被打断。1927年,国民党右派叛变革命,徐特立毅然加入中国共产党,从此走上职业革命家的生涯,与亲人、孩子一别就是10年。

在这10年中,徐厚本先读完了小学,上中学后,因家庭经济困难便于1935年从长沙县第一中学(次年改名长沙县立初级中学)辍学,到长沙大车修理厂当了学徒。1937年12月,徐特立作为国民革命军第十八集团军高级参议、驻湘代表,由延安回湖南主持八路军驻湘通讯处工作。通讯处的其中一项工作是组织、动员进步青年去延安参加革命,徐厚本知道后动了心,便跟父亲说了自己的想法。虽然徐特立第一次大革命时已有丧子之痛,但考虑到延安正需要汽车修理工,便毫不犹豫同意了儿子和儿媳一起去延安投身抗日战争的决定。可是,徐老太太舍不得他们远走,后来又只同意儿子去,要儿媳留下来。徐特立就做妻子的工作:"儿子和媳妇是去学习,去干革命,应该让他们一起去,我们怎么能将他们拆散呢?"又说:"儿子、媳妇,我们是要疼爱的,但叫他们总是蹲在自己身边,就会耽误他们远大的前程。父母疼爱子女,就要让他们到应该去的地方去,为社会做一番事业……"这是多么长远的眼光、多么深沉的父爱啊。

在徐特立的支持下,徐厚本夫妇于1938年春奔赴延安,两人在陕北公学学习

▶ 徐特立的小儿子徐厚本。

了 6 个月，于 1938 年 7 月被组织派回长沙。谁能料到，徐厚本在途中染上了伤寒，回到长沙时已是病情严重，虽经医治仍不幸去世。这对年已 61 岁的徐特立是一个多大的打击！

要多想群众和政府的困难

徐特立对子女的关心，对他们的爱护、帮助，从来不以宠爱、以物质上的关心为满足，而是从"革命第一、工作第一、他人第一"的崇高目标出发，言传身教，循循善诱，饱含深情。

徐特立的大女儿徐守珍出生于 1904 年，自幼爱好美术。在父亲的支持下，徐守珍去了男女合校的岳云中学。

中学毕业后，徐守珍于 1927 年考入上海新华艺术学校，是党领导的赤色工会的积极分子，1928 年因参加地下党外围组织的活动被捕，与家人失去了联系。出狱后不久，上海沦陷，面临失业的徐守珍经人介绍在上海某日伪机关找了一份看大门、送信件的差使，以谋生路。此后，她与父亲徐特立完全失去了联系。

1949 年，新中国成立，徐守珍得知父亲在新政府中担任高级领导，非常高兴地来到北京，失散 20 多年的父女重逢了。了解到女儿这些年的艰苦生活，徐特立心里非常难过，心底非常希望女儿能在身边，但想到中华人民共和国刚刚成立，百废待兴，国家在政治、经济、文化教育等方面困难重重，于是做女儿的工作，让她不要光想到自己的困难，要多想想政府的困难。徐守珍原以为作为共产党高级干部的父亲会答

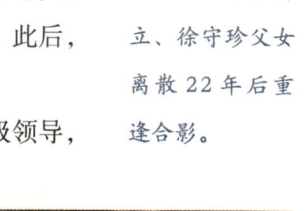

▼ 1949 年徐特立、徐守珍父女离散 22 年后重逢合影。

应她到北京来工作,听了父亲的话后,安心地回上海工作去了。

在给女儿的信中,徐特立说:"我已七十四岁,每天还要做八小时的工作。生活费公家尽量给我,但时局艰难,我不愿多开支,所以我不希望你北上。……你们如果需要我党录用,那么需要比他人更勤劳更努力,以表示是共产主义者的亲属。"此后,徐特立多次写信给徐守珍夫妇,鼓励女儿女婿政治上要求进步、关心国家的振兴。他说:"你们还不是共产主义者,这不是组织问题,首要的还是你们的思想问题和行动问题……我希望你们每一日、每一时都不要只为自己着想。上半晚想自己的困难,下半晚一定要想群众的困难,以及政府的困难,机关负责人的困难。这样去做人,自己的个人苦恼没有了,胸怀开阔了,就不知不觉变成了一个先进分子。"

随着"左"倾运动的开展,安心工作、积极上进的徐守珍再次受到影响。1957年,徐守珍受潘汉年案件株连,被定为"反革命"。徐特立得知这一消息后,非常担忧,忙叫徐舟去上海了解情况。徐舟找到当地组织,得到的答复是情况属实。徐特立一方面相信自己的女儿不会是反革命,但另一方面必须相信组织的认定。在亲人和组织二者之间,徐特立耐心地劝导孩子们相信组织。徐守珍默默地接受改造,1973年含冤去世。十一届三中全会后,随着潘汉年案件的彻底平反,徐守珍案于1985年平反昭雪。冤案终得平反,历史终究还人以清白,九泉之下的徐特立可以瞑目了。

"诚实地劳动,始终做有益于人民的人"

徐陌青是徐特立的小女儿,出生于1916年。这是一个从小就支撑家业的孩子。1927年秋,第一次国内革命战争失败,徐特立的大儿子徐笃本牺牲,年逾五十的徐特立跟着共产党走了,大女儿徐守珍被捕失踪。家庭的剧变,给熊立诚接二连三的打击,使她精神接近失常。那时，徐陌青年仅11岁，徐厚本才10岁。面对家庭的变故，11岁的徐陌青毅然挑起家庭的生活重担。她要烧饭、洗衣、种菜、养猪，要照顾母亲，照顾弟弟上学，还得带一个年仅4岁、还不懂事的外甥女徐舟。

因而，她连小学都没能完整念完，在繁重的家务劳动中度过了自己的童年和少年时期。在她的努力支撑下，弟弟上了中学，并于16岁时结婚，娶了刘萃英，这个家才由她和弟媳共同支撑起来，但生活是十分困难的。由于过度操劳，她自小得了哮喘病，却也没有钱治疗。

1937年，抗战全面爆发后，徐特立回到长沙，毫不犹豫地鼓励小儿子徐厚本夫妇去延安学习。徐陌青也想去，但想到年已61岁的老母亲熊立诚没有人照料，便放弃了这个机会。在父亲的建议下，她决定学医，以便为抗战服务。她进了长沙自治女校护士班学习，毕业后到长沙重伤医院工作。这所医院接收了不少从前线送回来的重伤员，护理任务非常繁重。徐陌青刻苦学习，勤奋工作，成了一名光荣的白衣战士，走上了救死扶伤的道路。在这里，她结识了一位热心抗日救亡、有学识才干的外科大夫卢振声，后来两人结为了夫妻。

抗日战争期间，徐特立曾两次派人来信说要接夫人、孙女去延安，并叫徐陌青与丈夫同去。但她想，父亲工作繁忙，母亲有病，还有外甥女需要照顾，于是询问母亲的意见后决定留在家乡，照顾和支撑整个大家庭。

解放战争时期，由于不时接到组织上送来的有关父亲徐特立及弟媳刘萃英的信息以及银元等生活补助，徐陌青在家里更是尽心地照顾母亲及外甥女，以便父亲和弟媳安心革命。

1949年全国解放，徐特立在北京定居下来后，马上安排人将留在五美老家的家人接到北京。徐陌青被分配到北京铁路医院工作。徐陌青一家本来可以和父母亲住在一起，但她觉得，父亲是党中央的领导人，自己只是个老百姓，还是另住一个地方好些。于是，他们一家居住在一个大杂院的一套两居室里，买了些旧家具，仍然过着俭朴勤劳的生活，同院的邻居甚至不知道她是徐特立的女儿。

在北京，徐陌青一家一直过着包干制生活。她积极参加机关干部学习，1952年到北京铁路总医院工作，1956年加入中国共产党，在护士岗位上默默工作、默默奉献，直至1977年退休。

徐陌青一生听从父亲的告诫，靠自己的诚实劳动生活，过着勤俭朴实的生活，她从不对组织提不合理的要求，即使是自己应该得到的，如果组织上没有考虑或有困难，她也从不提出。她经常对孩子们说："作为老人家的后代，要诚实地劳动，始终做有益于人民的人，才不愧对老人家，决不要给老人家脸上抹黑！"金玉之言，掷地有声。

正如徐特立外孙女徐舟所说："小姨的一生，没有惊天动地的业绩，也没有一串串辉煌的'名号'，只有诚实的劳动、简朴的生活、忠厚的为人。"北京铁路总医院在《徐陌青同志生平》中写道："（徐陌青同志）几十年从不计较职务高低，待遇高低，服从组织安排，党叫干什么就干什么，从未向组织提过任何困难与要求，一贯任劳任怨，做好护士工作，严于律己，默默地奉献，不愧为无产阶级革命家徐特立的好女儿……"

"你应该有自己的生活"

徐特立对儿媳、干女儿徐乾的悉心关心、教诲，更是显现出一位革命家、教育家的宽广心胸与感人情怀。

徐特立的儿媳刘萃英也是长沙县人，1933年与徐厚本结婚。当时徐特立正在江西中央苏区主持教育工作，与家里完全失去联系。因此，两人的婚事是由老太太熊立诚操持的。婚后，刘萃英协助婆婆熊立诚和小姑徐陌青一起操持家务，丈夫徐厚本则在长沙大车修理厂当学徒。1936年，刘萃英生下女儿徐禹强。

1937年，随着抗日战争全面爆发，国共实现第二次合作。年底，徐特立由延安回到长沙，主持八路军驻湘通讯处工作。当时徐老非常忙，根本没有空闲时间回家。刘萃英带着女儿，跟着熊老夫人一起去长沙城里找徐老，这才认识了老人家。由于通讯处刚成立不久，缺少服务人员，通讯处主任王凌波就将刘萃英留下来做勤务工作。

1938年春，在徐特立的支持、鼓励下，刘萃英将1岁多的女儿交给婆婆，和丈夫一起赶赴延安，在陕北公学学习6个月后毕业，和丈夫一起被组织上派回湖南工作。

◀ 徐特立的儿媳刘萃英。

不幸的是，丈夫徐厚本途中染病，回到长沙后医治无效去世，留下她们一对孤儿寡母，这使年仅23岁的刘萃英精神上遭受到极大的打击，陷入了无限哀思之中。刘萃英自己在医院因一时伤心过度，不慎摔伤，从此落下头疼症。失夫之痛加上时时发作的头疼症，折磨得她痛不欲生。她想到了死，想以死寻求解脱，有一天一狠心上了吊，幸亏及时被人发现。

徐特立一方面忍受着巨大的丧子之痛，另一方面要安慰儿媳，帮助她早点从痛苦中解脱出来。此外，为了防止老伴伤心过度，他还要与儿媳一起隐瞒儿子的死讯。他多次给儿媳写信，安慰她，鼓励她开始新的生活。在1938年夏的一封信中，他说："你是我们家里的人，你的孩子也是我们家的骨血，你还年轻，应该有自己的生活。你结婚以后，我们便不以翁媳相称，你做我的女儿也可以，作为同志也可以。在你结婚之前，你的生活我还是要负责的。"

为了解决刘萃英的后顾之忧，徐特立决定把她当作自己的女儿加以关心、照顾。1938年11月长沙文夕大火后，徐特立带着老伴、孙女和儿媳，随八路军驻湘通讯处，经衡阳、邵阳，一起转移至广西桂林。在桂林，有位男子追求刘萃英，要和她结婚。刘萃英思前想后，理不清头绪，感到心烦意乱、孤立无援。徐特立察觉这一情况后，立即有针对性地给刘萃英写了三封信，像对待亲生女儿一样地关心和教导。在信中，徐老为刘萃英指出解决婚姻问题的原则：青年人选择伴侣的条件，首要的是厚道、品行端正、不轻于弃妻、年岁相当。还帮刘萃英分析说："他（指那位男子）是党员，政治上很进步。在革命队伍里，选择配偶，不是为了钱财和地位，而是要选择先进的人。同时，你在他帮助下，可以继续前进，还有入党的希望。"就这样，徐老鼓励刘萃英勇敢地寻找自己的新生活。面对徐老的真诚关爱和教导，刘萃英很快从痛苦与烦恼中解脱出来："老人家对我这样真诚的关怀，使我感动。但我怎忍心离开这样慈祥可亲、德隆望重的老人呢？……我拒绝了这桩婚事，并且请求再去延安学习和工作。老人家理解我，信任我，他同意了我的请求。"于是，刘萃英又踏上了去延安的道路。

为刘萃英改名"徐乾"

在真诚关心刘萃英生活的同时，徐特立更是极力支持她的革命愿望，并为此费了一番苦心。一是想方设法瞒住夫人熊立诚。为了不使老太太因儿媳远离久别而悲伤，徐特立与刘萃英相约仍然瞒着她，只是对她说，让她和小孙女暂时回湖南，让刘萃英留在桂林。二是苦心孤诣地为儿媳改名。徐老送老太太和小孙女走的那天，特意来到刘萃英住的院子，亲切地对她说："你要走了，我把你的名字改一改吧。"他拿出一张纸片，上面写着"徐乾"两个字。当时，刘萃英虽然不能马上理解这个名字中的深意，却深深地体会到了老人家的一片深情，心里有很多很多话想向老人家倾诉，但是，刚要启齿却泣不成声了。

在徐特立的理解和支持下，徐乾于1940年1月踏上了去延安的路程，先是进入陕北公学学习，后入中国女子大学，正式走上革命道路。同年秋，徐特立回到延安，特地写了一封信，向徐乾详细解释"乾"的意义。他说："君子终日乾乾，夕惕若厉，无咎。乾，健也。终日乾乾，即终日健进不已；惕，警觉也。终日乾乾，至晚还加警惕，且若有凶厉

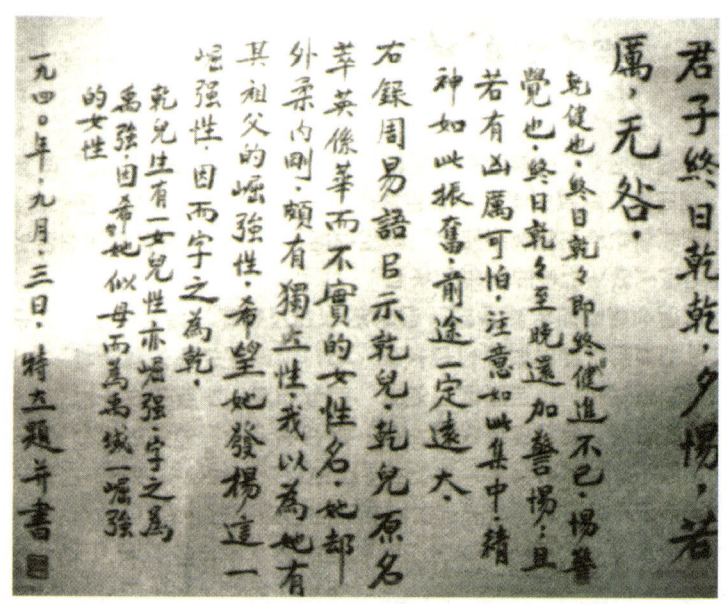

◀ 徐特立致信儿媳刘萃英,讲明为她改名"徐乾"的含义。

可怕。注意如此集中,精神如此振奋,前途一定远大。"

由此可以看出,徐特立为儿媳改名,不仅满含着老人家的一番情谊,而且寄予了父辈对儿女的厚望。正如徐乾所说:"一个人叫什么名字,并不含有重大的意义,名字的雅俗,更不能决定一个人思想境界的高下,但通过老爹爹为我改名这件事,使我体会到老人家对下一代成长的无微不至的关怀。"

徐老带着大家拔青稞。青稞又滑又粗又硬,可他却毫不在意。

第六章

一代师表，世之楷模

两个油粑粑

徐特立有一个非常难得的品质,这就是"他人第一"。正如李维汉所说:"毫不利己,专门利人,助人为乐,关心同志,这是徐老一贯的美德。徐老就是这样一个心中只有别人,而无自己,一事当前先替别人打算,把困难留给自己,把方便送给别人的人。"

1934年12月,中央红军占领湖南通道。在这里,党中央召开紧急会议,研究红军进军方向,决定放弃北出湘西与红二、六军团会合的原定计划,改向敌人兵力薄弱的贵州进军。

进入初冬时节,南方仍是雨水相对充沛的季节。徐老跟着部队在滂沱大雨中行军,已经整整一天了。这一天里,大家都嚼着生米爬山,翻过了一座又一座的大山,傍晚到达一个小集镇时,大家已经又冷又饿又累。

"这下可该好好休息一下,做顿热饭吃了吧?"大家心想。

可是,连长传达了总部的命令:"在这里休息片刻,继续赶路。"

即使只有片刻的休息,大家也想趁这个难得的机会,买点熟东西吃。小镇上人欢马叫,顿时热闹起来,镇上仅有的两家小店铺,一下子就挤满了人,围了个水泄不通。稍微慢了一点的,只好站在人墙外干着急。

一个警卫员费了很大的劲,才买来两个油粑粑,便赶紧给徐老送去。"徐老,快吃吧!"边说边往他手里塞。

"大家都在饿肚子,我怎么能例外呢!"徐老说什么也不肯接。

大家见他不肯要,都劝说:

"徐老,您年纪大,已经几天没吃热东西了,买来了就吃吧!"

……

徐老看见路旁的担架,想起担架上的高烧的伤员,已经几天没吃东西了,灵机一动,对警卫员说:"那就一人一个吧!"

徐老接过油粑粑,没等警卫员回过神来,已跑到担架旁边去了。他躬下身子，用亲切的眼光看了看伤员，然后，把油粑粑撕成一小块一小块，全都塞进了伤员的嘴里。

两张老羊皮

红军来到了川康边界的夹金山，这是长征途中第一座人迹罕至的大雪山。

雪山地区天气非常寒冷，可大家的衣服在过大渡河前为了减轻身上的负荷而丢掉了，再也没有可加的衣服。这时，先头部队给他们送来了两只羊，这可是难得的美味。他们先把羊宰了，让大家饱餐了一顿，又用篝火烘烤剥下的羊皮。

"徐老和谢老，年纪大，身体又不好，穿得那么少，怎么能过雪山呢？"李坚真说，"就把这羊皮给他们御寒吧！"

大家一致叫好。

"徐老，你来披上这块羊皮吧！"同志们拿着羊皮和绳子走到徐特立身边，准备把羊皮捆在他身上。

"不要，不要，我还能坚持。你们拿去给谢老吧！他的身体比我差。"徐特立忙摇着手说。

"徐老，您就披上吧！这里还有一块是给谢老的。"有人举起另一块羊皮说。

"一块不够，护了前面，护不了后面。他身体弱，又在生病，两块都给他吧！"他坚持说。

同志们看他这么坚决，又那么真诚，只好给谢觉哉送去。

"徐老不要，就给其他同志吧！我怎么好意思老让他照顾呢！"谢觉哉也坚决不要。

"觉哉，我们可是情同手足的同志呀，还说什么照顾不照顾的，你不要老放在心里不自在。"徐特立亲切地安慰道。

大家看他俩你推我让，都为两位老人的深厚情谊所感动，不知听谁的好。

"你们站着干什么，还不帮谢老把羊皮捆好。"徐特立急中生智。

大家把谢觉哉围起来，七手八脚地用绳子把两块羊皮捆在他身上。

徐特立看着，开心地呵呵笑了。

谢觉哉感动得热泪盈眶，也笑了。

这两位患难相交、生死与共的革命老人之间的感人情谊，很快就在红军队伍中传为佳话，成为鼓舞战士们不畏艰难、勇往直前的精神动力。

"现在是我们讲客气的时候吗？"

1935年夏，红军开始穿越荒无人烟、一望无边的草地。

过草地，粮食就是生命。对于红军战士来讲，一个非常关键的问题就是要准备粮食。可是，当地的藏族老百姓，由于不了解红军是支什么样的队伍，早就躲起来了，见不到一个人。

正好地里的青稞麦都熟了，还没有收割。总部就指示士兵们留下银元和字条，割田里的青稞麦来解决粮食问题。寨子里找不到镰刀，大家只好用手拔。

徐特立带着大家一蔸一蔸地拔。青稞麦秆又滑、又粗、又硬，只拔几下，手就被划破了，可他却毫不在意，跟没事一样，一边拔，还一边谈笑风生，坚持和大家一起把青稞麦拔完。

青稞麦拔完了，却又找不到脱壳的石臼和磨盘，于是，大家只好用手搓。

"您老年纪大，拔了几天青稞麦，双手都是伤痕，不要再搓了。"同志们劝他不要搓。

"为什么不要我搓？难道我不要吃饭？"徐特立装着生气地板着脸说，"要吃饭，当然有我的份。不让我搓，想饿死我呀？"

长征路上，同志们都摸熟了徐老的脾气，知道要劝住他是不可能的，只好加紧搓，以便快点搓完，好让他休息。

壳脱完了，徐老就撵着大家去休息，自己却到处察看，把散落在地上的每一颗青稞麦都捡到袋子里。他说："多几颗青稞麦，就有可能多使一个同志走出草地，多为革命保存一份力量啊！"

▲ 徐特立与谢觉哉的合影。

为了应对随时可能出现的粮食危机，徐特立不舍得吃发给他的青稞麦，尽量找野菜、草根、树皮等充饥。

这天，徐老发现正在患病的好朋友谢觉哉的青稞麦没有了。看着谢觉哉越来越苍白的面孔、骨瘦如柴的身体，赶紧拿出自己忍饥节省的全部粮食，毫不犹豫地倒给谢觉哉。

其实，在这种时候，在这样的环境下，谁心里都非常清楚，粮食意味着什么，更何况当时他也身患痢疾。

谢觉哉不肯要："徐老呀，你的年纪比我大。长征开始以来，不论是行军，还是宿营，总是你照顾我的时候多。进草地这么多天来，我看到你光吃着野菜和草根，没有吃粮食，现在你怎么能把干粮全部送给我呢？还是留给自己吧！"

"觉哉，现在是我们讲客气的时候吗？我的体质比你好，吃点野菜，还能对付，可你如果再不吃点粮食就不行了。我无论如何不能看着你倒下去啊！"

听到徐特立这肺腑之言，晶莹的泪珠从谢觉哉的眼角滚了出来。

对此，谢觉哉一直念念不忘。他说："要不是徐老让给我的那些粮食，鼓舞了我的精神和增强了我的体力，也许我已经永久地躺在草地上了。多少年来，我对此总不能忘怀啊。"

1937年在延安，党中央给徐老祝贺六十大寿，谢老在《寿特立同志六十初度》诗中写道：

> 漠漠沮洳地，峨峨暴冻冈。
> 是谁皆束腹，赠我竟倾囊。
> 攀石如猿上，趋蓬似鸟藏。
> 衣冠自缝缀，莫怪太郎当。

"我先下去试试"

每当面对方便、好处、名誉、利益时，徐特立总是坚持"他人第一"，可是，他也有"先己后人"的时候，这就是当面对困难、面临危险时！

草地行军快结束时，战士们脸上浮现出了难得的轻松。然而，新的困难还是随时可能出现。就在这时，一条弯弯曲曲的河，从齐腰深的草丛中钻了出来，横在大家的眼前。河水夹着腐烂的草块，泛着黑色的泡沫，哗啦哗啦地向前奔去。面对着这条河，大家都愣住了。

"我先下去试试！"突然传来的这一声，打破了周围的沉寂。大家顺着声音看去，竟是年龄最大的徐老。徐老话刚一落音，就卷起裤管，脱掉上衣，朝着河边走去。

"徐老！您不能下去，这太危险了！"战士们齐声劝阻。

"水流又急，天气又冷，您老的年纪这样大……先让我们去看看情况吧。"几个年轻的小伙子一边这么说着，一边赶紧脱衣服。

"你们先过去就没有危险了吗？"徐老反问了一句。小伙子们还没来得及下水，徐老就"扑通"一声跳到河里去了。他一边游，一边探索着河水的深度，终于找到了一条较浅的水道。就这样，伤员们骑在马上，女同志拉住马尾巴，安全地渡过了这条河。这时，每个同志的脸上,都露出了胜利的微笑。

奋不顾身救祖孙

1935年10月19日,徐老随党中央到达陕北靖边县吴起镇。徐老到吴起后街,首先遇到了一件意外的事。

洛河流经吴起,河水滔滔,水势急湍。一天早晨,一位老大娘和她的孙女不慎掉进河里,在水中大声呼救。由于水深流急,许多人站在岸边,束手无策,情况十分危急。徐老闻知此事,迅速赶到河边,不顾个人安危,纵身跳入水中,救起了那婆孙二人。从此,徐老奋不顾身救祖孙的事迹作为佳话,广为流传。

"马克思在保佑我们"

无论在工作、生活还是革命斗争中,徐特立总是充满革命的乐观主义精神,不仅以此自励,更用以激励同志们勇敢地同困难乃至危险作斗争。

1934年,红军在通过第三道封锁线时,一天,干部休养连行进到一座山坡上,停下来休息时,担任党总支书记的董必武趁机召开党总支会议,想给大家鼓鼓劲。这是一个光秃秃的山头,处在敌人的封锁线内。大家坐在一起展开热烈讨论时,突然一架敌机飞来,在山顶上盘旋几圈后,扔下一颗炸弹,正好落在他们围成的圆圈中间。炸弹一头栽进土里,泥土飞溅,落得大伙满头满脸都是土。幸运的是,炸弹没有爆炸。徐特立处变不惊,镇定自若。他抖了抖身上的泥土,风趣地说:"这是马克思在保佑我们,他叫我们继续干下去,因为我们的任务还没有完成咧!"谢觉哉笑得眼睛都眯成了一条缝。董必武是个诗人,他用毛巾擦了擦落在眼里的尘土，即兴编起了顺口溜："炸弹落地不开花，全凭马翁在保驾……"大家还想接着听，他却说："后面两句一时想不起来了。"他们挪了挪位置，继续开会去了。

"人老心不老"

长征是极其艰苦的，就是二十来岁的年轻战士，对于途中遇到的各种困难也常常觉得吃不消，更何况徐特立已经是年近六旬的老人了。可徐特立却人老心不老，他甚至表现出了比很多年轻战士更加强盛的生命力。

为了躲避敌人的围追堵截特别是飞机的轰炸，队伍常常夜间行军。在夜间行军中，尽管采取了种种办法，但人员还是时有走失。于是，部队便在白天利用敌机没来的空隙，进行军事训练，学习刺杀、夜间辨别方向和辨认岔道等方面的自卫本领。组织上认为徐特立年纪太大，需要多休息，就没有通知他参加训练。一天上午，敌机刚过，只见一个打着绑腿、头戴树枝编织的伪装帽的战士，从树林里跑了出来，要参加训练。教员一看，原来是徐特立，忙劝他说："徐老，您昨夜走了一通宵，还是回去休息吧。"徐特立拍着胸脯说："大家都一样，都很辛苦，很累。现在同志们都在这里训练，我当然也不能例外。难道你要取消我当红军战士的资格？"又说："光看表面，这可不对呀！我可是人老心不老啊！"说着，徐特立精神抖擞地站到了队列里。

三送鸡蛋

陕甘宁边区政府弄到一批鸡蛋，决定照顾年老体弱的同志，给他们发点"老年津贴"。

一个女同志负责给徐老去送"老年津贴"——十几个鸡蛋。徐老问清情况后，诚恳地说："组织上对我太关心了，不过我身体很好，用不着这些东西，请你拿回去，送给体弱多病的同志吃吧。"

组织上知道这个情况后，又派这个女同志第二次送去，徐老还是不收。这位女同志带着劝解的口气说："徐老，您已是六十多岁的老年人了，跟青壮年人不同，必须吃点有营养的食品，这是组织上的决定……"徐老不等她把话说完，大笑起来："哈哈，论年龄，也许我是你的三倍，说得上是个老年人了，但是，我的身体，不一定比你差。你看看，我穿多少？你穿多少？"说着，徐老把打满补钉的灰布单裤往上卷了卷："你看，我只穿单裤，你呢，穿的是棉裤！"

这位女同志一时被徐老说得答不上话来。她灵机一动，把鸡蛋往桌上一放，说："衣服穿多穿少是一回事，年纪大小又是另一回事，您还是把东西收下吧。"说完，赶紧转身出门，径直朝山下跑去。

没想到，她刚回去不久，鸡蛋又被送回来了，还有一封徐老的亲笔信，信上写明了不收的原因。大家看了信后，想来想去想出了一个办法——以组织的名义给徐老写一封信。

信写好了，还是这位女同志，带着鸡蛋和组织上的信，高高兴兴地来到徐老住的窑洞前："徐老，我又来了！"

徐老一见她来，笑呵呵地说："好孩子，你坐呀！"一边给她倒水，一边问："什么事这样高兴，是不是又来同我讨论'老年津贴'问题来了？"

女同志这回可有准备了，她不慌不忙地拿出组织上的信，交给徐老，说："今天我是来给您送信的，不是来同您讨论'老年津贴'问题的。"等徐老看完信，她故意问："徐老，这是组织上的决定，您该不会再叫我把东西拿回去吧！"

徐老没办法，只好说："既然是组织的决定，我应该服从，好，我收下。"

那位女同志终于完成了她的任务，欢欢喜喜地回去了。可是，徐老收下的鸡蛋，自己一个也没吃，又送给了有病的同志。

像马夫的教育部部长

为了事业,徐特立一生始终过着极其节俭的生活,但他从不以此为苦,反而以此为乐。正如他自己所说:"我生平过惯了俭薄的生活,觉得只有这样,才能使精神愉快。"

1935年10月,中央红军胜利完成了举世闻名的二万五千里长征,到达陕北。11月,中华苏维埃共和国临时中央政府西北办事处在瓦窑堡成立,徐特立担任教育部部长。

为了尽快了解当地的教育情况,在一个大雪纷飞的上午,徐老赶到瓦窑堡唯一的一所小学——市立列宁小学去听课。当时,王志匀正在给学生上语文课,突然,他发现一些学生的目光转向了教室外边。顺着学生们的目光看过去,原来,一个身穿破烂衣服、腰束一根黑羊毛绳,完全一副马夫模样的老头,正站在教室门外听课。

学生出于好奇,不断地往外看。王志匀怕影响学生听课,想叫他走开,然而看到他那充满诚实和智慧的眼睛和全神贯注听课的状态,又不好意思去赶他了。这是个什么人呢?他怀着疑惑不解的心情上完了这节语文课,"马夫"老头也直到将课听完才离去。

► 担任中华苏维埃共和国临时中央政府西北办事处教育部部长时的徐特立。

第二天,"马夫"老头又来了,一起来的还有三个同样衣服破烂的同志。其中一个知识分子模样的高个子,主动出来当介绍人,他指着面部表情诚实、严肃的老人说:"这是党中央纪律检查委员会书记兼中央党校校长董必武同志。"又指着另一个人说:"这是党校教务长成仿吾同志。"最后指着昨天来过的"马夫"老头说:"这是苏维埃中央政府的教育部部长徐特立同志,我叫冯雪峰。"王志匀一下子愣住了:这都是党中央的领导干部呀!"马夫"老头原来是毛主席的老师徐老呀,多么朴素,多么平凡,然而,正是在这朴素、平凡之中,却显现了他老人家的伟大和不平凡。

长征途中的"百宝衣"

在条件最为艰苦的长征中,徐特立将节俭作风发挥到了极致。长征途中,物资极度匮乏。为了解决吃、穿、住、用等方面的困难,徐特立发明不少"杰作"。例如:将一个马蹄钟用绳子系着,挂在脖子上,当作"怀表";用粗布缝了一顶八角帽,从帽盖、帽檐到红五星都精心制作……而在他所有富于心智的"作品"中,最让官兵难忘的是他的"百宝衣"。

长征途中,徐特立得到了一件长袍。这件长袍,白天可穿,晚上可当被子,不过,徐老为了充分发挥它的作用,又对长袍进行了改装。他将能收集到的哪怕是颜色各异、大小不等的布块儿,都缝缀在长袍上,缝成许多大小不一的口袋。他在里面分门别类地装着五花八门的东西,有图章、印泥、老花镜,也有文件、书籍,还有针头线脑,等等。常用的放在方便拿的口袋,不常用的则放在"偏远"的位置,重要的有重要的地方,不重要的也有"安身"之处……可想而知,这件长袍是多么的与众不同。随着时间的推移,长袍里的东西不断增加,品种也日渐丰富。

徐老"百宝衣"的作用,一开始并不为人们所重视,甚至他所在的干部休养连连长侯政还几次三番做劝说工作,希望他精简"百宝衣"中的"装备",以便轻装上阵。可每次徐老都只笑笑便罢了,并没接受侯政的劝说。部队打下桐梓后,没收了资本家的烟、糖、粮食等东西。这

▶ 长征中的徐特立。

时,侯政想,既然改变不了徐老长袍的容量,但总可以改变一些内容吧?于是,他又劝徐老将一些"无用"的东西扔了,换成吃的。可性格倔强的徐老依然我行我素,还将在桐梓得到的钉子、铁丝、锤子放入一个铁盒子,装入"百宝衣"中。这下可好,他走起路来就更多了一些"丁零当啷"的声响。

有一件事彻底改变了侯政对徐老"百宝衣"的看法。这一天,当走在后面的徐特立赶上侯政时,侯政正站在十二团政委钟赤兵的担架旁干着急。钟赤兵在娄山关战役中右腿负伤,被锯后感染,高烧不退。周恩来专门交代休养连,一定要抬着钟赤兵行军。可就在这时,担架坏了,在这前不着村,后不着店的地方,要修要买都是不可能的。侯政急得一时没了主意,额头上直冒冷汗。跟上来的徐特立见此情景,逗他说:"你快走啊,你怎么不走了?"心急如焚的侯政,再也按捺不住:"你这老头还不快走?这里没你的事。"徐老倒也不生气,不慌不忙地说:"你莫慌,我有办法。你去把挑药的扁担弄一根来。"此时此刻,侯政也只好照办。扁担拿来后,徐老"百宝衣"里的宝贝就大显身手了。只见他变戏法似的,从中取出了绳子、钉子、锤子,三下五除二,很快就修好了担架,这让周围的人佩服不已,侯政也心服口服了。这件"百宝衣"从此扬名于革命队伍中。

"身体是革命的本钱"

在革命队伍中,徐特立不仅是年龄最大的一位,而且也是非常长寿的一位,这与他非常注意锻炼、爱惜身体密不可分。徐老常说:身体是革命的本钱,革命的本钱越多越好,身体越健康,就越能为社会、为人民多做工作。徐老直到八九十岁的高龄,还能精力充沛地学习和工作,这正是他几十年来坚持锻炼的结果。

徐老52岁在莫斯科中山大学学习的时候,学会了游泳。他觉得这是一项能改善体质的运动,只要全身向水中"扑通"一跳,不论是潜入水底,或是漂浮水面,都能使筋骨得到舒展,还可以把全身皮肤冲洗得干干净净,真是爽快极了。

◀ 1961年8月,时年84岁的徐特立在北戴河游泳。

在延安的时候,徐老参加了青年同志组成的"跃鱼游泳队",在清凉山下延河最深的那一段,他经常和大家一起欢笑着下水游泳,动作舒展矫健,沉浮自如,而且速度很快,好多小伙子都比不过他。

有一年,延安举行运动会,其中有一百米游泳比赛的项目。当比赛开始时,朝气蓬勃的运动员行列里,站着一个须发银白、满面红光的老运动员——年近七十的徐老。裁判员令声一下,几个人一齐向前扑去,只见徐老仰着身子,手划足蹬,勇往直前。他满头的白发,像一簇洁白的银丝,漂浮在水面上,随波涌进。观众们纷纷拍手叫好,气氛热烈极了,都为徐老这种老当益壮的精神所鼓舞。事后,延安著名教育家续范亭同志特地写了一首诗:

曾记秋风八月寒,军民集会延河干。
七十老将水中舞,多少青年瞪眼看。

安步当车

中华人民共和国成立后,物质条件有所改善,中央专门为徐老配备了一辆小汽车,但徐老除了有急事和开会以外,一般很少乘坐。

1949年冬日的一个下午,徐老去北京医院看病,正排队等号时遇上了彭文龙。彭文龙和徐老多年不见,两人一见面就有说不完的话。这时,徐老的警卫员跑过来,向徐老请示:"徐老,我去看看汽车开来没有,如果没有,好打电话告诉他们,说你在北京医院,让他们来接。"徐老回答:"不用打电话,等等再说,没有来也没关系,可以搭别的同志的车回去。"听到他们的对话,彭文龙奇怪地问:"怎么?徐老,您是走着来的吗?"徐老点点头说:"我走惯了,走路是非常好的锻炼。"

还有一次,徐特立下午出门,直到晚上也没有回家。家里人一连查问了好些地方,直到很晚都没找到,家里人十分焦急。当时,徐老已经快80岁了,万一发生意外怎么办?家里人就把这件事报告了中央。周恩来总理知道后,非常重视,立刻通知当时的公安部长罗瑞卿,要求他想尽一切办法,尽快找到徐老。晚上九点钟,公安部打来电话,说找到了徐老,大家心里的一块石头才落了地。

原来徐老那天坐公共汽车到了西山,傍晚回来的时候,因为乘车的人很多,公共汽车又少,徐老就和大家一起排队等车。天快黑了,排队的群众见他满头白发、年纪很大,就请他先上车,但徐老谢绝了大家的好意,坚持要排队上车,直到公安部的同志找到他,他才离开那里。

徐老外出不坐小汽车,他的警卫员很有意见,有时在背后发牢骚说:"人家的警卫员出门都坐小汽车,跟徐老这个首长却常跑路,鞋子都得多穿好几双!"

警卫员的这些话,传到了徐老的耳朵里。有一天,他把警卫员叫住,和蔼地问:"你家现在是中农了吧,一年收入多少粮食,生活怎么样?"

警卫员说:"我家在太行山,土地薄,平均每年每人收大约500斤谷子，年景好时可收 600 斤，年景不好 500 斤不到。二三月份青黄不接的时候，还得掺着野菜吃，不过比'土改'前还是好多了！"

徐老又问："你知道开汽车的汽油从哪里来吗？进一趟城要多少汽油？值多少钱？"

警卫员一时答不上来，摇了摇头。

徐老耐心地告诉他："我们国家才解放，还不能生产汽油，现在用的汽车、汽油都是拿黄金和东西从外国换回来的，一加仑汽油要花几万元（旧币）人民币，大概可以跑三十来里路。你想想，西山到城里几十里路，坐汽车来回跑几趟，一个农民全年收入就跑光了。现在老百姓的生活还很困难，我怎么能一个人随便坐汽车浪费汽油呢！如果我们的生活和群众的生活相差太大了，群众是会有意见的！"

警卫员听着听着，慢慢地低下了头。徐特立慈爱地抚摸着他的肩膀，继续说道："小伙子，少坐车、多走路，有三大好处：一可以锻炼身体，二可以节约开支，三还可以密切干部和群众的关系。这不是三全其美吗？"

经过徐特立的耐心教育，警卫员心服口服，再也不抱怨了，还跟着徐老练就了一双铁脚板。

"自己的时间宝贵，别人的时间就不值钱吗？"

作为德高望重的老革命家、教育家，徐特立却从不倚老卖老，总是以普通一员要求自己，模范遵守规章制度。

有一次，徐老到北京医院去看病，候诊室里坐满了人，大家都坐在长靠背椅上等着叫号。徐老的警卫员一看这么多人，有点急了，心想：徐老是最爱惜时间的，就这么等着，得空耗多少时间哪。他走过去悄声问道：

"徐老，人太多了，我去跟医院张主任说一声，给您先看，好不好？"

徐老连忙摆摆手说:"不行,不行,不要告诉他,还是按次序看好,稍等一下没有关系。"

警卫员望了望墙上的钟,噘着嘴说:"那够等的啦……"

徐老看警卫员有点不高兴,便招呼他坐下,拍着他的肩膀耐心地说:"自己的时间宝贵,别人的时间就不值钱吗?我们要是不按次序看病,别人就要多等。无论做什么事,总要多替别人想一想,不能光图自己一个人的方便。再说,你去找张主任,咱们跟他熟,就特殊照顾,可以不按顺序看病。如果熟人都不遵守制度,他这儿的秩序还怎么维持呢?"

警卫员听了,觉得徐老说的很有道理,也就耐下性子和徐老一起等着喊号了。

"这是睁着眼睛说瞎话!"

徐老具有非常重要的一个思想品质,那就是实事求。他说:"实事求是,这是我的座右铭,也是马克思主义的精髓。"实事求是"这种作风对学习、对工作、对领导者和被领导者、对一切人、一切事业都是需要的","没有它,一切革命,一切建设,一切工作和学习,都会有偏差,都会有走歪路的危险"。

1958年,社会上兴起"浮夸风""共产

▶ 徐特立视察北京东郊农场。

风"，一些人大肆弄虚作假，欺上瞒下。这年秋天，徐特立南行途中，路过河南，在河南省委第一书记吴芝圃陪同下，到一个公社参观棉田。当时已经是晚秋时节，薄霜降过，又刚好赶上阴雨天气，棉桃儿大都没有绽开，但介绍情况的同志却信口雌黄，声称亩产皮棉能达几百斤。

◀ 1964年徐特立考察贵阳郊区中曹公社时，与农家孩子合影。

徐特立当即表示："我不相信，这是睁着眼睛说瞎话！等我回来还要到这里，看看到底摘了多少斤。"介绍情况的人还说稻子长得密不透风，亩产能上万斤。他听了，更加不高兴地对周围的同志说："这不可能！不透空气，稻子怎么能生长呢？这是常识嘛。"回到北京后，徐特立心情沉重。后来，有关方面通知他去徐水参观，他坚持不去。他说："我们要学习列宁艰苦创业的革命精神，也要学习美国人的求实精神。美国人搞经济，总是讲究合理。而我们国家封建主义的东西太多了；官僚主义，瞎指挥，导致人力物力的浪费！浪费是比贪污更大的犯罪！……"秘书徐乾劝他："在外面讲话可要注意啊，不然有人会说你反对'大跃进'。"他沉思片刻，说："实事求是说起来容易，做起来太困难了，但我们每一个共产党员必须坚持实事求是！"他还说："讲大话容易，到头还是老百姓遭殃！"事实证明，徐特立的担忧是完全正确的，浮夸风给社会带来了严重后果。这使他愤慨万分："浮夸风其目的是骗他人，结果把社会信用失掉，使自己孤立而垮台，并人格也丧尽。一切自谓聪明缺乏老实作风者，必遗害社会且害及子孙！"

生命不息，奋斗不止

1949年10月1日开国大典之际，徐特立登上天安门城楼，亲眼观看毛泽东主席升起第一面五星红旗，亲耳聆听毛泽东主席庄严宣告中国革命的伟大胜利，欢庆中国人民为之奋斗了一百多年的革命理想终于成为现实。

这一年，徐特立已经72岁，在常人看来实在可以颐养天年了，然而他却并不因年老而松懈。欢庆之余，他想到的不是革命大功告成，可以坐享清福，而是国家在经济、文化建设方面面临的艰巨任务。他在祝吴玉章七十大寿的诗里写道："……百年殖民地，从此永完结。前途之艰巨，基本在建设。幸勿过乐观，成功在兢业。您我励残年，尽瘁此心血。"表现出敏锐的眼光，对革命事业的高度责任感和"老骥伏枥，志在千里"的宏伟志愿。

为了学习新的知识，为中华人民共和国的建设事业多做贡献，徐特立根本没想自己年已古稀，竟雄心勃勃地制定了一个20年学习和工作计划。一心活到老，学到老，工作到老。他对好友谢觉哉说，人一天没停止前进，就没有老，一天停止前进就老了。

就这样，徐特立不顾年事已高，朝气蓬勃地投身于中华人民共和国的文化教育事业，领导一批党的宣传干部和史学工作者从事中国通

▶ 年逾古稀的徐特立在认真学习。

史、中国革命史和党史等的编纂工作，并继续以各种方式关心、指导教育工作：或报告讲解，或撰文著述，或视察调研，或接待来访，或书信交流，或应约题词……为发展社会主义文化教育事业不懈地奉献着光和热。这位坚强的老战士，生命不息，奋斗不止，直到生命的最后一刻。

最后的日子

徐特立生命中的最后一段日子，是在"文化大革命"的疾风暴雨中度过的。

"文化大革命"开始后，政治生活反常，社会动荡不安。在徐特立的寓所附近，每天都有好几个高音喇叭，轮流大吼大叫，要"造反"，要"革命"，要打倒一大批功勋卓著的老一辈革命家。平日心情愉悦、爱说爱笑的徐老，情绪变得很焦躁，他用手杖愤怒地指着门窗，让家人关门闭户，不让外边的声音传进来。

徐老变得沉默不语了。有时，他把家人叫到身边，好像有很多话要对他们讲，但刚动嘴就又忍住了。他常常一个人在屋里踱来踱去，长时间地沉思不语，实在憋不住，就自言自语地脱口而出："奇怪，怎么变成敌人了？……怎么个变的呢？不，我不信……我，我想不通……"

徐老有很多心里话想要对毛主席讲。他打过很多次电话，但总联系不上。有时，他焦急地要坐车直接去中南海，但被身边的工作人员劝阻了。忧愁和苦闷，严重地折磨着老人。有一次，他悄悄地对好友谢觉哉说，很想回乡下去养猪。谢老听了，很有感触，赋诗一首：

> 九十高龄力有余，身闲不住待何如。
> 老人又羡耕与读，想傍桑荫学养猪。

1966年国庆节那天，徐老早早来到天安门城楼，想在城楼上跟毛主席说几句话。开始检阅之前，他预先等候在电梯旁边的一间屋子里。当看到毛主席来了时，他想迎上去，但毛主席的身旁早挤满了一大堆人，年迈体弱的徐特立哪里挤得进去，只能远远望着毛主席挥挥手，看着毛主席走过去。徐老不愿意再继续观礼，便提前回家了。没想到，这竟是徐老与毛主席的最后一面……

1968年11月，徐特立病危。周恩来总理百忙之中挤出时间到医院探望他，并要医院全力组织抢救。可惜医生难有回天之力，11月28日，徐老因病医治无效，与世长辞。周恩来问一直侍奉在徐老身旁的徐乾："徐老有什么遗言？"徐乾说："徐老说，他过世后，把遗体送给科学部门。"听完后，周恩来久久没有说话，眼睛里闪动着泪花。

徐老逝世以后，中央为他举行了隆重的追悼会。党中央和毛主席都献了花圈，周总理亲自参加了追悼会。滕代远代表党中央致悼词。悼词给予了徐特立很高的评价，盛赞"他的一生是光荣的一生，伟大的一生，革命的一生"。

"平凡伟大马列真，一代师表启后昆。道德文章垂万世，堪称革命一完人。"这首诗对徐特立一生做了恰如其分的赞誉。徐特立无愧为中华民族的一代师表、世之楷模！

Chapter One

A Lifetime of Purposeful Hard Study

A Miserable Childhood

On 1st February, 1877 (19th December according to the lunar calendar), Xu Teli was born into a poor peasant household in Heyeduan, Wumei Village, Changsha County, Hunan Province.

His mother was a kind-hearted woman. Diligent and frugal throughout her life, she took care of the household chores, washed and starched and weaved and sewed.

His father was a simple plain peasant. Illiterate and clumsy with words, besides farming his own miserable patch of land he was obliged to do odd jobs for others during the slack season; never did he stop grafting and grinding.

His grandfather was a peasant too. Having pored over a few medical books, he knew a thing or two about the subject. In the countryside, where there was a crying need for doctors and medicines, he often magnanimously helped treat neighbours' and fellow villagers' ailments. He was also fond of reading *Romance of the Three Kingdoms*,[1] *Outlaws*

---

1 *Romance of the Three Kingdoms* (*San Guo Yan Yi*, 三国演义) is one of the Four Chinese Classics (the other three being *Outlaws of the Marsh*, *Journey to the West* and *The Story of the Stone* or *A Dream of Red Mansions*) and the first historical romance novel in which each chapter is headed by a set of couplets to give the gist of its content. The Three Kingdoms refer to the Kingdom of Wei (220 AD – 266 AD) established by Cao Pi, the Kingdom of Shu (221 AD – 263 AD) established by Liu Bei and the Kingdom of Wu (229 AD – 280 AD) established by Sun Quan. Attributed to the renowned novelist Luo Guanzhong (c. 1330 – c. 1400), the book depicts the historical winds and clouds which circulated during a period of nearly 105 years from the end of the Eastern Han Dynasty (25 AD – 220 AD) to the beginning of the Western Jin Dynasty (265 AD – 316 AD). Wars account for a major part of the book. The narrative relates how at the end of the Eastern Han Dynasty the heroes established separatist regimes and fought among themselves, how the three kingdoms of Wei, Shu and Wu waged political and military schemes against each other, and how Sima Yan (236 AD – 290 AD) unified the Three Kingdoms and established the Jin Dynasty (265 AD – 420 AD). The book also portrays all kinds of evolving social struggles and contradictions, summarises the historic changes of the age and creates a host of heroic images that lorded about the winds and clouds. The whole work might be roughly

of the Marsh² and other classics. After Xu Teli was born, he consulted the Kangxi Dictionary³ and gave his grandson the name "Maoxun (懋恂)." "*Mao*" means "diligent" and "*xun*," "honest." The old man hoped that he would grow into a model of diligence and honesty.

When Xu Teli was four years old, his mother succumbed to a disease. On the night she breathed her last, the dim paraffin lamp in their dilapidated cottage lit up her deathly pale face. His father and elder brother stood nearby in a trance. His elder sister clasped their younger sister to her chest. He leaned close to his mother, crying out for her, but there was to be no reply.

Soon after his mother's death his grandfather passed away as well. The expense of two successive funerals left the family with only fifty strings of coins as they sank into more embarrassing straits. In order to save them from destitution, his father bought a patch of mountain land and several thatched cottages, drawing on assistance from his father-in-law. The two families lived together and cleaved to each other for survival.

---

divided into five parts: the Disorder of the Yellow Turbans, the Disorder of Dong Zhuo, the Heroes Chasing after the Deer that Symbolised the Sovereign, the Three-way Division of the Realm and the Unification of the Three Kingdoms by Sima Yan.

2   *Outlaws of the Marsh* (*Shui Hu Zhuan*, 水浒传) is one of the Four Chinese Classics co-authored by Shi Nai'an (1296 – 1370) and Luo Guanzhong in the vernacular. Each chapter is headed by a set of couplets which provides a precis of the content. The book relates how a band of greenwood heroes headed by Song Jiang were forced to become outlaws in the Liangshan Marsh in what is now Shandong Province, how their forces developed and grew stronger until an imperial amnesty and enlistment had to be offered to them and how they then went on punitive expeditions to the east and west on behalf of the Court. The story draws on the peasant uprising headed by Song Jiang at the end of the Northern Song Dynasty (960 AD – 1127 AD). Many paragons of heroism such as Wu Song, Lu Zhishen, Lin Chong, Li Kui and so on are portrayed therein, the despotic cruelty and putrefaction of the feudal ruling class are exposed, and the social contradictions of the day are revealed.

3   The far-reaching Kangxi Dictionary was compiled by more than thirty scholars, including Zhang Yushu (1642 – 1711) and Chen Tingjing (1639 – 1712), under the imperial decree of the Emperor Kangxi (1654 – 1722). The dictionary includes a total of 47, 035 Chinese characters and is a milestone in lexicography.

The days that ensued grew harder and harder. Dogged by this hopeless situation, his father sent his elder daughter to another household to be a child bride and told his ten-year-old elder son to labour in the field alongside him. Xu Teli took care of his younger sister at home. The two siblings often dragged a long bench to the centre of the room and sat down there face-to-face to keep a constant eye on one another out of mortal dread that something insidious might befall them.

On New Year's Eve When He Was Eight

At the end of the year Xu Teli turned eight, a northerly wind was howling and a blizzard cascading down. Well-off households were slaughtering pigs and sheep and making preparations for Spring Festival; firecrackers were constantly to be heard pitter-pattering from inside the big courtyards encircled by tall walls. But Xu Teli's family had none of those seasonal boons. His naive younger sister kept crying at her father for sweets. Gazing at his children, his father felt an unbearable agony. He clasped his daughter to his chest and coaxed: "Don't cry, don't cry," but the sockets of his eyes were saturated with tears. How were they to get through this Chinese New Year? Suddenly it leaped into Mr Xu's mind that he had done odd jobs for a landlord whose surname was Yan during the year and hadn't received his pay yet. He promptly stood up and said: "First Sonny, Second Sonny, stay at home and mind your younger sister. I'll go and get some of what I'm owed so we can celebrate New Year." With these words, he draped a cape woven from palm bark fibre over his shoulders and hurried out of the door. It was already late at night. The northerly wind was roaring angrily. The heavy snow still drifted copiously and haphazardly, showing no sign of abating. The siblings sat fast together and waited for their father's return with longing eyes.

They had never expected that it would be the morning of New Year's Day before he would haul his exhausted body home. Young Xu Teli hurriedly stepped forward to help him remove the cape that was encrusted with snow. He then enquired in a worried voice if he had got his pay. His father's face was iron-black with fury. Shivering all over, he replied in indignation: "That heartless landlord flexed his muscles alright. He browbeat me and then simply brushed me off. I waited and waited until daybreak. Their steward did come out. Not only did he not acknowledge the debt. Worse still he swore blind that I was deliberately stirring up trouble on New Year's Day."

"That's too much to stomach. Can't we go reason with them?" an outraged Xu Teli protested.

"Kid, you have no idea. How can we reason with them?" His father heaved a long sigh. "*Humph*, I'm partly to blame for not being able to read and write. Had we signed a written pledge in the first place, I wouldn't have had to worry about the swine going back on his word. Next year I shall send you to school even if it means taking out a loan and begging."

Outside the window snowflakes were dancing on the wind. Although it was already daybreak, the skies and the earth remained dim. Trembling from cold and hunger, the whole family welcomed the Chinese New Year with a sense of grievance.

Studying Hard at an Old-style Private School

When Xu Teli was nine, his father, who had suffered on account of his illiteracy, scraped together a mite of cash to cover his tuition fees. Xu Teli duly enrolled at a primary school where he would receive the traditional "enlightenment" education.

Standards of education in the remote countryside were very poor. The teaching methods in rural enlightenment schools could be characterized as antiquated and uninspiring. A tutor in a long black-cloth gown and a pair of grandpa glasses would plant himself in front of the teacher's platform or sit squarely on a chair. His head quivering, he would recite ancient books such as *The Analects*[4] from the beginning to the end out loud. The students followed him, chanting in chorus repeatedly, but didn't have a clue about the meaning. The young Xu Teli felt this kind of learning was deadly dull. What is more, he had no interest in the content of the classes.

Half a year later, the old-style private school hired a tutor whose surname was Zhang. Their new teacher set great store by educating his pupils in how to be a man and chose Zhu Bailu's *Aphorisms on How to Run a Family* as the textbook. This included moral maxims such as "Rise at the break of day to sprinkle water on the yard and then sweep it clean" and "Even though we only have a bowl of porridge or rice, we should be mindful of how difficult it was to obtain it; even though we only have half a length of string or thread, we should always remember how hard it was to produce." Xu Teli felt that these words were catchy and melodious and easy to understand. What is more, they provided useful instruction in how to conduct oneself in this world. This was the catalyst he needed to throw himself into his study.

Later, Mr Zhang taught them to recite the testimony written by Yang Jiaoshan (1516 – 1555) the loyal-minded minister in the Ming Dynasty. Unable to turn a blind eye to the exploits of the treacherous minister Yan Song (1480 – 1567) and his clique, who brought calamity upon the country and its people and caused disruption to the Court, Yang Jiaoshan submitted a memorial to impeach Yan. Nonetheless, he found himself framed, thrown into prison and sentenced to death. This article was written to his son before his execution. In this article, he admonished his son that a man should have inspiration and never bow to the forces of evil; one should be modest and honest, just and honourable. It proved a

---

4   *The Analects* (*Lun Yu*, 论语) is a collection of writings that mainly records the words and deeds of the pedagogue Confucius (551 BC – 479 BC), his disciples and disciples' disciples during the Spring and Autumn period (770 BC – 476 BC). Compiled after the death of Confucius, the most important Confucian classic consists of twenty volumes.

very emotive piece. Xu Teli recited it time after time and was moved to tears; his heart couldn't be at peace for a long time afterwards. The image of Yang Jiaoshan, who held fast to justice and would rather die than yield, remained etched in his mind. From then on, he read avidly.

Being Adopted by His Great-uncle's Widow

When Xu Teli was twelve, his paternal great-uncle died from illness. The man's widow was already more than sixty and paralysed from the waist down. There was nobody close by to take care of her. His father then had her adopt Xu Teli as her grandson. Soon afterwards, she found him a child bride called Xiong Licheng. Eleven months younger than Xu Teli, the girl was smart and able-handed and could undertake all the household chores. Xu Teli and she addressed each other as "elder brother" and "younger sister." The two lived together harmoniously like bosom friends. She also showed great filial devotion to the great-aunt, who doted on her.

Throughout her life, his great-aunt was hardworking and frugal and good at running the household. Despite being disabled and awkward in her movements, she managed to put in order household matters both large and small. Wooden basins and tubs were treated with *tung* tree oil once a year so that they would last for dozens of years without ever cracking. The apron around her waist had been patched so many times that it was impossible to tell what the original cloth had been like.

She was a martinet when it came to home economics too. In order to save paraffin, she wouldn't allow Xu Teli to light a lamp to read at night. Nor did she allow him to go outside and pay visits. She required that he and Xiong Licheng sit down before her listening to her relate how one should organize one's life and run a household in a thrifty manner. She conveyed a clear explanation of why some family clans rose and why some crumbled. Every day, when it was barely daybreak, she urged Teli to get up, first sweep the courtyard and then recite poems and articles out loud. This helped him develop the habits of being thrifty, industrious and fond of learning.

"Teach and Prepare for the Imperial Examinations in the Meantime"

At fifteen Xu Teli was already a handsome young man. His eyes sparkled, his speech and behaviour were gracious and decent and he was eager to learn and practise calligraphy. People heaped praise on him without exception. However, it transpired in that year that his great-aunt's ailment was chronic and she passed away soon afterwards. He had to drop out of school and return home. But this didn't deter him from learning by himself. While trying to find a job so that he could make ends meet, he did his best to look for books to read so that his horizons would be broadened.

One day, he followed a monk about his business in a monastery. The monk was erudite. He taught him how to sit in meditation and to recite Zen Buddhist mantras. He also introduced him to the poems of Hanshan (dates unknown) and Shide (783 AD – 891 AD). Hanshan and Shide were two learned monks at the time of the Tang Dynasty. They used the vernacular to compose some intriguing poems that reflected the social reality of their day. Xu Teli liked these lively and cordial compositions very much and could recite many stanzas backwards fluently. Encountering such a learned teacher in a monastery even made him entertain the notion of joining the Buddhist sect. But then he dismissed the idea, reasoning that: "I have a family to look after, so how can I choose a religious vocation over them?"

He wanted to take a page out of his grandfather's book by practicing medicine and treating people's illnesses, so he brought home many medical books to delve through. However, despite being able to understand the procedure for taking a patient's pulse, he still had no idea how to analyse it. Having no mentor to guide him, he reasoned that it was better to abandon this plan rather than muddle through things like a quack.

Later, he thought about learning how to divine and study geomantic conditions. He read many books. When he tried to pass judgement according to the oracles written on the divination tallies, it frequently didn't work. A careful analysis of the oracles showed that they mostly consisted of ambiguous words. He could not rid himself of the suspicion that guesswork was involved, so he gave that up as a bad lot too.

When he was eighteen, Xu Teli finally made up his mind that he would "teach and prepare for the Imperial Examinations in the meantime." He set up an enlightenment school of his own and used his free time to study hard. In this way, not only was the problem of how to scrape by solved but he could go and sit the Imperial Examinations; perhaps he could gain an official post – whether it was an important one or not. During one spell, he gave his undivided attention to the writing of hackneyed "eight-legged" essays and composed eleven pieces back-to-back in half a year. But at the bottom of his heart he had absolutely no idea about how good his written efforts were.

One day, he selected several pieces he felt satisfied with and walked forty kilometres to the city proper of Changsha to seek out Mr Chen Yunfeng for instruction. Mr Chen was a widely-acclaimed scholar who was adept at composing poems and writing articles. After passing the Imperial Examinations at the provincial level, he lived an idle life at home and was unwilling to angle for personal gain or an official post. Moved by the modest way in which Xu Teli sought out advice, he earnestly outlined some learning methods and persuaded him that he should read extensively but not to waste his time on the rigid eight-legged essays. He also sent Xu Teli a fan. The lines written on it read: "Teachers are very important for people who want to read and learn, but how much more important are books. The countryside has neither teachers nor books. Nonetheless, books in fact are teachers. Zhang Zhidong's[5] *Answers to Questions on*

---

5 **Zhang Zhidong** (张之洞, 1837 – 1909) was born in Xingyi Prefecture, Guizhou Province. He was the leader of the "purists" in his early years and later a major representative of the Westernization Group. In the field of education, he founded insti-

What Books Are Worthy of Reading tells people what books should be bought and *The Words Gathered by the Emissaries in Light Carriages*[6] teaches people how to read. Poring over these two books will bring you lifelong benefits." Enlightened by Mr Chen's instructions, Xu Teli's mind was suddenly flung wide open and he studied more diligently.

Formulating "the Ten-year Reading Plan at the Expense of Insolvency"

Following Mr Chen Yunfeng's instructions, Xu Teli studied diligently for two years and gained a lot from this. But he soon encountered a problem: There were no books to read. Originally he didn't have many books at home. It was never easy to borrow them in the remote countryside. He had no other option but to buy them. However, books were too expensive for the poor at that time. His teaching job could bring him a dozen or more strings of coins every year, which was not enough to buy a copy of *Notes and Commentaries to the Thirteen Classics*.[7] What should he do?

---

tutions such as the Self-strengthening School and Sanjiang Normal School (the present-day Nanjing University). Politically he was an advocate of "Chinese learning as the base, Western studies for use." In the field of industry, he established the Hanyang Iron Factory, the Daye Iron Mine, the Hubei Firearms Factory and other bases. He was one of the "Four Renowned Ministers" at the end of the Qing Dynasty together with Zeng Guofan (1811 – 1872), Li Hongzhang (1823 – 1901) and Zuo Zongtang (1812 – 1885).

6   Before the Qin Dynasty (221 BC – 207 BC), the government would dispatch emissaries in light carriages to gather together local sayings, and then collate and record them. The title of the book *The Words Gathered by the Emissaries in Light Carriages* originated from this practice.

7   The **Thirteen Classics** refer to the thirteen Confucian masterpieces: the *Book of Songs*, the *Book of History*, the *Book of Rites*, the *Book of Changes*, the *Spring and Autumn Annals of Zuo Qiuming*, the *Spring and Autumn Annals of Gongyang Gao*, the *Spring and Autumn Annals of Guliang Chi*, the *Rites of Zhou*, the *Classic of Rites*, *The Analects*, the *Classic of Filial Piety*, the *First Dictionary of the Standard Chinese Language*, and *Mencius*.

He racked his brains and that little bit of farmland left to him by his great-aunt sprang into his mind: Could he buy the books that he wanted to and should read by means of selling a portion of the farmland every year and at the same time use his income from teaching to cover the expenditure of the family? He only had a small parcel of farmland. He estimated that if he sold a little bit off every year, he would likely be broke in ten years. On the other hand, if he studied hard for ten years, he would have become a learned man.

After thinking it over, he shared his plan with his wife Xiong Licheng. Following a moment of hesitation, she agreed with him. "We can live our life a little more frugally, but you must keep reading." Hence, Xu Teli started to carry out his "ten-year reading plan at the expense of insolvency" and sold his farmland to buy books. The others laughed at him, saying that he was a buffoon. Didn't everyone know that farmland was precious and only a fool would sell it to buy books? Xu Teli paid no attention to their jeers and carried on unswervingly with his plan.

Xu Teli was a very meticulous reader. It was never easy to memorise many words at once, especially since they were written in the seal script. He persisted in learning two or three of them every day and wrote on his palm from memory though it was already time for bed; he wouldn't fall asleep unless he could write them smoothly. Back then few people knew anything about algebra and geometry and other newfangled systems. When he encountered something he didn't know, he had nobody but himself to turn to. Frequently he kept a maths book in his pocket. First he opened it and studied one theorem. When he was travelling somewhere, he tried to lodge it in mind. Then he would turn to another one. During this process of self-study, not only did he scrawl all kinds of marks and note down his opinions and reflections in the margins, but he also copied out the main content.

Later he would often share with others his experience to the effect that: "There is no shortcut to pursuing knowledge. I had no choice but to resort to clumsy methods. Whenever I struck upon a word or a sentence on a book, I would close my eyes and think: What knowledge did it teach me? I wouldn't read on until I had figured it out. In this way, after I had read through a book, I would know the key ideas and I could keep the knowledge in my mind."

Xu Teli studied assiduously and brought in a bumper harvest. As well as surveying all the representative works of the Confucian classics, historical records, philosophical writings and miscellaneous works, he learned knowledge of natural science including physics, chemistry, and maths and new knowledge about the social sciences. Thus he transformed himself into a learned young man.

Sitting the Metropolitan Examinations at Yueyang City

In 1905, the ten-year reading plan at the cost of insolvency reached its eighth year. His family was already on the brink of bankruptcy. Xu Teli found himself on a knife-edge, but good luck hailed him at this time: The Metropolitan Examinations at Yueyang City were open to anyone who wanted to sit them! "He who excels at learning can be a government official." This was the dream of every scholar. Sitting the Metropolitan Examinations was without doubt a rare opportunity for the ambitious 28-year-old Xu Teli. If he passed, he could realise his aspirations; if he failed, however, that would draw into question the efficacy of his "reading plan at the expense of insolvency."

After supper one day, Xu Teli compared notes with Xiong Licheng: "Licheng, I want to go to Yueyang to take the Metropolitan Examinations. What do you think?" "This is a good idea, but where can we get the money for the journey?" Xiong Licheng of course knew her husband's mind, but the travel expenses put the husband and wife in an awkward position. Xiong Licheng planned to borrow from her neighbours. Unwilling to see his wife beg from the others, Xu Teli scraped together several strings of coins, packed up his belongings and embarked to

Yueyang with some dry rations.

When he reached Yueyang, numerous other candidates had already arrived and many taverns were filled to capacity. Many were brats from rich households and were pumped up with confidence; some were the offspring and younger brothers from poor families. In spite of wearing tattered clothes and hats, their aspirations were obvious. A candidate by the name of Wu was staying in the room next to Xu in the tavern. Wu was a rich brat. Xu Teli greeted him, but he acknowledged him in a cursory fashion and appeared very arrogant.

The examinations were set in motion. First came the preliminary round. After laying his hands on the examination papers, Xu Teli scanned the topics and found that they were rather ambiguous and hard to understand. The geography topic was: "Please discuss: Parthia in the Han Dynasty refers to the present-day Persia and Antakia refers to the present-day Arabia." The history topic was: "On Zhang Juzheng's destruction of the academies throughout the country."

According to his knowledge, the history books of the Han and Tang Dynasties took Chang'an (the present-day Xi'an City) as the centre of the world when speaking about the Western Regions. Xu Teli surmised that Parthia and Antakia must lie to the west of the Pamirs and to the east of the Red Sea, that they should be so many miles away from Chang'an and so on and so forth. After analysing like this, he finished answering the question on the first examination paper.

As to the second examination paper, he didn't know how Zhang Juzheng (1525 – 1582) had destroyed the academies throughout the country, but he knew that Zhang was the prime minister under the Emperor Wanli in the Ming Dynasty. Back then the eunuch officials monopolised power and the competition between the scholar bureaucrats and the eunuchs was cruel. Therefore, destroying the academies didn't serve to suppress the discontent that the scholar bureaucrats felt towards the Court. The corruption of the Ming Dynasty (1368 – 1644) came about mainly as a result of the fact that the eunuch officials and Buddhist monasteries held the power. Taking this as his proposition, he also produced a voluminous paper. But the way he saw it, he felt that the content of his argumentation bore no relation to the remit. Therefore, he didn't hold out much hope for this round of examinations.

Against all expectations, the eyes of the examiners fell on Xu Teli's answer sheets. Out of more than 3,000 candidates, he ranked 19th and so qualified for the next stage. However, in order to sit the subsequent examinations, a one yuan fee for the paper had to be handed in. He was put in an awkward position again: His money for the journey had been used up. Where could he find money to cover the exam paper fee? In the midst of his worry, the fellow Wu sidled over and said "Congratulations!" On knowing of his plight, he wanted to loosen his wallet string and help. Such was Xu's loathing of snobs like that he declined.

He thought: "It is hard for a person to stand in the Court if he has received too much kindness. He can't uphold justice if he has accepted too many personal favours. If I do pass the exams, he might cosy up to me and request that I grant him a favour in return. I shall never associate with such people."

He therefore decided to give up on the supplementary exams and packed up his luggage to go back home. He wrote a poem to express his aspirations:

A gentleman feels empty when he is down-and-out.
But beyond the ninefold azure sky his aspirations hover about.
Unlike those weak willows in the marshes and those tender shoots,
Accidentally fondled by a spring wind they bend low without any doubt.

The Restless Student

In 1906, Xu Teli accepted the invitation of Zhu Jianfan (1883 – 1932) the Headmaster of the Zhounan Girls School to come to the city proper of Changsha to teach. He worked there for four or five successive years. He was erudite and his lectures were lively. He was welcomed and loved by his students and became a renowned teacher who soon all the schools were vying against each other to employ. But he was not satisfied with his accomplishments and often single-mindedly applied himself to the issue of how to improve the teaching quality. He visited many schools in counties including Changsha and Liuyang and found out that although primary school education was meant to be the base of all learning what was on offer was inadequate. He could detect many limitations in areas such as the curricula taught, the textbooks used and the teaching methods employed. Worse still, few people even had access to primary education in those days. He felt that if matters went on like this, there was no hope for improving basic learning. Believing that he should shoulder this responsibility, he decided to visit a wide range of junior high schools and primary schools, seeking out what experience and advanced methods were being employed. It became his ambition to improve and enhance Hunan's elementary education. This idea found support from Zhu Jianfan, who accepted his resignation and what is more, funded his travels.

After the Spring Festival of 1910, Xu Teli left Changsha by boat and went down along the River Xiang to Lake Dongting. This was the first time in his 33 years that he had been able to leave his home province. The boat docked near Yueyang City for three days. He scaled the Yueyang Tower to feast his eyes on the splendid scenery and appreciated the writings inscribed in the stone tablets. Repeatedly he recited the widely-acclaimed line "Be the first one to worry about the country and its people and be the last one to enjoy life" written by Fan Zhongyan (989 AD – 1052 AD) and resolved that he would dedicate his mortal life to making an extraordinary contribution in his ordinary teaching post.

When the boat reached Hankou, Xu Teli transferred onto a ship bound for Shanghai to join the primary school teachers' training class organised by the Jiangsu Province Educators Association. On the first day he came to the school, the two teachers leading the training class Yang Baoheng (1873 – 1916) and Yu Ziyi (1886 – 1970) were unable to hide their surprise at seeing a student who looked older than them. They made enquiries and discovered that he was a well-known junior high school teacher from Hunan, who had come to Shanghai at his own expense for the sole purpose of examining the local primary school education. They couldn't help but admire him very much. Xu Teli requested that the two teachers Yang and Yu should be strict with him, taking him as an ordinary student, but also give him a little free time so that he could call in on and investigate the primary schools in Shanghai. The two teachers assented warmly and complied with his request by adding every possible convenience to his visits.

During his inspection, Xu Teli paid much attention to familiarising himself with the operational methods and characteristics of these schools. For example, when he visited the East Shanghai Girls School, he heaped praise on Mr Yang Boming for how he was able to make the best use of existing facilities to run the school. Mr Yang used his main room as the lecture hall and a tea table as the teacher's platform. The screening wall in front of the main room was decorated with many news materials, reports and periodicals for the students to read. Wooden boxes were used to hold those items that the students couldn't bring into the classroom. Mr Yang was the headmaster-cum-teacher. Besides teaching the Chinese language and sewing skills, he was also the editor of a magazine, and so did the work of several men simultaneously. Xu Teli thought that he should learn and carry forward his hard-working and painstaking spirit in running the school.

Another school he visited was the Wanzhu Primary School in the suburbs. He lauded the close relationships between the teaching staff and the parents of the students: A teacher came to a student's home and chit-chatted on a squat bench with the student's parents. He set no store by ceremony. When tasting the pickled vegetables being hung out to dry by the door, he didn't make a fuss about them being grubby. Xu Teli thought that this kind of interaction was an important means of maintaining the close ties between the school and the students' families.

Xu Teli stayed in Shanghai for more than four months. Almost every day he engaged in these investigations and skipped some lectures delivered by the training class with the consequence that later on he didn't pass the examinations. He summed this up by saying: "I was a little restless and unwilling to read psychology and moral philosophy books or their like. I was fond of taking part in all kinds of educational activities in Shanghai. Whenever there was a sports meeting or an exhibition, I would be there. The classes lasted five or six hours every day, but I had run off after four hours at most to carry out my visitations and investigations. And so it was, I failed the exams, which were based on the knowledge found in the textbooks." In fact, what he had gained from his investigation could never be gleaned from attending the classes listening to Pedagogy and Psychology. "Being a little restless" perhaps was one important reason why he dared to reform and create something new and original in the educational field and why he was able to achieve something later on.

Learning from Japanese Primary School Education

While he was studying in the training class in Shanghai, Xu Teli admired Mr Yu Ziyi, who was younger than him. Mr Yu had once studied in Japan. He introduced Xu Teli to the conditions of the Japanese educational system at length and encouraged him to go to Japan to investigate. In his heart, Xu Teli had always wished to undertake some learning in Japan. Therefore, after completing his inspection of the education system in Shanghai, he set sail again in July, 1910 and took a sea-voyage eastward to Tokyo.

Prior to visiting the schools in Japan, Xu Teli read some books on the education in Japan, for example *Collection of Primary School Affairs*, *Three Thousand Excellent Primary Schools* and so on. Following the instructions and hints provided by these books, he went to investigate some schools on the spot. During his tour, what impressed him most was how Japanese schools set the greatest store by the frugal use of human, physical and financial resources and strove to improve efficiency. Take the Practice Girls School as an example. The school's administrative personnel consisted of only the Headmistress Natsuda Kako. The other staff was all dedicated to teaching. Their daily business was managed entirely by the students. The premises and facilities were all put to best use. For instance, when the desks were moved away, a sewing classroom would be transformed into an indoor playground. The curricula also corresponded to hands-on needs. The whole campus was neat, elegant and well-regulated. Xu Teli appreciated the smart, able-handed headmistress very much and thought her experience of running the school should be made widely known.

What is more, some Japanese schools arranged their class schedules according to the students' everyday circumstances – something which also left a deep impression on him. For example, the students in a certain Tokyo primary school were mostly factory apprentices and their shift hours differed. In order to suit their regimen, the school conducted several classes with different curricula at different time periods and allowed them to select the ones which suited them best. Their method of running the school was flexible. When they were understaffed, students could act as teaching assistants. Such good experience not only enriched the content of his investigation but also provided an object of reference when he later carried out educational reforms.

After having stayed in Japan for more than two months, Xu Teli embarked on his homeward voyage filled with the sense that his journey had not been fruitless. On-board ship, he gripped his suitcase like grim death and was in mortal dread of what mischief might come to it because inside were his diaries written during his educational investigation – a treasure trove in his eyes.

"The Aged Foreign Student in France"

One day in the second half of 1919, following the long-drawn-out wail of the steam whistle – *toot!* – a steamer from China was berthed at a wharf in Marseilles, France. A group of sallow-skinned young men in plain clothing climbed down. These were Chinese students who had come far away from their motherland to France for a work-study programme. Xu Teli stood among their number.

Xu Teli was already forty-three. After working for more than twenty years as a teacher, he already enjoyed prestige and had achieved a considerable amount. But in order to pursue new knowledge, he was still obsessed with coming to France for a work-study programme.

His friends dissuaded him: "You are already so old. Why do you still want to learn? Why must you run to France to be an apprentice and student?"

"It is wrong for you to say that a man who is long in the tooth no longer needs to learn," he answered. "You should know that the elderly wield considerable power in this society. If they don't want to learn at all and don't gain some new knowledge, society will suffer much harm …"

Some relatives and friends enquired with a puzzled face: "But aren't you already a very learned man?"

Shaking his head, he replied with a smile: "My present store of knowledge is far from sufficient. I am forty-three this year. Forty-four, forty-five will creep up without me knowing it. If I muddle through my days, my sixtieth birthday will come around soon. I might have reached sixty, but my knowledge would remain as shallow as when I was forty-three. Wouldn't I have lived those seventeen years in vain? Sixty is too late to start repenting. Why don't I start to learn from today?"

His relatives' and friends' dissenting voices failed to sway him. He sold his books and borrowed here and there to raise a sum of money for the journey, kissed goodbye to his wife and children and hopped on the steamer that was bound for France.

After Xu Teli arrived in France, seeing that he was at an advanced age, the man in charge of the work-study programme persuaded him to live outside the campus and hire someone to tutor him alone. This would give him more freedom.

Xu Teli declined, explaining: "I came to France with the intention of familiarising myself with the rules of French schools. In this way, I can apply that knowledge after I come back to China. If I didn't stay at school and experience things in person, how could my wish be fulfilled?"

"You are not getting any younger," the man then reminded him worriedly. "The school rules are too strict. I am afraid that you wouldn't be able to tolerate them."

Xu Teli replied: "Others respect me precisely because I am in my dotages; if I have any bad habits, they won't tell me to my very face. If I live on campus, for one thing I have the teachers' instructions and for the other, I can gain help from my classmates."

In this way, he succeeded in talking that comrade round and went to Moulins Collége to take remedial French lessons. Meanwhile, he worked as an operator of tongs at an iron and steel foundry. He also cooked for the Chinese students who were working and studying in France.

Xu Teli's memory was bad. His mouth had two missing front teeth, which made it very hard for him to pronounce French words. The obstacles on his route to learning the language were acute, but he was filled with confidence.

"If I start to learn French from this year onwards, there are still seven years left before I turn fifty," he said. "Even if I learn only one new word per day, I can master 365 words in one year. Seven years means more than 2,500. Wouldn't I have become a man who knows a thing or two about the French language? If I learn two words per day, I will be able to read French books by the time I am forty-six and a half years old."

The students at Moulins Collége were mostly young men and quick learners. Xu Teli took them as his teachers and asked them for instructions modestly. One fifteen-year-old student by the name of Xiong Xinwu, who hailed from Hunan, was the son of Xu Teli's student Xiong Jinding. The young man ought to have addressed Xu Teli as his "Grand-teacher," but Xu Teli invited him to be his "young teacher" and teach him the French language. After catching sight of this scene, someone poked fun at him, laughing: "You ask for directions from your student's son. Haven't you brought yourself down several rungs on the ladder of seniority?"

Xu Teli replied: "Yeah, I have brought myself down several rungs. But you should know that it is already a shame to be a 'grand-teacher' if you are not knowledgeable. Now I don't know even a single French word. It would be more shameful if I were to remain as proud as a peacock and yet be afraid of losing my status. As long as the student doesn't loathe how decrepit I am and is willing to help me with my French language, I need to be a progressive old man though I have been kicked down several rungs on the seniority ladder."

His industrious and humble spirit of learning moved his French teachers. They all heaped praises on the diligent aged student. Through hard efforts, he had overcome one obstacle after another and had finally succeeded in understanding science books written in French. One year later, he was admitted to the University of Paris to study courses including maths and physics. He had truly become an "aged student."

Studying Marxism and Leninism at Sun Yat-sen University, Moscow

In May, 1928, the CPC dispatched Xu Teli to Sun Yat-sen University in Moscow to study Marxism and Leninism. The school accepted only Chinese students and offered introductory and intermediate courses. After the failure of the First National Revolution (May, 1924 – 12th April,

1927), veteran comrades such as Dong Biwu,[8] He Shuheng,[9] Lin Boqu,[10] Wu Yuzhang[11] et al had studied here. The school respected these highly

---

8   Dong Biwu (董必武, 1886 – 1975) was born in what is now Hong'an County, Hubei Province. He was one of the founders of the CPC. After the establishment of the PRC, he served variously as Director of Central Commission of Finance and Economics, Vice-Premier of the Government Administration Council, Director of Political and Legal Affairs Committee of the Government Administration Council, President of the Supreme People's Court, Vice-Chairman of the National People's Congress, Secretary of the Supervisory Committee of the CPC Central Committee, Vice-Chairman of the PRC and Acting Chairman. He, Lin Boqu, Xu Teli, Xie Juezai and Wu Yuzhang were hailed as the "Five Reverend Elders of the CPC."

9   He Shuheng (何叔衡, 1876 – 1935) was born in the present-day county-level city of Ningxiang, Hunan Province. He was a proletarian revolutionary, a key member of Xinmin (meaning the "new citizenry") Society and a member of the Changsha Communist Group. He graduated from Hunan First Normal School. In 1930, after returning to China from abroad, he was a key player in charge of the Communist International Relief Federation and the National Mutual Aid Society. In the autumn of the following year, he went to the Soviet areas under the governance of the CPC Central Committee. There he became a member of the Central Executive Committee of the Soviet Republic of China, a People's Commissioner of the Workers' and Peasants' Procuratorate, Acting Minister of Internal Affairs and President of the Provisional Court of the Central Government, to name just a few of his roles. When the Central Committee was dominated by the "left-leaning" mistakes, he was removed from all his posts. After the major force of the Red Army embarked on the Long March, he was left behind at the base area to continue fighting. In February, 1935 when he passed by Shanghang County in Fujian Province, he was hounded down by the enemy and sacrificed his life heroically.

10   Lin Boqu (林伯渠, 1886 – 1960) was born in modern-day Linli County, Changde City, Hunan Province. He was a renowned proletarian revolutionary and educationist and a key leader of the Party and the country. He joined the Revolutionary Alliance in his early years. In 1921, he became a member of the CPC. He participated in key revolutionary activities such as the Nanchang Uprising and the Long March and was appointed Chairman of the Government in the Shaanxi-Gansu-Ningxia Border Region. After the establishment of the PRC, he was the Chief Secretary of Central People's Government Commission and Vice Chairman of the First and Second Standing Committees of the National People's Congress.

11   Wu Yuzhang (吴玉章, 1878 – 1966) was born in Rong County, Sichuan Province. He was a veteran revolutionary who had experienced first-hand the Reform

virtuous elders and held a special class for them. Xu Teli studied in this special class.

Xu Teli's diligence left a very strong impression on people. In order to delve deeper into Marxist and Leninist theories, he studied the Russian language hard with old age being no deterrent. His missing front teeth meant it was very difficult for him to pronounce Russian syllables accurately. His memory was rusty too. Today he would read them over and over again, but tomorrow he would have forgotten them clean. He lay down a rule for himself that he should get up early to recite out loud every day. Whether it was windy or rainy, every morning one shadow would pace to and fro on a secluded quiet corridor in the school babbling loudly. Every syllable or word was recited dozens of or even one hundred times until they were finally lodged in his mind. His industriousness allowed him to forge outstanding achievements within a short period of time. Some teachers also realised how Xu Teli was anxious to treat them with proper respect, never taking advantage of his seniority and vast knowledge. Rather, he always listened all ears to their lectures and sought out their teachings earnestly. They admired and respected him.

The winter days in Moscow were frigid and people were fond of holing themselves up at home. Especially in the morning, few were willing to go outdoors. Xu Teli, however, would go out running early in the morning and do physical exercises on the shadowy avenues at noon. He also often

---

of 1898, the Revolution of 1911, the Punitive Expedition against Yuan Shikai, the Northern Expedition, the Anti-Japanese War, the Liberation War and the establishment of the PRC. From being a member of the Revolutionary Alliance to being a member of the CPC, from being a participant in the "Old Three People's Principles" Revolution under the leadership of Mr Sun Yat-sen to being a participant in the "New Three People's Principles" Revolution and the socialist revolution under the leadership of the CPC, he fought throughout his life for social progress, national liberation, socialist construction and the Party cause. After the establishment of the PRC in 1949, he served as the President of Renmin University of China for seventeen years and his students migrated throughout the world. He also acted as Director of the Committee for the Reform of the Writing System attached to the State Council, Chairman of China Educators Union and Chairman of China Natural Sciences Publicity Association.

invited his classmates to join in, claiming that they should build up their bodies for the revolution.

"It Is Very Important to Beat the Clock"

In December, 1940 after he came back from the Communications Service of the Eighth Route Army in Hunan, Xu Teli was appointed the President of the Yan'an Academy of Natural Sciences (the predecessor to the Beijing Institute of Technology) – the first college of science and engineering established by the CPC. The school was newly set up and every aspect of its work was in need of standardisation. The school-running conditions were rather unfavourable. Xu Teli had a tight schedule every day. He needed to consider all aspects including the guidelines to run the school, the building of the curricula and teaching plans, the fostering of the teaching staff and so on. He also needed to squeeze out time to learn mineralogy and geology and to organise people to compile relevant textbooks. Every day he had numerous items of business to attend to and always felt that his time was pinched.

Back then he lived at Yangjialing or "Yang Family Ridge." Whether he had a meeting to attend or some work to undertake, he needed to run down the mountain. Originally an ancient route consisting of flights of stone steps led to the base of the mountain from Yangjialing, but those travelling on foot would have to take a lengthy detour. Fearing that it was too far and too much time would be wasted, he blazed a trail through the weeds and bushes. Following the lie of the mountains to zigzag up and down, the new route was very treacherous and steep and beset with brambles in some places. By the time he had covered this distance, he would always break into a full-body sweat and pant heavily. The secretary who followed him was a young man. His head too would be drenched in perspiration.

"Your Honour, you're not being made to take the Long March,"[12] he persuaded Xu Teli. "There are no enemies in the sky giving chase and no enemies on the earth hounding us. Why should we hurry like this? Let's take the main road next time even if it is a little circuitous."

"One second of time is worth one inch of gold," Xu Teli explained humorously. "Taking the route I've chosen does take some exertion, but much time can be saved because it is only one third as long as the old one. It is very important for us revolutionaries to beat the clock. The time squeezed out can be used to accomplish many things or read many books."

He persisted in taking this road every day. A growing number of people followed his lead gradually.

---

12 In October 1934, after the failure of the Fifth Counter-campaign against the KMT "Encirclement and Suppression," the bulk of the Red Army under the direct command of the CPC Central Committee (the First Front Army of the Chinese Workers' and Peasants' Red Army) was forced to carry out a great strategic shift, abandoning the CPC Central Committee base area and embarking upon the Long March so that they could shake off the KMT army's encirclement, pursuit and attack. The Long March was a great miracle in human history. The Red Army fought a total of more than 380 battles, occupied more than 700 county cities and routed several hundred KMT regiments. Their travail extended 25,000 *li*, during which they passed through 11 provinces, scaled 18 great mountains (including rolling snow-crowned eminences), and negotiated 24 big rivers, as well as barren grasslands. 430 battalion-commander-level-or-above cadres – with an average age of no more than 30 – sacrificed their lives. In October, 1936, they reached Northern Shaanxi and joined forces with the local Red Army. In October, 1936, the Second and Fourth Front Armies of the Chinese Workers' and Peasants' Red Army reached Huining County, Gansu Province and teamed up with the First Front Army. The three major forces of the Red Army joined together, which announced the successful end of the Red Army's Long March.

The Skeleton on the Sick Ward

Logistics in Northern Shaanxi were far from convenient. The land was barren, there was a dire need for all kinds of materials and the living conditions were appalling. Even so, Xu Teli never complained and took care of every single matter personally. Because he was so busy, he often had no time to take his meal. Sometimes when the mealtime was over, being unwilling to trouble the cooks, he would go to the kitchen and eat a little leftover rice and side dishes soaked in boiled water. Exhausting work and irregular meals gave him a relatively severe stomach condition. He had to receive treatment as an in-patient in the Central Hospital. The doctor stressed it into him: "You must take it seriously. Rest well and never tire yourself out." But how could Xu Teli stay idle? He remained busy with his study and work despite being hospitalised.

One day, some comrades came to see him. They pushed the door of his ward open and were shocked at the sight of a human skull at the head of his sickbed. What appeared to be a full skeleton was also draped over the sickbed.

"Venerable Xu, what are you doing here?" they asked in great surprise.

"Nothing. I find it too uncomfortable to lie here for long. I am making use of the time and equipment available to learn a little new knowledge!"

In this way, Xu Teli turned the sick ward into a classroom.

He was hospitalised for more than twenty days, but ended up dabbling in a new subject – physiology.

"These Books Will Be Put to Greater Use Later in the Future"

At the end of 1946, the KMT army swarmed to attack Yan'an. According to the arrangements of the CPC Central Committee, Xu Teli headed one section of the comrades from the Educational Research Office that was affiliated to the Propaganda Department of the CPC Central Committee to retreat. His seventieth birthday was around the corner by then – few people in ancient times could reach that milestone.

When he was to leave Yan'an, considering that it must be a long trudge, the Organisation especially allocated a "sedan-chair" drawn by three mules to him to save his labour.

He declined by saying: "The Organisation cares about me. I can still walk right now, so there is no need to extend any special concern to me."

No matter how he declined, the other party would never accept it.

Thinking awhile, he suggested: "Then let's do it this way: give me an animal to carry my books."

Books were Xu Teli's treasures. He had several big crates full of books. One animal alone couldn't take care of them. He racked his brains and finally hit upon an idea: Every book has margins. If the margins were sliced away, wouldn't a book become smaller and lighter? Then couldn't more books be carried?

Since he had made up his mind, he rolled up his sleeves and used a kitchen knife and scissors to cut. His palms blistered.

Someone persuaded him to stop.

He replied: "These books will be put to great use in the future. The more margins have been cut off, the more books can be salvaged!"

In this way, with his books being carried by the animal, he trudged on foot with his team to march towards their new journey.

Wherever He Went, He Would Learn

After they retreated from Yan'an, whenever their team halted to take a break, Xu Teli would take out a book to read. It didn't matter how turbulent that stage of their march was. Sometimes he would gather all kinds of samples of ores to study on the spot. Some comrades didn't know what had hit them as they watched how in spite of clambering up mountains and scaling ridges, he remained fond of picking up stones, observing them this way and that and knocking at them here and there.

"These are all ores," he explained. "We should study them early on. Later when our revolution is successful, we need to produce and construct. They will be put into good use."

In this way, wherever he went, he would learn. Knowing that these stones would be made great use of, his guard also helped him gather them warm-heartedly and learned by the way. Now he too could recognise several kinds of ores.

One day, a comrade asked him what the glistening stone in his hand was.

The guard answered: "It is called quartz stone."

The comrade commented in great surprise: "You're a little rascal who's not to be messed with. You also know one thing or two!"

"I have been following Venerable Xu on the march for more than a fortnight. How could I not know this?" the guard replied.

"Live and Learn"

In October, 1949, the People's Republic of China was established. Xu Teli was already seventy-two.

When he thought about the hard tasks faced by the country in fields such as economic and cultural construction – which were, it should be noted, mostly brand new challenges for the newly-born regime – Xu Teli realised clearly: "Some knowledge I knew in the past might not be of much use now. To take on new battles, one needs new knowledge. Only through learning new knowledge can one keep up with the pace of the time and never age. A man who stops learning and allows his brain to stop functioning really has aged!" In order to encourage and spur himself on, he drew up a twenty-year-long study and work plan and made up his mind to live and learn so that he could continue making contributions to all kinds of causes in the New China.

Xu Teli continued to be the Vice Head of the Propaganda Department of the CPC Central Committee. Simultaneously, he was also the Director of the Educational Research Office and the Party History Research Office, which were affiliated to the Propaganda Department of the CPC Central Committee. He had been elected the Honorary Chairman of China History Association and, together with the historian Fan Wenlan (1893 – 1969), led a batch of historians and cadres from the Propaganda Department of the CPC Central Committee and Party School of the Central Committee of CPC to compile a general history of China, a revolutionary history of China and a history of the CPC and other data. Though he was erudite, he remained ever-modest, like an empty valley, and was prepared to start from scratch in any task. All kinds of books were stacked up on his writing desk. Even though he might only need to write a short article or draft a speech, he would consult many books and magazines and weigh his words repeatedly so that he could make the problem at hand clear and so that his article or report would benefit the people or a cause he was taking up presently.

He developed a habit. If he failed to clarify a problem in the daytime, he would continue thinking it over at night after he woke up from his slumber; sometimes he would get up at midnight to note down what he had been thinking about. Such occurrences were frequent: At night, his secretary Xu Qian had put the items on his writing desk in good order, but early the next morning there were again many slips of paper cramped with words on the desk.

"Venerable Xu, you wrote all of these?" she asked in surprise.

"Yeah. Something struck me at midnight. Worried that I might forget it on the next day, I got up and noted it down," he explained.

With this tireless enterprising spirit, Xu Teli overcame all kinds of difficulties and learned insatiably. He lived up to the phrase that one should "live and learn."

Chapter Two

Sacrificing His Family Life to Run Schools and Saving the Country through the Promotion of Education

"Blazing a Trail in Establishing New-style Schools in the Countryside"

After the Metropolitan Examinations in Yueyang in 1905, Xu Teli's knowledge and integrity won the admiration of countless people. Some schools beat a path to his door to employ him. Many students also sought him out especially for his teachings. But he was not satisfied with pottering through his days by teaching just a few students in the remote countryside. He wanted to give full play to his talent in a vaster world and to explore a path of salvation for the country and its people. Soon afterwards, he was admitted with excellent examination marks into Ningxiang Accelerated Normal School, which stood at Wangluyuan (or Mount Yuelu Gazing Garden) within the city limits of Changsha. This was a freshly-established new-style school. The headmaster of the school Zhou Zhenling (1875 – 1964) was a member of the Revolutionary Alliance. He frequently propagandised to the students on the truth of the national revolution. The revolutionary atmosphere on the campus was palpable. Xu Teli studied there for four months and gleaned a lot of new scientific knowledge and advanced ideologies. At the graduation ceremony, Headmaster Zhou Zhenling harangued and incited the graduating class by saying: "We established this school not only to nurture you into good teachers but, more importantly, we hope you will create a cause that will benefit the country and the nation."

Headmaster Zhou's words stirred up Xu Teli. He compared notes with his classmates including Jiang Jihuan and He Yunong and decided to establish a new-style school in the countryside so that more people could read and know the truth of how to save the country and its people.

In the summer of 1905, Xu Teli, who had barely wrapped up his studies at Ningxiang Accelerated Normal School, established a new-style primary school – the Lijiang Senior Primary School – together with his good friends Jiang Jihuan and He Yunong at Langli Town, which was fifteen kilometres away from the city proper of Changsha. This was hailed as having "blazed a trail in establishing new-style schools in the countryside."

Langli Town lay along the River Liuyang to the east of Changsha City. It was a big town with numerous shops and restaurants doing a booming business to match. But the place was rather backward in cultural and educational terms. Many children from poor households couldn't afford their schooling. A senior primary school was newly established there. The news soon spread far and wide.

"It's said that the school charges only a little. Now the children of us poor households can go to school as well."

"Hey, it's said that they recruit girl students too."

"It's said that new knowledge will be taught there."

…

Yes, this was a new-style school!

Rushing One Hundred *Li* Every Day

After Lijiang Senior Primary School was in session, besides teaching the Chinese language, maths, history, geography and some other courses, Xu Teli actively took charge of many chores. Every day he was as busy as a bee, but he didn't ask for one cent's salary. He threw himself into the educational cause and never allowed his personal affairs to influence his teaching. His home was fifty *li* away from the school, but he seldom had time to take care of his family alongside running the school well.

On one Mid-autumn Festival, Xu Teli hurried back home from school. His wife had barely given birth to their third child. His three-year-old daughter had contracted dysentery and suffered from loose bowels for several days. Both his wife and children needed to be taken care of by someone. His household was in a desperate state, but he was unwilling to ask for leave due to his personal businesses and disrupt the students' schoolwork. What was he to do? While putting the house in order and tending to his wife and children, he racked his brains and finally struck upon an idea. After coming back to the school, he made the following arrangements: All his classes would be taught in the morning. After class, he would rush back home to cook, decoct medicinal herbs and take care of his wife and children. Before dawn of the next day, he would head back to school.

One morning the students were all in the classroom and the bell had already rung for class, but there was still no sign of Xu Teli. Jiang Jihuan was puzzled: Mr Xu was never late or dismissed his class ahead of time. But why was he still not in class today? Who should he look for to take his place? While he was on this knife-edge, Xu Teli rushed in through the school gate soaking in sweat. With no time to explain, he strode into the classroom to begin his class.

Later, when Jiang Jihuan and He Yunong heard tell of what happened at Xu Teli's home and knew that he needed to dash several dozen *li* to teach every day, they were deeply moved and persuaded him to stay at home for a few days to take care of his family. But Xu Teli declined. In this way, in order to neglect neither his home nor the school, he covered about one hundred *li* in a round trip and couldn't sleep for three or four hours every day. One day passed by. Two days passed by. Eight or ten days passed by. In no time at all the excessive fatigue had made him bony. But during that fortnight, he persisted in repeating the process every day and never missed one class – be it blowing a gale or raining.

Building up Changsha Normal School from Nothing

In 1912, the Republic of China was established. Jiang Jihuan became the Head of Changsha County. He spared no efforts in developing the educational cause and planned to establish 1,000 schools in Changsha City. In order to solve the teaching staff problem, he invited Xu Teli to establish a normal school first. Xu Teli promised without hesitation.

Operational funds were needed to establish and run a school. Xu Teli fixed his eyes to a batch of nitramide stored at Shanhua Academy by the Xiang'an Tea, Wine and Salt Commission. Changsha County First Senior Primary School with Xu Teli by then serving as Headmaster was rebuilt out of the Shanhua Academy. He went to the Commissioner and sold the nitramide after managing to get him to promise to solve some of the financial problem.

The to-be-established school had no classrooms at the very beginning. Xu Teli emptied some dilapidated rooms of the Shanhua Academy, gave them a facelift together with the passageways and corridors and converted them into classrooms. The classroom dilemma was solved.

By March, 1912, Changsha Normal School was formally in session. In total six classes were enrolled with a cohort of more than three hundred students. Among them two were for students who would graduate after studying there for five years, two for students who would graduate after receiving lectures for one year and two for students who would graduate after receiving lectures for half a year. Even under such adverse circumstances, Xu Teli managed to enrol batch after batch of able students and the fame of the normal school spread far and wide.

There were no experimental chemical facilities at school. During the chemistry classes the teacher taught only and the students couldn't understand. Xu Teli was worried. One day, toting a basketful of scrap metal and glass tubes bought from rag-and-tag shops and recycling stations, he informed the chemistry teacher happily: "Today I only had to spend very little to obtain a basketful of stuff we can use in chemistry class!" Under his directions, a simple and crude but comparatively practical chemical laboratory was finally set up. Someone asked him how much money he had spent on it. He answered smilingly: "Very cheap. I resorted to the poor man's way."

In order to find a permanent location for Changsha Normal School, Xu Teli went to every corner of Changsha City and finally set his eye on the

Letan Temple near the Lotus Pond in the north of the city. The ancient Letan Temple had been deserted long ago after the scourge of war. Once he had made up his mind, he submitted a request to the County Head of Changsha, Jiang Jihuan, and gained his generous support. The land was then allocated to Changsha Normal School.

The school grew by and by, but it was more and more difficult to raise the operational funds. In order to prevent the students from dropping out, Xu Teli had to fight back his pain and rented out the premises he had been shaping into a campus to Hunan Province First Junior High School to cover the expenditure with the several hundred silver coins of monthly rent income. His own school, however, was transferred to the dilapidated City God Temple to keep rolling on.

In this way, Changsha Normal School, which was run painstakingly and inspired by Xu's spirit, weathered the storm that lasted more than one hundred years and surmounted one difficulty after another. In the present day, the sound of music and singing still echo here.

Where Has the Headmaster's Salary Gone?

All things prove difficult before they become easy. Xu Teli started from scratch to set up Changsha Normal School and took the post of Headmaster himself. In order to provide conditions for the poor students to study with their minds at ease, he donated the better part of his salary to helping them out. Sometimes several months didn't see him send any money back home.

Once, Xiong Licheng was put in an awkward position. Her son Xu Duben caught a high fever and had been lying on bed for several days; even the sockets of his eyes had become sunken. She needed to chop firewood, carry water back home, brew tea, cook and invite the doctor, decoct the medicinal herbs and look after the patient. The doctor's bill and the charges for medicine swallowed up all her savings and there was no rice to be tipped into the wok. With no other option, she had to leave her son to her neighbours and went into the city proper to look for her husband herself.

She reached the road before daybreak, alternating between confident strides and a slow dawdle. When she reached the downtown area, it was already afternoon. She made enquiries anywhere along the street and finally found her way to the newly-established Changsha Normal School.

Seeing that Mrs Xu had come, the school caretaker Old Wang wanted to help her find the Headmaster.

She thanked him all the same hurriedly: "You are very busy. I will go look for him myself."

Exactly at this moment, some students came to Old Wang to ask for some brooms, saying that they saw Headmaster Xu was sweeping the rear yard.

But another student denied it by saying: "The foot of one of my classmates is festering. He's lying in bed and can't walk. I saw Headmaster Xu go to fetch some water with a bucket to wash his feet."

Clustered around by the students, Mrs Xu reached the dorm room. The student with a festering foot was warming his feet, but her husband was not there. With no other option, Old Wang had to settle Xiong Licheng down in Xu Teli's room for a rest. The students went separate ways to look for their Headmaster Xu. While Xiong Licheng was on tenterhooks, Xu Teli hurried in.

"Old man," Xiong Licheng fired a question at him head-on. "You haven't been home for months and haven't forwarded any money either. How do you expect us to live!"

"*Ayiah*, you make it sound like there's been a death in the family." Xu Teli teased her on purpose.

"Duben is ill. The doctor's bill and the expenses for the medicine have used up all the money. Now there is no rice to be tipped into the wok at home, but you still laugh? Ah! I don't know where your Headmaster's salary's gone?" Xiong Licheng complained.

Xu Teli let out a snort of bitter laughter and explained: "I didn't become a headmaster because I wanted an official post or riches. You don't know how difficult it is to keep a school running. The government is unwilling to allocate funds. Our income can't cover our expenditure. Everything beyond what I have to spend on meals for myself goes on subsidising students from poor households. How can I have money to send home?"

"Then what should we do about Duben's disease? What should we do now we don't have rice to eat?" Xiong Licheng was worried sick.

Thinking awhile, Xu Teli said: "Let's do it like this! Curing Duben's disease must be the first priority. I shall try to borrow some money for you to take back home. You must go back home first early tomorrow morning. As to the rice, I shall find a time to send some home. And take a look at Duben."

His words gagged Xiong Licheng's mouth.

Early the next morning, Xu Teli saw his wife out of the city and then went back to school to teach. After school was over on that afternoon, he borrowed a few bushels of rice from the kitchen and sent it back home that very night.

The Disturbances at the "Foreign School" at Wumei Village

One night in 1913, a raging fire shattered the serenity of Wumei Village. A small compound suddenly caught ablaze. The cluster of rooms at the centre of the courtyard together with the desks, chairs and benches were burned to a frazzle. The next day, Xu Teli, who by then was teaching in downtown Changsha, hurried back home.

The compound was the Wumei Junior Primary School established by Xu

Teli in his home village. Not long prior to that, he came back to Wumei from urban Changsha and found out for himself how backward the local education provision was. Across several dozen square kilometres, there was only a smattering of old-style private schools and not one new-style school. He therefore decided to raise fund and set up one. He dipped into his own pocket and purchased some writing desks, chairs and teaching aids to establish this primary school. The new educational system was implemented and new textbooks were adopted in this school; the usual old stuff taught in the old-style private schools was discarded. As a consequence, he was subject to concerted attack from reactionary folks.

"It's said that the 'Four Books and Five Classics'[1] are not taught there, only some 'foreign books!'"

"What kind of a school this is! It has become a foreign school through and through! Our ancient ancestors' traditions will all be discarded."

"Alas! They also enrol girl students! A boy and a girl can share a desk. Where is the precedent for that!"

...

One night, the diehards incited some people who didn't know the truth of it to devastate the campus and torch the classrooms. Xu Teli hurried back to Wumei Village. On the one hand, he went to look for those diehards to reason with them. Being on the side of right and consequently having strong lungpower, he lectured them: "What the new-style school teaches to the children is truly useful knowledge." On the other hand, he went to look for the teachers and encourage them: "Nothing in this world will always go smoothly and so does running a school. As long as it is beneficial to the folks and to the country, you should straighten your backs and carry on with it."

One teacher was perplexed with doubts: "Mr Xu, we could manage to

---

1   The Four Books refer to the *Great Learning*, the *Doctrine of the Mean*, *The Analects* and *Mencius*. The Five Classics refer to the *Book of Songs*, the *Book of History*, the *Book of Rites*, the *Book of Changes* and the *Spring and Autumn Annals*.

carry on. But our school has been burned down now and the folks are so scared they don't dare to send their children to us. What should we do?"

Xu Teli thought it over and suggested: "Isn't the Guanyin Temple at the entrance to the village a very good place? Let's move our school there to carry on with our classes! As to the students, let's put them all to work."

He swung into action the moment his words left his mouth. He led several teachers to the students' homes to make domiciliary visits and propagandised towards the folks why the old-style private schools should be abandoned and new-style schools be set up. The scales fell from the eyes of those who were not aware of the truth. They again sent their children to the school one after another. The number of the pupils rocketed up to more than seventy from the original thirty or so.

Emptying out His House to Serve as the Campus

After the failure of their sabotage attempt, the diehards were still unwilling to desist. The next year, a plague struck their village and claimed lives. They took advantage of this so as to spread a rumour: "The temple was changed into a school. The Goddess of Mercy was deprived of the sacrifices offered to her. The Bodhisattva meted out this disaster in a rage." Back then many people didn't have a clue about science and were convinced that the rumour was true. Hence, they assembled a gang of people to the school to stir up things, disturbed the classes and demanded that the school be moved out of the Guanyin Temple.

In order to solve the classroom problem, after gaining his wife's consent, Xu Teli decided to move the campus to his home. He emptied out a comparatively spacious tiled house, which was converted from an old building belonging to his family, and used it as the schoolhouse. He also raised money to build another two classrooms. His family, however, had to move into two newly-built thatched cottages. The school once more surmounted fresh difficulties. Thanks to his persistence, the rural primary school finally clung on, again setting an example to the whole of Wumei Village. More than fifty other national primary schools or teaching facilities were established in turn. Taking Changsha Normal School as the propagation site, he had nurtured a batch of qualified teachers for these schools within a short period of time.

He wrote out the four words "diligent," "frugal," "public-minded" and "honest" as the school motto with his own hands. During one speech, he expounded the connotations of the four words to the teaching staff and students. He said: "'Diligent' here is synonymous with being 'assiduous' and 'hard-working.' We should study hard at school and work hard at home – we should each of us be a hard-working student. 'Frugal' here is synonymous with being 'economical' and 'simple and plain.' No matter what time it is, we should practise frugality and oppose extravagance. We should develop this habit from an early age. 'Public-minded' here is synonymous with being 'just,' 'selfless' and unbiased in everything. No matter what we are doing, we should first and foremost think of the others but not consider ourselves only and sink into selfishness. 'Honest' here is synonymous with being 'sincere,' 'earnest' and true to one's words. When we study and work, we should always be honest and wholehearted but never resort to fraud, lying or cheating; after we have grown up, we should never do anything that offends the Heavens and reason. If you can fulfil the above-mentioned requirements, you are a good student. "

New-style teaching methods were adopted and practical knowledge was taught at Wumei Junior Primary School. People welcomed it warmly and the reputation of the "foreign-style" school echoed through the vicinity. Never did those diehards dare to come and make trouble again.

"Xu the Second Tinker"

In his home village, folks addressed Xu Teli by his nickname – "Xu the Second Tinker." He was the second son at home. "Tinker" is a Hunan local saying that refers to someone who solders together a broken wok with melted iron. This nickname can be traced back to the manner in which he established his schools.

In the summer vacation of 1924, a group of girl students who entered their names for Hunan First Girls Normal School but failed found Xu Teli and expressed their eager wish of attending school.

"Don't worry. Let's set up another school." After hearing them out, Xu Teli sympathised with them very much. He contacted some colleagues in the educational circles, compared notes with them on the establishment of a girl's school and gained their unanimous support. He was elected Headmaster of this school and immediately started the preparatory work. He commandeered a number of empty rooms from Changsha Normal School and again gave a face-lift to and whitewashed several old rooms in a nearby vegetable garden. These became their classrooms, office and dorm buildings. He stuck a sheet of white paper to the panel of a narrow side door. This read "Changsha Girls Normal School" and was to become their school gate. At the door of one room was positioned a single writing desk on which there was laid out a writing brush, Chinese ink and a registration book. This became their registration office. As to those office and teaching items such as desks, chairs, teaching aids and so on, they were either borrowed or second hand items temporarily put into use. A new school soon took shape like this. Some poked fun at him by saying that "Headmaster Xu has started from scratch again."

The school was so financially straitened they couldn't afford to hire a caretaker. Xu Teli was the Headmaster-cum-teacher-cum-janitor. In the daytime he taught, rang the bell to signal the beginning and the end of class, swept the floors and performed all kinds of chores. After class, he tutored the students. At night under a paraffin lamp he marked the students' homework. He was so busy he didn't have one moment's break. However, he wore a smiling face throughout the day. When another teacher was absent, he would cover his class. Not only could he teach Chinese language, history and geography but he was also proficient with maths, physics and chemistry. The others admired him not only because he loved the students and was scrupulous in his work but also because he was learned and his classes were very lively. Back then one Changsha newspaper reported: "The Headmaster of a certain school is aged but erudite. No matter which colleague is absent, he will go take over his class. He is good with every course except for music because he is short of two frontal teeth. If he sings, wind will gush out." The Headmaster described in this report was none other than Xu Teli.

In order to save expenditure, Xu Teli held school property very dear and would never waste anything – even if it was only a piece of paper or a stick of chalk. Every day he patrolled the campus several times. When he saw the desks and benches were not put in their due places or the flowers and woods and teaching aids were not well protected, he would put them in order in person. When it was windy or rainy – be it in the daytime or at night – he would lead the teaching staff and stress it into the students that they must shut the doors and windows tight. Books, newspapers and magazines purchased by the school would be taken charge of by people appointed by him especially. They should be stapled monthly with the table of contents well-made and stashed away respectively. Sometimes the other teachers might drop the ends of the chalk they had used on the floor. He would pick these up and put them in his pockets; when he was teaching, he took them out and put them to use.

Some felt that he was too penny-pinching.

"The chalk stubs can still be used to write," he explained. "Isn't it a pity to discard them! From small increments comes abundance. A lot of office expenditure can be saved in this way. Later after you have become a teacher, you must cherish diligence and frugality anytime and anywhere. You should help the children and teenagers to develop the habit of saving trivial property."

Xu Teli established many schools in Changsha, Hunan Province. Every time he did so he encountered many difficulties and setbacks. But undaunted and never deflated, he managed each one of them well by making the best use of all the facilities available.

Later Mao Zedong commented that: "Mr Xu often passed things that were of convenience to others but always hauled hardships up onto his own shoulders. He was good at managing broken-down stalls and knew only too well how to wear a coolie hat woven from tattered bamboo strips. When neither one classroom nor one coin was available, he still managed to start a not so small normal school. That was the tinker's spirit."

Allowing Paupers to Receive a Schooling

After the Revolution of 1911, Xu Teli was for a time employed as a Section Head in the Department of Education of the Provincial Government. Seeing that the children of numerous working people didn't have the chance to receive a schooling, he strongly advocated the development of mass education and the establishment of some half-day or night schools. Some people in the educational department, who were still in the grip of the old way of thinking, disagreed with his advocacy and retorted: "These wild goons are like the dog tail grass in the fields – they are not worthy of being educated. Why should schools be set up for them?" Infuriated by their words, he gave back his certificate of appointment and left the educational department.

In order to fulfil his advocacy of mass education, Xu Teli made an appointment with some like-minded friends to establish a night school so that the toiling paupers and their children could also have the opportunity to become literate. In the daytime he taught at school. At night he and several teachers took turns to teach at the night school. The night school stood in the Shrine of Governor Li outside the Northern Gate of Changsha. There were several factories around there and it was convenient for the workers to come and learn. Every day after nightfall, the students scurried here from every direction. Among them there were rickshaw-pullers, porters, sedan-chair bearers and shop apprentices – all "low-class rowdies" despised by the others back then. But Xu Teli liked them very much and was also liked and respected by them in turn. The night school offered classes in a number of disciplines, including the Chinese language, arithmetic and geography. Propaganda was also shared with the students so that they might keep abreast of current affairs.

When the night school was first in session, not many came there to learn. But the teachers' passion and advanced teaching methods and content soon won people's approval and were welcomed. More and more people requested to study there. Their number gradually increased to more than two hundred. Under their influence, many schools in the urban and rural areas of Hunan also started to set up night schools and half-day remedial schools. Mass education slowly became popular.

The New Ethos Was Established at Hunan First Girls Normal School

Xu Teli was the Headmaster of Hunan First Girls Normal School (popularly known as Daotian Normal School) from the spring of 1925 to 1927. Here he blazed a trail in establishing a new school ethos by blending some management systems drawn from schools in the West with the existing teaching management system. His reforms were brave. After taking on the role of Headmaster, the first thing he did was to quash the bans imposed by the school: In the past, the students were not allowed to go out of the school gate freely. Now they could go in and out freely during the period after class. In the past the students were banned from taking part in politics. Now they could participate in social activities. He even escorted them to go sightseeing in the vicinity and smashed the shackles the school had imposed upon the students.

Meanwhile, he opposed the harmful practices of forming cliques and small factions at school. He always treated competent and well-learned teachers with courtesy and severely criticised those who wanted to control the school through factionalism.

"It is a great shame to form small factions at school and transfer the practice of forming cliques for private gains from the realm of officialdom onto the campus."

He also clearly expressed his view that he would never be a "puppet headmaster." He sought out upright seasoned colleagues in the educational world in person and entrusted them to introduce excellent teachers untainted with factionalism to teach in the school. He loved his subordinates and fought those forces that were hostile to progressive teachers.

Once, some students, instigated by a factional force, stepped forward to stir up trouble and requested that the school dismiss a physics teacher. He sent people to make clear the ins and outs and then explained the truth to the students and warned them of the consequences. He pointed out that the physics teacher was indeed a fine teacher and shouldn't be fired. In short, he nipped the incident in the bud.

Soon afterwards, those factional instigators again posted anonymous letters to some progressive teachers and demanded that they resign, resorting to the force of threat. Such despicable tricks were also tackled head-on by Xu Teli. Those progressive teachers thus could give full play to their key role at school and the school could go from good to better.

Braving the Blizzard to Employ Teachers

In order that the students could master useful skills, Xu Teli stopped at nothing to employ all kinds of experienced teachers. Despite being the Headmaster, he was easy-going and never got on his high horse to boss his subordinates about. Even though the wages on offer might be a little low, many teachers were still willing to teach at the schools over which he presided.

One winter morning a cold wind was moaning and a heavy snow was drifting down. In a pair of wooden clogs and with an umbrella in his hand, Xu Teli braved against the blizzard and trudged several *li* to offer a post to a geography teacher with the surname Lu. When he reached Mr Lu's home, he knocked at the door. The door was opened by Mr Lu's wife.

"Where are you from?" she asked Xu Teli.

"Hunan First Girls Normal School."

"What are you here for?"

"To look for Mr Lu."

"It is so early! Mr Lu hasn't got up yet. Sit down here and wait awhile!"

With these words, Mrs Lu went into the kitchen to prepare breakfast.

Sitting down alone on the oblong wooden bench for half an hour, Xu Teli still couldn't see Mr Lu and had to go to the kitchen to probe: "Has Mr Lu gotten up?"

"It is snowing so heavily. How can Mr Lu get up so early! If you can't wait that long, you can go back first and come another day!" Mrs Lu replied impolitely, believing that Xu Teli must be a hired hand from the girl's normal school.

"No problem, no problem. I will wait a bit longer."

Xu Teli didn't feel her words offensive but stepped back and continued to wait.

After waiting for the better part of another hour, Mr Lu got up for his meal. Not until then did he know that Headmaster Xu had been sitting there waiting for him for more than an hour. Moved deeply by his patient and sincere attitude, Mr Lu gladly accepted his invitation despite having already accepted a post with another school.

The "King of Changsha" in Hunan's Educational World

In order to utilise the wisdom of the people and accomplish his wish of saving the country through the promotion of education, Xu Teli rode a beaten-up cart in tattered clothing. Sparing no efforts, he blazed a trail throughout his life. When he was sixty, he recalled: "Teaching has been my lifelong vocation and career. From enlightenment school to junior primary school, senior primary school and secondary normal school up to advanced normal school, I have taught at every one of them. Even when I was a teacher at an advanced normal school, my love of teaching pupils meant I couldn't tear myself away from my post at a primary school."

In his early years Xu Teli set up two senior and one junior primary school in Changsha. One of the two senior primary schools operated for fully thirteen years. He established a junior girls normal school that could boast two hundred students, but this nonetheless remained open for only three years and had to close down due to the failure of the Great Revolution. He had also started a men's normal school of more than four hundred students, however later on this had to be handed over to the Government of Changsha County because he couldn't maintain its operations.

Latterly, he felt able to laugh at himself by saying: "I have never owned any personal property, nor held any public office that could be plied for a fortune. So how was it that I could keep my schools in operation? My methods included: First of all, teaching two hours of overtime every day. In this way I could earn an extra sixty yuan every month, which would be divided up between the two senior primary schools to cover their expenditure. I left my family in the countryside, cut down my daily expenditure, declined any social engagement and never invited my friends to drink wine or dine on meat and snacks. Secondly, the primary schools charged no fee and the fee charged by the normal schools was less than that charged by a common private school. I set about improving the teaching methods and making myself into a model of assiduousness that would inspire the teachers and students to love their school, redouble their efforts and win over every possible personnel and material support."

You reap what you sow. Under Xu Teli's painstaking management, incremental progress was made in the name of education in Changsha County. By the eighth year of the Republic of China (1919), there were eighty hundred primary schools in Changsha. Many teachers had previously received short-term training from his schools. On account of his distinguished merit and reputation and his outstanding contribution to the learning in the province, he was hailed as the "King of Changsha" in Hunan's educational world back then.

Chapter Three

Loving the Students as if They Were His Own Children and Nurturing Their Talents

Carefully Fostering the "Modern-day Guan Hanqing"

Xu Teli cared very much about his students and committed his very lifeblood to his work. He never spared any efforts in helping and looking after young men who came from poor households yet aspired to gain knowledge. Tian Han stands out as a prime case.

Hailed as the "modern-day Guan Hanqing," Tian Han (1898 – 1968) became a renowned dramatist and poet, and was the composer of the Chinese national anthem. When he studied at Changsha Normal School, he was the beneficiary of Xu Teli's earnest teaching and intense loving care.

In 1912, fourteen-year-old Tian Han was admitted into Class One for undergraduates at Changsha Normal School. Having lost his father in his childhood, his family was trapped in grinding poverty. In order to support his schooling, his mother came from the countryside to the city. She first set up a small tea stall outside the Northern Gate and later washed other people's laundry at the Pengjiajing (the Peng Family Well) to earn some pocket money.

Owing to the straitened financial circumstances, Tian Han had no money to buy a mosquito net and was destined to face sleepless summer nights in bug-infested and mosquito-ridden Changsha. When he inspected the students' dorm rooms, Xu Teli found out that Tian had buried his head under the quilt and a rash had erupted all over his body. The next day, he purchased him a mosquito net and said: "If you run into any difficulty, you should tell me! If things carried on like this, you wouldn't get a minute's rest at night. Then how would you manage to study properly in the daytime?"

Tian Han liked reading very much, but he had no money to buy books and had to head to Changsha Library in the holidays to pore over them. The library charged one copper coin as the admissions fee. In order to save money, he frequently had just a single sesame-seed pancake for breakfast and left one copper coin behind to buy the ticket. He then stayed there reading throughout the day and was unwilling to leave for lunch.

Observing how the penniless Tian Han loved reading like this, Xu Teli gave him his own book-purchasing card and told him to buy whatever he pleased. The fee would be written down on the card and Xu Teli would go and pay the bill at the end of the year.

Tian Han was a lover of literature and often composed nonsense verses and dramas. Xu Teli encouraged him to edit a "windowpane newspaper." When Ouyang Yuqian and some of the members of Spring Willow Society Repertory Company came to the Confucian Temple in Changsha to rehearse modern drams such as *Hot Blood*, *Better Come Back*, *A Backward Jerk of the Head* and so on, he escorted Tian Han and some other literary-minded students to go over there to watch and encouraged them to boldly compose and rehearse dramas.

Supported by Xu Teli, Tian Han gave full play to his literary talent at Changsha Normal School. In 1913, he finished composing his first work of drama *How a Widowed Mother Taught Her Son – A New Story*, which was published in *Changsha Daily*. In 1914, he took charge of editing the journal *Youth* together with his classmates including Huang Zhigang. Two of his own dramas were featured in its pages. In 1915, he completed the drama *The New Peach Blossom Fan* after the style of *The Peach Blossom Fan* composed by Kong Shangren in the Qing Dynasty. In this work he also drew from *The New Roman Legends* written by Liang Qichao. *The New Peach Blossom Fan* was serialised in the supplements of *The Shanghai Times*. Tian Han later became a renowned dramatist and man of letters. He owed much of his ultimate success to Xu Teli's support and help.

Tian Han always kept Xu Teli's teachings lodged in his mind. In 1947 when Xu Teli celebrated his seventieth birthday, he took the trouble to post a long poem from Shanghai. This sang the praises of his teacher's brilliant achievements in education. Several lines from it read:

Your students spread everywhere beneath the sky.
Like a spring breeze to caress everything you try.

...
Now please raise your gold goblets high.
Let's toast the aged gentleman from Shanghai.

The Windowpane Newspapers

When he was the Headmaster of Changsha Normal School, Xu Teli advocated education and democracy and extended his greatest care and solicitude to the students. In addition, he sought to seize on every opportunity to stimulate their activity.

Back then, the fourteen-year-old Tian Han could number Huang Zhigang, Cao Bohan, Zhou Zhu'an, and Zhang Huai as fellow literature lovers in his class. They would pen nonsense verses and hang their manuscripts on the windowpanes of their self-study classroom.

One day, they composed two poems which included the names of the Headmaster Xu Teli and two other teachers – Shou Yuanlong and Huang Zhucun. One read: "Stand (*li*) loftily (*te*) among the raging billows and tumultuous waves. Behead (*shou*) the most huge (*yuan*) dragon (*long*) with a precious sword." The other one read: "Chickens and dogs are making a raucous din at Huangzhu Village (*cun*)." After the two teachers spied them, they flew into a rage, surmising that "the students show no respect to their elders and betters and their deed brings disgrace to the educated class." They requested that the Headmaster severely scold the students.

After consoling the two teachers, Xu Teli sent for Tian Han and the others.

Tian Han explained: "We meant no ill intentions to Headmaster Xu and the two teachers Huang and Shou. We composed them on the spur of the moment. It was a joke only to humour the guys."

Xu Teli first criticised their disrespectful deed but again felt that the poems demonstrated the children's wisdom. He then said to them kindly: "It is a good thing that you like writing. But you shouldn't waste your time and efforts fiddling about with your brush and ink. You should throw your intelligence, wisdom and writing skills into doing the right things. It would be best if you were to write some meaningful articles which would help you to hone your abilities."

Xu Teli's words energised the students in their compilation of "windowpane newspapers." Like the bamboo shoots after a spring drizzle, the windowpanes of almost all the self-study classrooms were instantaneously hung with newspapers. What is more, each one gave a name to the newspapers they edited. For instance, *Morning Toll* and *Evening Toll*. Tian Han called his newspaper *Zu's Whip*, in reference to the words of a letter Liu Kun wrote to his family and friends in the Jin Dynasty. The portion quoted read: "My dagger-axe serves as my pillow as I await the break of day, ready to try and crush the treacherous barbarians from the north. I am always afraid that Zu Ti might vault into the saddle and whip the horse in action before I've had the chance." Articles and poems published in these windowpane newspapers mostly adopted an impassioned and forceful tone in order to give vent to their anxieties about the situation of the country and its people. Later the newspaper *Antan*, which was conservative by comparison, came into circulation. Tian Han and his partners then united the other newspapers to argue against it and the atmosphere became very lively.

Xu Teli was a most ardent reader of the windowpane newspapers and often read through them carefully; sometimes he reprinted some good articles in his *Education Weekly*. Motivated greatly, the students threw themselves into their writing. Suddenly, all kinds of literary styles began to appear in the windowpane newspapers. Book reviews, commentaries on current events, poems, stories, essays and so on burst into view like an array of flowers. The campus became a garden awash with the splendour of spring. Even the two teachers Shou Yuanlong and Huang Zhucun who had once felt "humiliated" changed their attitudes and nodded their heads happily to heap praises on the students' endeavours.

The Headmaster and the Demobilised Soldier

After Xu Teli opened Changsha Normal School and assumed the post of Headmaster, he strained every nerve to keep it going and single-mindedly wanted to nurture more excellent teachers for Changsha's fundamental education.

One day while he was busy in his office, a demobilised soldier by the name of Liao Yi came over to make enquiries. Originally, Liao had made his living as a coolie labourer in the city. After the Revolution of 1911, he joined the New Army, but he knew only two to three hundred Chinese characters. In 1913 after he was demobilised, he felt the pains of being illiterate and wanted very much to go to Changsha Normal School to study. He therefore descended on Xu Teli and expressed his eagerness to expand his knowledge.

Moved by the visitor's spirit, Xu Teli arranged an entrance examination for him to decide which class he should attend. However, after his marks were returned, he found out that Liao Yi's basic knowledge was too meagre and his foundation was too weak. Every class would pose a big challenge for him.

Looking at his marks, Liao Yi insisted: "Mr Xu, I am willing to study hard. I have the aspiration to learn. Please do take me in."

Deeply moved, Xu Teli replied, "I shall make an exception and enrol you simply because you say you *have the aspiration to learn*. But you must study hard."

"I surely will. But I don't know how to," a worried Liao Yi answered. "I don't know how to study so that I am able to catch up with the other students. I hope Teacher, that you will give me more instruction."

"Put your mind at ease." Xu Teli promised. "As long as you want to study, I can tutor you every night."

"Really?" Liao Yi asked in disbelief.

Xu Teli nodded his head.

Thanks to Xu Teli's concern, support and encouragement, Liao Yi studied hard and made rapid progress. Later he followed Xu Teli to France for a work-study programme. After coming back to China, he established a civilian craft factory. Never would he forget how Old Headmaster Xu Teli had nurtured him. "But for Venerable Xu's earnest teachings and solid support right at the very beginning I would surely have dropped out long before. Now I must be muddling through my days in goodness-knows-where and living by my own muscle."

The Blacksmith Student

The blacksmith Li Shengzhou had an even more pitiful schooling than Liao Yi, but he too wanted to enrol for study. One day, with his blacksmith's kit on his back, he came to Changsha Normal School and requested that he might be admitted there.

Sizing up Li's attires, Xu Teli asked: "Are you here to study?"

"Of course!" Li Shengzhou answered. "It is said that Mr Xu Teli never despises the poor and curries favour with the rich and never detests how low a student's origins might be. So what? I am a blacksmith and I can't go to school?"

Xu Teli smiled. "Of course you can. But you should take an entrance examination first so we can assess your knowledge. We can then arrange which class you should attend."

Li Shengzhou dropped down the tools from his shoulder and sat at a writing desk to sit the entrance examination obediently. He was very serious and answered the questions on the paper meticulously.

When he marked his paper, Xu Teli found out that Li Shengzhou had received schooling for several years, but apparently he had clean forgotten what he had learned long before. His answers were seldom correct. But he took his handwriting very seriously and the overall appearance of the paper was neat and tidy.

He summoned Li Shengzhou over and said to him: "This is your answer sheet, but the results are not satisfactory …"

"I did learn a thing or two in the past." Li Shengzhou was now seized with panic. Believing that Xu Teli didn't want to take him in, he explained in a hurry: "But these years I've seldom been able to brush up on what I know and so it's gone from my mind. Teacher, please give me a while. I am sure I can answer all these questions."

With a smile, Xu Teli encouraged him: "Don't worry, don't worry. That much I can tell, but you won't be able to catch up with the others in this term. Let's do it this way: You pick up your lessons at home during this period of time and come to get registered directly next term."

"But if I stay at home these days, I can't pick up anything. Can you give me a dorm room? Can I be your student and board here as I swat up?" Worried sick, Li Shengzhou's face turned pale.

But all the rooms at school were filled to capacity and really couldn't accommodate another person. Xu Teli thought a little longer and said: "Let's do it this way: I know someone at the repair shop of the ordnance depot. You go there to lend them a hand and earn a little money to cover your living cost in the daytime. Come to me at night. I shall help you make up your lessons."

Not only would he now have a job but he could also learn from Xu Teli. Li Shengzhou's gratitude towards Xu Teli knew no bounds.

After learning for half a year, Li Shengzhou finally made up his missed lessons. At the beginning of the next term, he was admitted into Changsha Normal School without a hitch.

Later he became a widely-acclaimed biology teacher and was elected an Excellent Teacher in Hunan after the liberation of China in 1949.

Fetching Water for a Student to Bathe His Feet

When he was the Headmaster of Changsha Normal School, Xu Teli showed great care and concern to his students and never struck the posture of a Headmaster. Frequently he sat at the same dinner table with them to experience how their food was and see if the situation could be improved at any time. During one spell, he shared a dorm room with them and supervised and urged them to go to sleep on time.

One day, he went to inspect the students' dorm rooms and found that one student was lying on the bed moaning. He asked about this and was told that he had an excruciatingly painful sore on his foot. He immediately fetched some hot water, helped him to wash his feet clean and again applied some ointment. "It is best that you don't move about for the time being," he stressed into him. "You'd better rest well and have a break from class!"

Nobody knows how word of this situation got out. Back then someone in the educational circles jeered at him unstintingly and felt astounded that Xu Teli, being the Headmaster of a public school, would actually stoop to such a menial deed. After hearing of this, Xu Teli dismissed it as nothing and defended himself with a grin: "A headmaster or teacher is duty-bound to care about and love their students. I only did one small good work, but it's been blown out of all proportion." The way he saw it, those acts he did which were deemed "unorthodox" were precisely what people in the world of education should be doing but rarely did or never had done.

"Grandma Xu"

In January, 1925, Xu Teli was appointed Headmaster of Hunan First Girls Normal School. After assuming office, he set about overhauling the teaching, wielding mighty swords and broad axes to achieve his purpose. He selected and recruited a batch of teachers who were virtuous and talented and advanced in their ideological thinking. He also rescinded many bans, for example the prohibition on girls coming in and out of the school gate freely, on them not being allowed to take an interest in politics, on them participating in social activities in public and so on and so forth. The girls were thereby freed from many feudal-style shackles.

In the autumn of that year, a girl named Xu Deyao came to Hunan First Girls Normal School from the countryside of Xiangtan. In floods of tears she sought out Headmaster Xu, introduced to him her family situation and confided to him that she wanted to go to school. She told Headmaster Xu that her love was studying at Hunan University. The young man wanted her to break free from the bondage of her family and come to Changsha to attend school. Xu Teli sympathised with her plight very much and admitted her to the school roll. Beside herself with joy, Xu Deyao studied judiciously and didn't fall behind her classmates in any respect.

Unfortunately, Miss Xu soon afterwards discovered that she was pregnant. Unwilling to sacrifice the hard-won chance to study, she had to keep the truth to herself. But the baby would be born sooner or later. At midnight in the depths of winter, she went into labour without there being any time for her to be sent home or to a hospital. On learning of this, Xu Teli decided without hesitation to let her give birth at school. The baby came to this world smoothly.

The next day, Xu Teli summoned all the teachers, students, staff members and workers for a meeting and explained to them what had happened to Xu Deyao. He told them not to be apprehensive and not to succumb to prevailing prejudices or pressure. The girls were more readily attuned to a fellow woman's difficulties. They toed their headmaster's line and adhered to his standpoint from the bottom of their hearts. Crowding around him to offer their congratulations one after another, they cordially addressed him as "Grandma." The nickname "Grandma Xu" soon spread all over the campus.

At the same time, rumours were rife and not a little criticism was vented in educational circles. Some gossiped and maligned the ethos of the first girl's school. But Xu Teli stood firm in the face of pressure and persisted in allowing Xu Deyao to complete her schooling.

In 1956, Xu Teli came back to Hunan. Some graduates from the first girl's school went to see him and told him that Xu Deyao was now a teacher in Xiangtan. The baby born thirty years earlier had now become a government cadre. The venerable Xu smiled in relief.

The Amiable "Grandma" Headmaster

Xu Teli gained the nickname "Grandma Xu" not only because he was kind to Xu Deyao but more because he was benevolent to every student as if they were his children – he extended to every student his "grandmotherly" warmth and forbearance.

Whenever winter came around, he drilled it into the students at Hunan First Girls Normal School that they should put on extra clothes so as not to suffer from chills; charcoal braziers were lit in the classrooms very early in the morning. On the arrival of summer, he pushed the classroom windows open for ventilation. After self-study sessions at night, he required that students take care of their health and go to bed on time; they should do no more reading. Frequently accompanied by the female counsellor, he patrolled each dorm room to check out if someone was still chit-chatting or doing something else. Whenever he came across a student who hadn't gone to sleep on time, he would always ask: "Why are you not in bed? You'd better rise early than retire late." He often shared a dinner table with the students to find out how their meals were. His meticulous love and concern made them think that Headmaster Xu was as amiable and benign as their maternal grandma. Therefore, the nicknames "Grandma Xu" or "Grandma" spread out throughout the campus.

Back then the renowned writer Xie Bingying was a student at Hunan First Girls Normal School. She later recalled: "He really was a great educator! His arrival transformed the school into a brand new one. Some students who had been used to learning by rote sprang to life like the little birds in the spring. We all addressed him as 'Grandma.'"

It was this selfsame Xie Bingying, who felt indebted to both Headmaster Xu's support and the atmosphere of democracy and openness to learning that reigned at Hunan First Girls Normal School. She devoured numerous advanced literary works, for example the poems and prose works of Guo Moruo, Yu Dafu, Cheng Fangwu and the works of Maupassant, Zola, Tolstoy, Dostoevsky and Eroshenko and so on. Her thought gradually matured and she was beholden to a perspicacious view of the world. In the winter of 1926, she entered her name for the entrance examinations of Wuhan Central Military and Political School and became a female soldier, which was something of a rarity back then. Subsequently, she became a renowned writer and published a body of works amounting to more than twenty million Chinese characters and including *The Autobiography of a Female Soldier* and *Army Diaries*.

Teaching the Students Kindly through Poems

When he was the Headmaster of the Hunan First Girls Normal School, Xu Teli often taught the students kindly through poems. He hung up a big blackboard in the corridor through which the students often passed. Whenever he found out the students had done something praiseworthy or below par, he would praise or criticise their conduct by putting their names into poems which were easy for all to understand. This way they were given yet further ideological and moral education. These poems, later known as "One Hundred Poems Composed on Campus," reflected how Xu Teli loved and cared about the young generation.

One day, being disgusted at the standard of the food from the school canteen, one student went to the kitchen after supper and took the opportunity to smash some bowls. Xu Teli criticised this wanton vandalism and wrote out a poem on the blackboard early the next morning to educate all the students:

I hope that the students are a cut above their teachers just like indigo surpassing its parent blue.
But they should never squander human resources, materials or finances too.
What on earth was it that happened last night,
To send her into the kitchen and stir up such a to-do.

In his running of the school, Xu Teli practised frugality in every area. When he saw a fragment of chalk on the floor, he always picked it up and pocketed it for his personal use. Some students couldn't understand why. He explained by telling them how an ancient government official cherished even chips of wood and how meaningful that was. He wrote a poem on the blackboard to teach them to form the habit of frugality:

Even half a length of chalk is a treasure.
Saving public property is always a pleasure.
Unable to tune in to my heartfelt ardour,
The students, on the contrary, presume that I am a miser.

Every day Xu Teli would patrol the dorm rooms at bedtime in the company of the female counsellor. One day, he found out that some students hadn't gone to sleep on time but were still chit-chatting; one student was knitting a sweater under the lamp light from the washroom. He admonished them that they should go to bed on time. Realising they had breached the work-and-rest system, the students expected a severe reproach and disciplinary punishment. But he didn't do as they anticipated. Instead, he wrote two poems on the blackboard on the next day.

The clock has already struck midnight.
But someone is still knitting a sweater with poached light.
I agree that you do love the others.
But you don't love yourself and that can't be right.

Running from east to the west,
They not only knit but also jest.
Don't defend yourself by saying that your voice is low.
It is already late and others will still protest.

After reading through the poems, the students were affected. From then on they were conscientious about keeping the curfew and never let behaviour of that kind happen again.

Two students with the surnames Tang and Yu were not mindful of their physical health and were always to be found with their heads buried in books. Their health deteriorated accordingly. Xu Teli wrote a poem on the blackboard especially for this reason and taught all the students to set greatest store by physical exercise to be both healthy and excellent in their studies:

I exhort the students Tang and Yu hereby.
Please stop studying so hard – don't ask yourselves why.
Both of you are a mass of skin and bone.
Because you know nothing but books and have no lusty tone.

After snacking on oranges and peanuts and such like, one student left the floor strewn with peel and shells. Xu Teli criticised her severely:

Peanut shells and orange peel have been tossed everywhere.
The stone steps are awash with them but she doesn't seem to care.
Students should be the cream of the human race.
But her carelessness is proving a shabby disgrace.

Because Xu Teli loved his students so much, they addressed him as "Grandma Xu." He also composed an interesting poem touching on himself:

Fearful that the students might go short on sleep,
I patrol the campus nightly, no matter how cold and deep.

I am in fact the grandfather to the kids in my company.
So why is it that everybody always calls me their "granny"?

The Literacy Campaign Launched by the Minister of Education

At the end of 1930, Xu Teli came back to his motherland from the Soviet Union and reached the Soviet Revolutionary Base Area in Jiangxi Province that was under the direct jurisdiction of the CPC Central Committee.

Back then, the vast districts under the jurisdiction of the CPC Central Committee Soviet Area were remote and uncultured. Ninety people out of every one hundred couldn't read even a single word. After the establishment of the revolutionary regime, impoverished people became their own masters. They were eager to learn to read and write. After his arrival in the Soviet Area, Xu Teli was appointed Deputy-Minister and then Acting Minister of China Soviet People's Commission for Education. He made up his mind to address the situation.

Hardships piled up upon hardships. With the flames of war raging across the land, sowing and nurturing the cause of education became an ever taller order. Back then books were few and far between. Even finding a newspaper was not easy. Sometimes it took the Red Army taking control of a county city so that people could lay their hands on newspapers. Paper for writing was in extremely short supply too. Even a palm-sized piece was precious. Under these most adverse of circumstances, Xu Teli made painstaking plans and preparations and started basic literacy and training classes. There were not enough teachers. He adhered to the principle that whoever proved themselves qualified could be a teacher. Moreover, he put forward the very effective anti-illiteracy guideline that "A husband can teach his wife, a son can teach his father, a secretary can teach a chairman, a stable hand can teach another stable hand, a cook can teach another cook, those who know more Chinese characters can teach those who know fewer and those who have learned to read already can teach those who haven't learned how to read yet." A magnificent mass literacy movement was set into motion like this.

Every night, uncles and aunts studied the new words laboriously but meticulously beneath the dim light of paraffin lamps. Xu Teli often went to the classes to teach the students to read word by word and to recite the texts sentence by sentence. Any good experience would be publicised immediately. Taking up his lead, people worked out many fantastic methods for learning how to read: Sand was used as paper and tree switches were used as writing brushes to practice how to write; word-teaching boards were hung on the wellheads and lookouts were planted at the entrances to villages. In this way people were given supervision and urged to learn more.

Xu Teli also compiled textbooks and personally created teaching aids and established primary schools. The children happily stepped into the classrooms with schoolbags on their backs and opened the mimeographed textbooks to recite loudly:

The sun is brightly shining.
Illuminating everything.
Members of the Children's Corps
All go to school with their faces beaming.
Learn how to read and write.
Wipe out illiteracy outright.

In addition to these operations, Xu Teli established normal schools and agricultural schools. He seized every moment of free time to pen screenplays and direct them. In this way, he nurtured a clutch of talented individuals equipped to undertake cultural and artistic work and propaganda.

Back at that time, fighting on the battlefield was the No. 1 task. In order to channel more hands to the front to join the battles, the government organs at home were drained of personnel. During one period of time, the Ministry of Education had only two members of staff: one being Xu Teli the Minister in charge and the other one being a fourteen-year-old orderly. The school staff was cut back to a bare minimum. Besides teaching, Xu Teli was required to sweep the floors, ring the bell, grow vegetables and cook. He worked like a Trojan every day.

The KMT army blockaded the Soviet Area tightly from all four sides. Salt and the other daily necessities couldn't be brought in and their lives were gruelling. Their school frequently went for months without a taste of salt. Once, Qu Qiubai obtained a mite of salt through great effort. He especially invited Xu Teli over for a meal and used it as seasoning. That might be counted as a real treat.

Despite the adversity of the circumstances, Xu Teli grafted with pleasure. The causes of culture and education prospered in the Soviet Area in little time at all.

The Minister of Education "Who Didn't Know How to Accrue Wealth"

In 1935 after the Red Army reached Northern Shaanxi, Xu Teli took the post of Minister of Education of the North-western Office of the Soviet Republic of China and took overall charge of the educational work in the Shaanxi-Gansu-Ningxia Border Region. Though he was the Minister of Education, he never left the first front of education, participating in the establishment and running of schools, taking on teaching tasks and caring about and assisting students from poor households. Many widely-known stories were left behind.

One young man called Yan Jingshan single-mindedly wanted to come to the border region to study, but on his way he had to pass through the blockade imposed by the KMT army. It was a tough and perilous journey. Many items of his hand luggage ended up being discarded. His quilt was lost en route. When he was admitted to the Lu Xun Normal School, he had no quilt to keep him warm but was forced to share a bed with someone else or put on several items of upper clothing. It was becoming colder every day and he was on a knife-edge. He threw everything he had into his study. Before dawn every day he got up to start cramming.

Xu Teli rose early each morning to patrol the campus as usual. He found out that one student was always studying diligently on the stone bench in the self-study classroom. Feeling curious, he made enquiries among other students and knew of Yan Jingshan's situation.

"This is a good kid," he praised. "I will give my quilt to him!"

He carried his quilt over and gave it to Yan Jingshan.

"Jingshan," he said. "It is getting cool. Take good care of your health and don't let the cold make you ill! Health is the seed money of revolution!"

Greatly moved, Yan Jingshan vowed that he would study even harder to return Xu Teli's kindness. After he sent his quilt to Yan Jingshan, Xu Teli had to use the raincoat sent to him by Premier Zhou Enlai as the quilt every night.

One further tale concerns a student named Luo Jinhua. Luo came from Huangling County in Shaanxi Province and studied at a local junior high school. Single-mindedly he wanted to go to Yan'an. One night he fled from his school quietly. In order that his footfall was not to be heard by anyone, he pulled off his shoes and reached Lu Xun Normal School in his bare feet. The moment he spotted this, Xu Teli took off his shoes and gave them to him without thought.

Luo felt very apologetic and refused by saying: "Venerable Xu, how can I accept your shoes? What is more, if you give your shoes to me, what will you have to wear?"

Xu Teli waved his hands and insisted: "Student Jinhua, you must put them on. I have shoes in my dorm room. I will go back and change into another pair after a while."

Luo put on the shoes gratefully. After sending out his shoes, Xu Teli, however, wore a pair of hempen shoes for a long time. Later Cai Chang noticed that and told Li Fuchun about it. Li Fuchun gave a pair of his shoes to Xu Teli. Again Lin Boqu, Chairman of the Government of the Shaanxi-Gansu-Ningxia Border Region wrote out a brief note and solved the problem of Xu Teli's quilt.

Generous, warm-hearted and sincere, Xu Teli loved the students as if they were his children and cared about the others more than about himself. People back then praised him: "Venerable Xu doesn't know how to accrue wealth. If he hasn't given his quilt to someone else, he has given them his shoes."

Nurturing the Sapling of the Natural Sciences

In August, 1940, Xu Teli came back to Yan'an and at the end of the same year was appointed President of Yan'an Academy of Natural Sciences – the first college of science and engineering established by the CPC.

Back then, some comrades did not want to endorse the establishment of an academy of natural sciences. Their reasoning was that Yan'an was rather weak in terms of its personnel and material resources, making the conditions less than favourable for the development of the natural sciences. But Xu Teli was resolute about establishing the school.

He reasoned: "While engaging in revolutionary work, we should never merely take care of what is under our noses and neglect the bigger picture. When scientific talents are to be nurtured, it takes a dozen or so or several dozen years for results to be shown. This is what the ancients meant when they said, 'It takes ten years for a tree to grow tall, but it takes one hundred years to raise a generation of people.' If we don't seize the day, what is to be done in the future? If we just sit on our hands waiting for the conditions to become ideal on their own without creating those conditions, are we to expect scientific and technological talents to fall down from the skies?"

He stuck to this view: despite the fact that back then our nation lacked strength, the tragic history that our national science and technologies were backward, the country was weak and the people were poor should never be left to slide. He published many articles in the newspapers to propagandise how important it was to develop science and technology. He harangued: "We have suffered too much from our backward science and technology! The cart in the front has overturned; the following ones should learn a lesson from the tragedy of their predecessor. How can the Yan'an of today neglect such a great cause!"

Back at that time, Northern Shaanxi was a remote and insignificant place with inconvenient transport links and backward culture. Scientific and technological talents had little chance to reach that place because of the Japanese imperialist invaders and the KMT blockade. There was neither scientific apparatus and equipment nor necessary books and data. Even the common classrooms, blackboards, paper and pens were in very short supply. However, Xu Teli was not thwarted. He led the teaching staff and students to excavate caves and used them as school buildings; they created teaching aids and experimental apparatuses; they compiled textbooks … Their determined sweat nurtured the sapling of natural sciences on the barren wasteland, allowing it to thrive.

The school which boasted several hundred students stood on a series of mountain slopes. Each mountain slope had a number of layers of caves. The students scattered in the not so bright cave classrooms to hear the lectures. When a meeting was convened or a big class was conducted, they gathered together on the empty terrace outside the caves. Xu Teli personally looked into the school's teaching guidelines, the curricula, the ideological work and the logistical supply piece by piece. Every day he needed to clamber up and down several mountains. On rainy days, the roads on the steep mountains were slippery. He then trudged with bare feet supported by a walking stick. When a large class was being conducted, he delivered his lecture on the earthen terrace. Be it high summer or the dead of winter, he never put on a hat but wore a bald pate and lectured for several hours at a time. He was the President of the school. According to the rules, he was entitled to occupy his own cave house. But he persisted in summoning two other teachers to live and share the small paraffin lamp at night together with him.

"Everyone's living space is cramped," he explained. "Why should I be the exception?"

The teachers and students of the academy were mostly young people from all over the country. At the very beginning, they couldn't get accustomed to the hard life. But taught by Xu Teli through both his words and actions, they gradually did. Using bricks as benches, their knees as writing desks, tree switches as their writing brushes and the earth as their paper, they threw themselves into the nervous study. Their conditions were very straitened, but everyone was in good spirits and enjoyed their life. Whenever class was over, merry songs would echo both inside and outside the cave classrooms:

Our life is hard and fast-paced.
But our revolutionary zeal soars high each day.
Who says we have no classrooms?
We have the best in the world.
The clear blue sky is our rooftop.
The high mountains are our perimeter walls.
Who says we have no teaching aids?
Our self-made kit is more beautiful.
Who concludes "country bumpkins" don't know how to run a big school?
Our confidence is more solid than Mount Tai.
Our will is stronger than steel and iron.
For the rebirth of our motherland,
And for the liberation of our nation,
No hardship can stop us ...

Under the leadership of Xu Teli, the Yan'an Academy of Natural

Sciences that was born in the flames of war nurtured batch after batch of scientific and technological talents and made a great contribution to the development of science and technology after the establishment of the PRC.

"Be a Gardener but Never a Woodcutter"

Xu Teli began teaching in an old-style enlightenment school in the countryside at the age of eighteen. Until he departed from this world at the grand old age of ninety-one, he was constantly engaged in his beloved cause – education. He held the view that a teacher is a transmitter of truth and an engineer of human souls. He emphasised repeatedly that a teacher should "be a gardener but never a woodcutter." A teacher should be prudent and serious, treat his work meticulously and throw himself into the nurturing of the saplings and flowers. When a student had violated the school regulations or done something wrong, they shouldn't be dealt with using disciplinary punishments or be expelled casually. Instead, starting from the perspective of loving them, they should be subject to meticulous and patient ideological persuasion. As to how to punish them, he was against corporal punishment or corporal punishment in a disguised form and held the view that "corporal punishment is a barbarian act."

In the first several years after the liberation of the country in 1949, great progress was made in primary school education, but corporal punishment was still commonplace. In the winter of 1952 when Xu Teli listened to an educational work report, the reporters told him how the pupils were punished in the primary schools, saying that one teacher strained a student's wrist by tugging at him and that one teacher even forced a student to lick up the phlegm he spat out on the floor. In a towering rage, Xu Teli bellowed: "These people are not qualified to be teachers! Not only do they not love and protect the children but they mistreat and crush them! Such violations should be punished! The educational administrative departments and the school leaders haven't instructed the teachers well and haven't taken actions to stamp out corporal punishment on their campuses. This also highlights their lack of responsibility!"

The more he fumed, the angrier he became. The expressions of all present changed because they knew that Xu Teli rarely lost his temper at ordinary times and, in fact, was always amiable; they all judged that they had never seen how Xu Teli became so worked up! Deeply moved by his love towards the students, they hoped that the teachers would refrain from resorting to coercion and humiliation in future and adopt new methods suited to nurturing the next generation.

"My Teacher Forever"

At a meeting held in January, 1937 the CPC Central Committee resolved to hold a celebration to mark the sixtieth birthday of Xu Teli. Mao Zedong attended the meeting and delivered a speech. He said: "While I was studying at Hunan First Normal School, two teachers won over my deepest admiration: one of them was Mr Yang Huaizhong and the other one was Venerable Xu."

Having passed the entrance examinations, Mao Zedong had originally entered the Hunan Fourth Normal School in the spring of 1913. One year later, the school was merged with Hunan First Normal School. He was allocated to the eighth class. Here he grew acquainted with many erudite and virtuous teachers, among whom was Mr Xu. Many students had already heard about Xu Teli. They knew that this Mr Xu was a great personage: He was the Headmaster of Changsha Normal School and had once served as Deputy Speaker of the Hunan Province Provisional Parliament and Section Head in the Provincial Educational Department – he was a man of social reputation; he had received only six years of schooling, yet he was versant in prose written in the classical literary style, history, geography and maths, teaching himself fields of knowledge required in other courses; he had become a tutor at an old-style private school at eighteen and later established many new-style schools with his own hands – his disciples had spread throughout Changsha … The students all felt it a great honour to learn from renowned teachers such as Xu Teli. So did Mao Zedong.

A new school year began in the spring at Hunan Fourth Normal School but in the autumn at Hunan First Normal School. The length of schooling back then was one year for the preparatory courses and four years for the undergraduate courses. Mao Zedong studied for an extra half a year and didn't graduate until the summer holidays in 1918. He had therefore studied there for a total five and a half years. Xu Teli worked at Hunan First Normal School from the spring of 1913 to the summer of 1919 and taught pedagogy, self-cultivation and other subjects to twenty classes – a total cohort of 762 students; he was also the Director in charge of their internship. At Hunan First Normal School, the teacher Xu Teli and the student Mao Zedong were very close to each other for four and a half years.

One day after class, Mao Zedong came to Xu Teli, who was reading in the staff room, and asked: "Mr Xu, would you please share some of your reading experience for us to follow?"

Xu Teli eyed the student Mao Runzhi, who by then was already a bit of a somebody, and answered: "Runzhi, I hold the view that while reading, one should abide by the principle of 'quality' rather than 'quantity.' The key lies in that one should understand what you are reading and read it through. You should improve your ability to distinguish and know the value of books. While reading, one should extract the wonderful parts from the books and copy them down on a notebook. In a word, I don't read unless I am able to throw my pen and ink into work. Reading like this, my progress might be slow, but every line and every book I have read through count. Not only will the knowledge be firmly lodged in my mind, but I can also understand it thoroughly."

Mao Zedong listened carefully and followed Mr Xu's maxim that "One must throw the pen and ink into work while reading," practising it for the rest of his life. With his noble character and vast knowledge, serious attitude towards scholarly research and excellent learning methods, Xu Teli greatly influenced Mao Zedong, who back then was pursuing knowledge like a parched man craves water, and became one of his most cherished teachers at Hunan First Normal School.

On 30th January, Mao Zedong wrested a break from his hectic schedule to offer his sincere returns by writing a letter and dispatched someone to deliver it into Xu Teli's hands that very night. The first line read: "Venerable Comrade Xu: You were my teacher twenty years ago. You are still my teacher now and you will surely still be my teacher in the future." Such was his highest esteem for his respected teacher.

Chapter Four

"You Should Study Hard but Never Forget about Our National Salvation"

Cutting off the Tip of His Finger and Writing down a Petition with His Blood

Xu Teli was an educator, but he never confined himself to the small circle of schools and education. Rather, he always paid close attention to the future and destiny of the country and nation. He told his students explicitly that they should "study hard but never forget about our national salvation." Meanwhile he himself always practised what he preached: Teach but never forget our national salvation and save the country through the promotion of education.

Before the Revolution of 1911, the imperialist powers bullied and humiliated China more ferociously with every passing day. The corruption and incompetence of the Qing government practically gave the foreign oppressors a free hand. Foreign missionaries thronged to the hinterland of China and at times had strained relationships with the local people. These grievances resulted in Chinese people up and down the country petitioning for reparations in so-called "missionary cases." During one missionary case in Nanchang City, Jiangxi Province, a high-ranking local official was murdered by foreigners because he insisted that foreign missionaries must be subject to the rule of Chinese law.

Facing all those kinds of humiliations to which the country was then subject, Xu Teli's grief and indignation reached extreme. One day in December, 1909, Xu, who by then was teaching at Xiuye School, gathered together the students and teachers on the big playground and delivered a speech to them on the current political situation. Quoting from recent "missionary cases" all over the country, he listed how the invading imperialist countries committed atrocities in China and how the Qing government suppressed the people internally and had lost sovereignty and suffered humiliation externally.

The more he harangued, the more vehement he became until his words were punctuated with sobs. Suddenly, he rushed down the speaker's platform, darted into the kitchen and brought back a kitchen knife.

Chapter Four "You Should Study Hard but Never Forget about Our National Salvation"

"I, Xu Teli, would like to summon up all my courage to join with my compatriots in killing the enemy. I shall never turn back my head even if I am threatened with death!" With these words, he raised the kitchen knife, sliced into his left finger and used his fresh blood to write down the words "Drive out the Manchus and restore China!"

All those who were present and witnessed this heroic and patriotic undertaking felt stirred up. "Down with the foreign powers!" "Restore China!" Slogans like these resounded throughout the place.

Finding out that the whole campus was rife with indignation and worrying that something might go wrong, the Headmaster of Xiuye School hurriedly used the blood from Xu Teli's wounded finger to write the words "Cut off the tip of my finger to see you off. Please request the government to convene the parliament" on another sheet of white paper and gave it to the representatives who were preparing to go to Beijing to beseech the Qing government to draft a constitution.

Several days later the news that Xu Teli had cut into his finger and written down a petition with his blood hit the newspapers all over the country. This made for striking headlines. His patriotic action soon became known across Changsha proper and electrified the entire province. More people were motivated to wake up and throw themselves into the struggle against imperialism.

Hearing of this news, young Mao Zedong admired Xu Teli very much. When he recalled this episode later on in Yan'an, he said in a respectful tone of voice: "… After making enquiries, I knew that this middle-aged gentleman was called Xu Teli. He won my respect. For the first time I was given some true insight into revolution. He was my teacher when I came to study at Hunan First Normal School. He was also the teacher who led me to take the revolutionary road!"

A Fighter during the Revolution of 1911

In the middle ten days of October, 1911 (the year was called *Xin Hai* according to the lunar calendar), the atmosphere within the city proper of Changsha crackled with tension. The Qing government dispatched soldiers to patrol the main streets and small lanes. Notices stating that revolutionaries were being hunted were hung everywhere. Machine cannons were installed in the hall of the Governor's residence. The reasons for this can be summarised as follows: On 10th October, the revolutionaries in the New Army in Wuchang rose up and occupied the three towns which made up Wuhan City. They established the Hubei Military Government and announced their independence. Fearful that the revolutionaries in his own province would feel incited into action, Yu Chengge (1856 – 1926) the Governor of Hunan, fortified defences and wilfully hounded out rebel elements. Shops and restaurants were harassed to shut their gates and all the households secured their doors; the citizens didn't dare go outdoors.

One night in the Changsha County Educators Guildhall, a crowd of people began to argue in low voices around a paraffin lamp. This was a clandestine meeting attended by the headmasters of all the local schools. They were talking about how to respond to the Wuchang Uprising.

During the impassioned argument there was deadlock. They could not reconcile two contrasting viewpoints: A portion of the group claimed that the Hunan educational circles should take action immediately to answer the Wuchang Uprising and join the revolution; another portion held the view that the present revolutionary situation was not yet clear and they had better wait and see.

At this time, Headmaster Zhou of Shiye School said in a low voice: "You gentlemen have all aired your brilliant opinions just now. We should reinforce Wuchang immediately. But at the moment we have no weapons to hand. How can we respond to the Wuchang Rising with empty hands and bare fists? My opinion is that we should first wait a few days and see which way the wind is blowing. If all the other cities have risen up in the meantime, it won't be too late for us to take action."

Barely had he spoken, when several others echoed: "Headmaster Zhou is right. We should wait for a while and then take action!" "Yeah, more haste, less speed!"

"I don't agree!" A middle-aged man in a long blue-cloth gown stood up straight. The others took a look. It was Xu Teli the Headmaster of Zhounan Girls School. Two years ago, he "cut off the tip of his finger and worte a petition with his blood." This heroic deed catapulted him to fame. The others all waited in silence to hear what he had to say.

Xu Teli harangued: "Fellow headmasters and colleagues: Revolution is a dangerous thing. Bloodshed and loss of life are unavoidable. Now the situation is critical. If we don't answer the uprising, the revolutionary action in Wuchang might fail and the Qing Court will kill off every last one of our revolutionary brothers. By then I am afraid we won't even be able to summon enough hands though we want to rise up!"

He continued: "Considering the present situation, we should answer the Wuchang Rising immediately. Those who are afraid of death, stay put here; those who are NOT, follow me. Take advantage of the present moment. The rattled spirits of the authorities haven't had chance to calm down, so let's lead the progressive students to the New Army's barracks outside the city ASAP. There we can propagandise and provoke. We should do our best to rise up while the time is ripe."

Xu Teli's resonant voice, resolute facial expressions and fearless spirit moved all the attendees. The meeting sprang to life as everyone concurred with his message and resolved to take action at the earliest opportunity, answering promptly to the call of the magnificent Wuchang Uprising. After the meeting, Xu Teli made an appointment with and summoned together some progressive teachers such as He Yunong, Ling Zhenjia, Liu Mingyi, and Li Dongtian to propagandise and deliver speeches everywhere calling for support for the revolution, irrespective of the dangers to themselves.

On 22nd October, the Changsha Uprising succeeded and the new military government was established. Jiao Dafeng (1886 – 1911) and Chen Zuoxin (1870 – 1911) were elected Governor and Deputy Governor respectively. All the soldiers and people who rose up wore smiling faces and rushed about telling the others the good news. Xu Teli went here and there and everywhere. He gathered together sedan-chair bearers, rickshaw-pullers and transport coolies and explained the revolutionary truth to them in the plain language. He also ran outside the city to buy bullocks, had the animals slaughtered to feast the army of insurrection and relayed messages for them.

Refusing to Serve as Speaker and Remaining as a Teacher

After the Changsha Uprising, Xu Teli was elected Deputy Speaker of the Hunan Province Provisional Parliament in respect to his pragmatic response to the Wuchang Uprising.

The new government was established. Xu was filled with enthusiasm. He thought that the feudal emperor had been overthrown, the democratic government realised, restoring hope to China. However, there was an about turn for the worse in the revolutionary situation. On 31st October, 1911, the two revolutionary leaders Jiao Dafeng and Chen Zuoxin were murdered by the renegade soldiers. Tan Yankai the leader of the constitutionalists became the Governor. Not only did he turn a blind eye and a deaf ear to the murderers who killed Jiao and Chen but he also put forward the administrative guideline that the government should "maintain security and preserve order." Xu Teli's confidence towards bourgeois democratic revolution started to wane.

Soon afterwards, he proposed that county heads should be elected by the people, something which aroused impassioned argument within the provincial parliament. His proposal was finally accepted, but the

Speaker shelved it without proper reason and didn't forward it to the Governor's Office to be enacted. This was a heavy blow to Xu Teli. He, moreover, observed that from the Speaker to the ordinary Members of the Parliament, the majority were eager to gain official promotion and rake in money, tussling over power and wealth. Corruption and degeneracy pervaded and shrouded an organ of government that ought to have represented the will of the people. Feeling great disappointment towards the provincial parliament, Xu Teli resigned from his post as Deputy Speaker in disgust.

He then accepted the invitation from Chen Runlin (1879 – 1946) the Head of the Department of Education to be a Section Head in the provincial educational department. He advocated the vigorous development of general education so that the children of the poor could all go to school. But he could never gain the support of his superiors. He again felt deep disappointment. All his endeavours and struggles since the Revolution of 1911 were wasted. All the hopes seemed to have burst like a pricked bubble. Government seemed an intrinsically bad institution. Once revolutionaries became government officials they would betray their course. He racked his brains and concluded that the country couldn't become prosperous and the masses were not enlightened. The key reason lay with the uncultured people. To truly save the country, he thought, education must be used to reform people's hearts and more schools must be established to enlighten the population. He therefore resigned from his Section Head post and again returned to the educational world to be a teacher.

The Daring Vanguard to "Oust Zhang Jingyao"

In March, 1918, Zhang Jingyao (1881 – 1933) one of the major warlords of the Anhui Clique assumed the post of Military-cum-Civilian Governor of Hunan Province. Zhang was despotic, imperious and grasping. He ganged up with his three younger brothers – Zhang Jingshun, Zhang Jingyu and Zhang Jingtang – to implement a rampant dictatorship and wield their power all over Hunan. Their subordinates marauded throughout the lands, persecuted ordinary folk and committed all kinds of crimes. Everyone in the province was seized with fear and uncertainty and their complaints rang out everywhere. One popular ditty that did the rounds back then complained:

Their surname is the dignified and imposing Zhang.
They claim they respect Yao, Shun, Yu and Tang.
One, two, three and four.
They are tigers, leopards, jackals and wolves to the core.
If their malice can't be mopped clean.
In Hunan Province no hope will be seen.

In August, Zhang Jingyao abused his power to suspend the Hunan Students Association and closed down the *Xiangjiang Weekly Review*, the editor-in-chief of which was Mao Zedong. Demonstrations, involving Changsha residents drawn from all walks of life, who torched Japanese commodities in process, were forcibly suppressed. Zhang dispatched soldiers to occupy schools, destroy teaching equipment and burn up books. He also froze the funds to cover running costs. His savage acts infuriated the people. Mao Zedong and others made the best of the circumstances and united the various forces from both inside and outside the province to initiate a battle to oust Zhang Jingyao.

Xu Teli was teaching at Hunan First Normal School at that time. He was simultaneously the Head of the Hunan Provincial Orphanage. Having long hated to his marrow the atrocities of the Zhang brothers, he threw himself into this battle.

One day, he gathered together the progressive headmasters and teachers of all the schools for a meeting and incited them: "Fellow headmasters and teachers, don't we want to establish schools? Don't we want to promote education in Hunan? Well, the Zhang brothers have dispatched soldiers to occupy our schools, withdrawn our funds, docked our wages and devastated the educational cause. If such mean predatory beasts are not driven out, not only the education in Hunan would be hopeless but all the people might be eaten up by them."

The headmasters and teachers became indignant.

Some suggested: "Let's go look for Zhang Jingyao the lout to settle the score!"

Some shouted: "I'll quit! Whoever wants to take my headmaster's post can have it!"

Xu Teli took the opportunity to call upon them all: "That is right! Those of you who are headmasters should look for Zhang Jingyao to tender your resignations and those who are teachers should look for Zhang Jingyao to demand your wages!"

A campaign aimed at tendering resignations and claiming back wages erupted like this.

Xu Teli also organised the teachers in all the schools through the educators association to establish speech groups. After being trained uniformly, they were sent to all the counties and towns to wage patriotic and anti-imperialism propaganda campaigns and called upon the people to boycott Japanese commodities and punish dishonest businessmen, the flunkeys of imperialism and others of that ilk. He himself shuttled between the urban and rural areas to deliver speeches, exposing the Zhang brothers' crimes to the students, teachers and people and calling upon them to rise up and oust Zhang Jingyao. Zhang Jingyao issued an explicit order and put him on the *Wanted* list for the crime of "being in cahoots with the bandits." He furthermore declared that he would close down the Wumei School established by Xu Teli.

In the face of the atrocities of Zhang Jingyao, Xu Teli decided to go to Europe for a work-study programme. Before his departure, he wrote a letter to Zhang Jingyao in the name of the Head of Hunan Provincial Orphanage, in which he listed all the crimes Zhang had committed after his arrival in Hunan.

The letter read: "Since the northern soldiers came south, they kidnapped, killed, raped and plundered, stopping at nothing. The old and the weak were exiled or died. The strong and the young had to turn to banditry because they were suddenly deprived of their livelihood. The so-called 'banditry' was in fact the dregs of those marauding soldiers and never consisted of Hunan natives. When the situation had calmed down slightly, the authorities held meetings and proposed to purge the countryside. The campaign came into full swing with the vigour of a roaring wind and scudding clouds. Now the bandits are gone but the countryside-purging teams have come. Those so-called bureau heads and their acting deputies are in fact nothing more than hooligans and thugs. They try to curry favour, offer and take bribes, buy and sell official posts, and feather their nests. The vices of extorting and threatening have therefore been taken to a new level …"

Finally, Xu Teli warned that if Zhang Jingyao was not ousted, he would bring this matter to the attention of the "media from both home and abroad."

This letter was published in the *Morning News* in Beijing on 20th November, 1919, which further pushed forward the campaign to oust Zhang Jingyao.

When he saw this letter, Zhang Jingyao was furious. However, while he was growling hysterically, he realised that the special correspondent of the *Morning News* had described Xu Teli in a truthful way in the article: "He has already gone to Paris!"

In 1920, with the people's anti-Zhang movement gathering momentum, the Zhang brothers – a pack of jackals, wolves, tigers and leopards – were finally driven out of Hunan.

Throwing Himself into the Peasant Movement

In January, 1924, the KMT convened their first national congress and formulated the policy "to associate with Russia and its Party and to help the peasants and the workers." The Nationalist and Communist Parties cooperated for the first time. This not only boosted the workers' movement nationwide but also propelled the development of the peasant movement. Presently, the Northern Expedition was savouring victory after victory. The peasant movement in Hunan, promoted by Mao Zedong in person, was thriving like a tempest. "Down with the local tyrants and evil gentry!" "All the power belongs to the Peasants Association!" Such slogans were echoing throughout the vast countryside.

In the middle ten days of December 1926, Xu Teli met up with Mao Zedong at Wangluyuan. Mao had come back to Hunan to investigate the peasant movement. He suggested that Xu Teli should go to the countryside to make inspections. In the spring of 1927, Xu Teli went back to Wumei Village to check out how the peasant movement was unrolling. After coming back, he found out that despite having been away from home for only three months, the countryside he had known was almost changed into another world:

The peasants association had reformed everything there. Gone were the local tyrants; gone were the thugs, opium smokers and gamblers; phenomena like the rich bullying the poor, men bullying women and the wise bullying the poor had been eradicated.

A new righteousness could be observed in the countryside. All the lawsuits taken up by the peasants association were being settled without one cent of legal cost being charged. The eyes of thousands of people were now watching and thousands of hands were pointing. The rights and wrongs were judged in public and no one dared to challenge their judgements.

The poor peasants, women and children, who used to be looked down upon, were organised to be their own masters with their chins up and their chests sticking out.

None of the evil-doers dared to stir and none dared to commit abuses …

Xu Teli couldn't believe this was true. For the first time he witnessed such an unprecedented new world. He told anyone who came his way that: "The peasant movement is fantastic!" Whenever he bumped into someone, he confided that: "The peasants association is great. The little people have accomplished what the emperors can't do; the 'mere ciphers' have fulfilled what the 'big shots' can't do." He started to truly realise the potential of people.

Soon afterwards, he came to read the "Report on an Investigation of the Peasant Movement in Hunan" written by Mao Zedong and felt the content was very profound. For so many years, he had constantly been searching for a road by which to reform society. He had previously backed up reformists and participated in campaigns, but none had succeeded in fundamentally changing the fabric of society. But now, the peasant movement did it in one go and realised his long-cherished wish. He made up his mind to throw himself into the dynamic peasant movement and apprentice himself to be a pupil of the workers and the peasants.

During this period of time, Xu Teli was not only the Head of the Workers and Peasants Department of the Nationalist Party Headquarters in Changsha City, the Head of the Educational Section of Hunan Province Peasants Association and the Director of the Lecture Office for Peasant Movement that was affiliated to Hunan Rural Normal School but also the Headmaster of Changsha Normal School and Hunan First Girls Normal School. Every day he busied himself until he was short of breath, but he threw himself into his work with great revolutionary gusto. With regularity, he went to all the towns under the jurisdiction of Changsha County in a short-sleeved shirt and a pair of grass sandals to get into the swing of the peasant movement and dived deep into the peasant ranks to see what was really going on. He laid his hands on a great quantity of data about the peasant movement and trained many stalwart members for the grass-roots peasants organisations in all the counties in Hunan.

Under his influence, his eldest son Xu Duben played an active part in the peasant movement. He took the post of Head of Liling County Peasants Association and joined the CPC soon afterwards. Later he lost his life at the age of twenty-one when the Great Revolution (1924 – 1927) foundered.

"A Wordless Textbook"

One very sullen afternoon, a slow, persistent drizzle fell with a *pitter patter*. Holding a paper umbrella in his hand, Xu Teli dragged his feet forward along a muddy road. With a heavy heart he finally reached Lituo, ten kilometres away from the city proper of Changsha. What was he doing there?

The cooperation between the Nationalist and Communist Parties had fallen apart. The rightists in the Nationalist Party initiated a campaign to purge the Party: In April, 1927, Chiang Kai-shek started the "12th April" Counterrevolutionary Coup in Shanghai and raised his butcher's cleaver against the Communist Party members; in May, Xu Kexiang (1890 – 1964) initiated the "21st May Incident" in Changsha and pounced upon the revolutionaries and workers and peasants like mad. Shanghai and Changsha, and the whole country for that matter were shrouded in a white terror. The counterrevolutionaries destroyed revolutionary organisations such as the workers associations, the peasants associations and the students associations and freed local tyrants and evil gentry from prison. Everywhere they hunted down and slaughtered CPC members, workers and peasants and other progressive elements. Many CPC members had to work in a clandestine manner. Some weak-willed people broke away from the Party. The revolution sank to a low ebb.

Xu Teli was not a CPC member yet at this time, but observing how the counterrevolutionaries had betrayed the revolution and instigated savage massacres, he felt shocked and outraged beyond words. Before this turn of events, he had nursed a warm feeling towards the CPC. He was fond of reading their books and magazines and liked associating with supporters. In the schools established by him, he had been known to employ many CPC members such as Chen Zhangfu, Luo Xuezan, and Zhou Yili as teachers. Many of his students were CPC members. Especially after having taken part in the peasant movement, he had come to know the CPC better and endorsed the Party. Frequently he delivered speeches to sing the praises of the Communists and gave coverage to the activities of the CPC and the Communist Youth League.

After the "21st May Incident," the KMT rightists didn't dare to arrest him but even tried to win him over because of his reputation in the educational world in Hunan. But Xu Teli was not swayed. He left the city secretly, first hiding at his home at Wumei Village for a while and then relocating to Lituo to take boarding at the home of his female student and CPC member Li Shangjin. The Li family was a large household. They had more than one hundred old rooms. Li Shangjin's father Li Xuequ had once taught in the Lijiang Senior Primary School established by Xu Teli. He was very close to Xu Teli and often lent financial support to the revolution. Therefore, this was an ideal hideout.

Also in this place, Xu Teli unexpectedly ran into Luo Mai (a.k.a. Li Weihan), who was Xu Teli's student when he was teaching at Hunan First Normal School. Luo Mai was once a leader of the CPC Hunan Provincial Committee. He had resigned from his post by then and was getting ready to go to Wuhan. But the railroad was blockaded by the counterrevolutionaries and he was temporarily hiding at the Li family. Teacher and student were reunited at such a critical moment. Xu Teli and Luo Mai both felt overjoyed. They exchanged their points of view on the Great Revolution. Luo Mai also told Xu Teli that after the "21st May Incident," the CPC was profoundly concerned about his safety and had tried to dispatch hands to look for him everywhere.

Facing his esteemed teacher, Luo Mai asked in a low voice: "Teacher, would you like to join the Communist Party?"

"What?" Xu Teli thought that he misheard him.

Gazing at his mentor's surprised face, Luo Mai said word by word: "The Organisation told me to ask for your opinion and see if you are willing to become a member of our Party?"

Not until now did Xu Teli understand fully. He answered in excitement: "I adore the CPC. They are active, never scramble for personal power and work heart and soul for the society. But the CPC members are all promising young people. I am already long in the tooth. Will the CPC accept an old buffer like me?"

"Teacher," Luo Mai explained. "Revolution doesn't discriminate between the old and the young. But now the revolutionary situation has fallen to a low tide. If you join the CPC, you not only need to leap through hoops but your life might also be in danger anytime."

Xu Teli replied: "Bloodshed and loss of life are unavoidable in the pursuit of revolution! I AM willing to follow the CPC. As long as the Party needs me, I am willing to sacrifice anything."

Luo Mai nodded his head and took grip of Xu Teli's hands firmly. "Teacher," he said. "The Provincial Committee has for a long time paid attention to and studied your attitude towards revolution and towards our Party. We are also very familiar with your inner requests. Previously, we did instruct Comrade Xue Shiguan to contact you. But we had never expected that the revolutionary cause would suffer such a severe setback. Teacher, since you have made up your mind to follow the CPC, we are comrades-at-arms who will fight shoulder to shoulder from now on! I will be your referee for joining the CPC. From now on you are a CPC member!"

In this way, when the revolution was at a most critical moment and when Changsha was engulfed in white terror, the aged educator Xu Teli, who by then was already fifty years old, formally became a member of the CPC. He felt that he had "gained my rebirth since then."

Lu Dingyi later commented: "... The people's educator Comrade Xu

Teli delivered his first lecture to all the comrades of the Party like this: Never sway when the situation is desperate but fight more resolutely and revolution will surely succeed. Sometimes a good example can teach us more than a textbook full of fine words. The Venerable Xu set such an example to us all in requesting to join the Party."

Achieving Outstanding Merit during the Nanchang Uprising

After he joined the CPC at the recommendation of the CPC Hunan Provincial Committee and Luo Mai, Xu Teli first went to Wuhan and boarded at the Lecture Office for Peasant Movement in Wuchang. There he met up with individuals including Mao Zedong, Fang Weixia, Zhou Yili, and Zhang Guoji. They had never expected that the situation in Wuhan would also alter suddenly like the winds and clouds. On 15th July, Wang Jingwei betrayed the revolution in Wuhan in public. The Nanking and Wuhan National Governments converged into one. The revolutionary situation took a turn for the worse. On 18th July, the CPC Central Committee convened a meeting in Wuhan and made the preparatory plan to stage an armed uprising in Nanchang. Xu Teli, Fang Weixia, Zhang Guoji and Yi Lirong first reached Jiujiang by steamer disguised as businessmen and then hurried to Nanchang by train. Before the uprising, Xu Teli settled down in the Grand Jiangxi Hotel, which was also the Headquarters of He Long, the Commander-in-chief of the uprising.

Nanchang by then appeared very peaceful even though the political climate was in fact especially perilous. On the enemy side, Zhu Peide the Chairman of Jiangxi Province was holding an anti-CPC meeting at Mount Lu together with Wang Jingwei, Zhang Fakui et al, at which they conspired to clandestinely suppress the revolution. On the revolutionary side, according to the directions of the Headquarters of the Uprising, the troops that participated in the uprising were coming close to and revolutionaries and hot-blooded young people from all over the country were gathering towards Nanchang like the clouds. The city was like a volcano that would erupt at any time; a life-or-death war was imminent. Both the Nationalist and Communist sides were doing their best to win over the local armed forces of Jiangxi Province.

Zhu Peide was not in Nanchang. Jiang Jihuan the Department Head of Civil Affairs took over his post as Chairman temporarily. Therefore, Jiang's attitude and actions played a decisive role during the battle. However, Mr Jiang was Xu Teli's classmate and good friend during their adolescence. They had once studied together at Ningxiang Accelerated Normal School and established the Lijiang Senior Primary School and Changsha Normal School together; they were very close.

Xu Teli reported his years-long friendship with Jiang Jihuan to Zhou Enlai, who by then was Secretary of the CPC Committee in Front of the Enemy. Zhou Enlai immediately instructed him and Lin Boqu to do some homework on Jiang Jihuan by making use of their old friendship.

Xu Teli wrote a letter, which was sent to the Government of Jiangxi Province. After receiving the letter, Jiang Jihuan sent hands to collect Xu Teli to live in his residence. Xu Teli went over there gladly and moved to the Jiang Mansion. There he talked with Jiang throughout the night for many times.

One day, Jiang's good friend Lin Boqu and student Guo Liang (1901 – 1928) came to pay Jiang a visit. The arrival of these three old friends pleased Jiang greatly. The host and guests took their respective seats one after another. After a round of civilities, they seemed to have been transported back to the old days. Xu Teli took the advantage to divert their topic to the subject at hand.

"Jihuan, do you still remember those days when we studied together at Ningxiang Accelerated Normal School? Headmaster Zhou Zhenling is upright and righteous. He is a senior member of the Revolutionary Alliance. At our graduation ceremony, he harangued us emotionally: 'Students, we established this school not only to nurture you into good teachers but more importantly we hope you will create a cause that will benefit the country and nation and save the country and people from torture by water and fire.'"

"Yeah! Yeah! Back then we were both hot-blooded young men. All the days long, we were obsessed with how to do something big enough to shock the heavens and startle the earth. We established Lijiang School together in the hope that more people could read and know the truth about how to save the country and people until finally the country would be saved through the promotion of education." Jiang Jihuan was eloquent.

"*Ai*! Skip 'save the country through the promotion of education!'" Xu Teli took over his words. "I've been engaging in education for several dozen years, lecturing on both education and history. Frequently I insinuated that Yuan Shikai was the usurper Wang Mang or Dong Zhuo. But I still couldn't find a way to reform the current odious government and failed to find a bright highway to save the county and people. However, I went back to my home village this spring, witnessed the power of the peasant movement with my own eyes and finally found a realistic path for our national salvation." With these words, he smiled. Judging from the changes of Jiang's facial expressions, he concluded that he had already got what he implied and thus didn't carry on with what he had been saying.

"Yeah! Yeah! Mr Jiang, we two share this feeling as well." Lin Boqu and Guo Liang echoed in tacit agreement.

Jiang Jihuan meditated awhile and then said slowly: "I know what you gentlemen meant. Let's open the window and talk frankly in the sunshine. I too have witnessed for myself the peasant movement under the leadership of the CPC. Their deeds are in tune with the mood of the people. What is more, I sympathise with their political views. But the present political situation is very unfavourable towards them."

"Brother Jihuan, this depends upon how you put it." Xu Teli laughed out loud. "Chiang Kai-shek and Wang Jingwei have betrayed Dr Sun Yat-sen's three wise policies and the revolution. They kill CPC members and revolutionaries and have reduced themselves to being the enemies of the people. Their brutal irrationality can only last for a brief time but will never be long-lived. You should know that the CPC and all its members can never be wiped clean away. The Peasants Associations and the Workers' Red Guards in Hunan and Hubei have been reorganised. The raging revolutionary fire is burning ever more fiercely."

"You have right on your side. The CPC have the support of the people and represent the interests of the nation. But there is still cause to be circumspect." Jiang Jihuan was still a little hesitant.

"Circumspect about what?" Xu Teli stood up greatly perturbed. "Is Brother Jihuan afraid that the risk might be on your head? Or are you unwilling to kiss goodbye to the high official post with a salary to match? You are no longer who you used to be! At this critical moment when the country, nation and revolution are at stake, following the CPC adamantly is the only way to save the country and nation from the disastrous trials by fire and water! I hope you will step forward and set up a role model for future generations to learn from. You must never step back from it!"

Swayed by Xu Teli's sincerity and passion, Jiang Jihuan stood up and paced to and fro several times around the living room. Suddenly he turned around and gripped Xu Teli's hands tight. "How could I not know what kind of a man you are?" he said. "Whatever you have said, goes! I will follow the CPC and outlast the hardships and difficulties together with you."

Won over by Xu Teli, Lin Boqu and Guo Liang, Jiang Jihuan became a part of the Nanchang Uprising. Persuaded by Jiang Jihuan, three of the four Department Heads of the Government of Jiangxi Province joined the uprising. This paved the way for the success of the uprising, ensured that social order was maintained afterwards, that grain was raised, troops were successfully transferred and all other kinds of critical events.

"Marching by Night Was No Big Deal"

In October, 1934, owing to the failure of the Fifth Counter-campaign against the KMT Encirclement and Suppression, the Red Army under the direct command of the CPC Central Committee, which consisted of more than eighty thousand soldiers, was forced to carry out a huge shift in strategy. The army started off from Ruijin with plentiful equipment and stores as well as a large company of porters. They trudged forward slowly along narrow snaking mountain tracks that resembled sheep's intestines. Sometimes they could cover only twenty to thirty *li* or even a dozen or more *li* a day. Frequently they found themselves in a passive position and subject to enemy bombardment.

In order to avoid being decimated by the enemy bombers, shake off the enemy pursuit on the ground and prevent the enemy scouts from knowing their whereabouts, the Red Army often marched quietly at night.

Xu Teli recalled: "We had several dozen stretchers, twenty to thirty horses and dozens of medicine boxes. They could only be moved very slowly so stood out as sitting targets. If the enemy bombers came, we had no way out. If we tried to run away, the stretchers were too heavy and clumsy. If we wanted to hide away, the grasses and bushes were too short to provide any cover. Therefore, marching by night became a regular habit."

However, marching by night was also very arduous and perilous. Afraid that they might expose themselves, they were prohibited from talking or lighting a fire; neither could they allow their belongings to knock against each other. One after another they marched forward. When the distance between two soldiers grew a little too great, a low voice would be heard urging the stragglers to: "Hurry and keep up!" In those nights when they couldn't see their five fingers if they reached out their hands, a strip of white cloth would be bound around their arms to prevent someone from dropping out of the procession. These methods could prevent them from being discovered by the enemy or dropping out, but they could not avoid natural threats on the way. There were dangerous slippery roads, deep holes, perpendicular slopes, cliffs and rivers and so on. Any carelessness might lead to disaster.

However, what were these like in the eyes of Xu Teli? "Marching by night was no big deal. Rainy days, slippery roads and pitch-dark nights were our common obstacles. We had got accustomed to them and could overcome any hurdles. So too could our women and children. There was nothing strange. Marching by night was no big deal."

Conquering the Three Great Snow-crowned Mountains

In June, 1935, the Red Army breached the enemy line of defence in Lushan and Baoxing Counties, which were both under the jurisdiction of Ya'an City in Sichuan Province and next scaled the first great snow-crowned mountain during the Long March – the Mountain Jiajin.

The Mountain Jiajin was called the "Mountain of the Immortals" by locals. This was in reference to the fact that not even birds could fly over its summit and so only an immortal would be able to climb to the top. It was the subject of many remarkable legends. For instance: If a man opened his mouth as he climbed, the chilly hand of the "mountain god" would reach out and throttle him. Likewise, if the same deity heard him raise his voice too loudly, he would change the complexion of the sky and assault him with either a downpour or hailstones. After he had climbed up nine folds and thirteen slopes, the sons of the devil would yank at his exhausted feet; even so, he knew if he sat down that would be the last thing he ever did.

On the thirteenth day of that month, Xu Teli reached the Mountain Jiajin together with the army. On the night before they were to scale the mountain, the army camped at its foot. Xu's umbrella was broken. There was neither oilcloth nor stable hand nor horses. Night fell. He found a hollow place between two stone slabs because it was comparatively safe to sleep in this way. However, sleeping between two stones, he felt so cold as if he was lying in a coffin. He added a roll of blue cloth on top as a cover. It rained during the night and the blue cloth became sodden. Luckily, the blanket and his clothes were still dry.

Early the next morning, the army started to scramble up the mountain. The heavy snow that capped the mountaintop could be seen from down below. What is more, those big patches of accumulated snow didn't seem too far away. At first, they didn't sense that they needed to climb so high. After entering the snowy world, they were already spent and broken. Prickled by the boundless white snowfall, it was too painful to open their eyes. There was no road under their feet. The higher they ascended, the thinner the air was. Chills pounced upon them. They were seriously short of oxygen. Breathing became increasingly laborious. Their lips were frozen blackish blue. A mixture of rain and snow fell on their way . The wet clothes and blankets became stuck to their bodies and felt ice-cold.

Xu Teli edged forward step by step with the help of a red-tasselled spear that he had used as his walking stick ever since leaving the Soviet areas. On his way he constantly greeted the others: "Comrades, never sit down and never halt. Sit down and you'll never get up again." It took great efforts for them to reach the mountaintop against the sleet, but they didn't take a break and started to go down immediately. The snow abated slowly. Descending the other side of the mountain proved not so strenuous, but the wet clothes and blankets became stuck to their bodies and felt frigid. Xu Teli made simple work by picking up speed and strode and trotted down. In this way he kept warm. By the time he reached the foot of the mountain, the warmth from his body had dried out his clothes. That night, they camped in a valley of the great snow-crowned mountain.

After successfully negotiating this hoop, Xu Teli felt very spirited and happy and believed that his powers of resistance must surpass those of any ordinary soldier. Unconsciously he was filled with more confidence. Many comrades praised him, commenting that he should live to be at least ninety.

On the 24th day of that month they reached another snow-crowned mountain between Lianghekou or "the Estuary of Two Rivers" in Hubei Province and Zhuokeji in Sichuan Province. Known as the Mountain Mengbi, the summit was more than 4,100 metres high. People had to cover ninety *li* to scramble up and down it. The local Tibetan elders said this snow-capped mountain was a god or demon. When it was angry, it was more lethal than the Mountain Jiajin. The Red Army soldiers were now already experienced in scaling a snow-crowned mountain. They conquered it comparatively smoothly.

The third snow-crowned mountain conquered by Xu Teli was called the Mountain Changban. It stood more than 4,800 metres above the sea level. People had to cover eighty *li* to scramble up and down it. The sheer cliff in some places made this near impossible to climb. On his way to clamber up, Xu Teli stood there resting awhile after trudging several dozen steps to save his strength; when it was time to climb down, he picked up speed to catch up. Originally they decided to pitch camp at Matang after they had covered seventy *li*. When Xu Teli reached there, the army had marched on. The words written on a flag that was poked in the bridge read: "March another thirty *li* and set up camp at Kangmao Temple."

The comrades from the Political Work Section all persuaded Xu Teli: "Venerable Xu, it is already evening. You have trudged more than seventy *li*. There are no households on the way from here to Kangmao Temple. We'd better camp here and try to catch up with the major force tomorrow!"

But what about Xu Teli?

"I think I should be a role model and not fall behind. I shall try to catch up with the major force alone."

"There Is No Need to Fuss about Me"

Xu Teli was among the eldest of the long marchers and highly respected as a virtuous educator by the Organisation and the other comrades. Thus, they always took good care of him. Every time when they reached a new campsite during the Long March, the other comrades would often take his food and boarding into consideration first.

But in order to alleviate their burden as much as possible, Xu Teli always beat them to it and tried to save them from raising their hands. Every time when he was on the point of reaching the campsite, he picked up some dry brushwood and plucked some wild vegetables. When he reached the campsite, he improvised a stove out of two stones and took out his small wash basin to boil some water to wash his feet. Then he cooked some paste mixed with the wild vegetables. Next he would inform the others with a smile: "I've had my meal and washed my feet. There is no need to fuss about me." If the other comrades arranged a room or a door panel for him to sleep, his reply would always be, "I have found a better place." The room or door panel would then be given to the wounded or diseased or to the other comrades. He and the stable hand would squeeze into the doorway or corridor of some household with a small bundle of rice or wheat straw and bunk down there after spreading out their bedding. When his clothes were tattered, he did the darning himself. When his shoes were broken, it was he who repaired them. When he was hungry, he gnawed at wild grasses and tree roots. When lodgings were unavailable, he slummed it on a slope or in the wilderness.

A Performance of How a Monkey Hunts For Lice

The Long March was littered with difficulties and hardships, but Xu Teli was always brimming over with optimistic revolutionary spirit.

Before the Spring Festival of 1935, the army fought here and there about the border region between Yunnan, Guizhou and Sichuan Provinces. The taxing march and the hostile environment left the generals and soldiers spent and broken. On New Year's Eve, Li Bozhao and some others arranged a party. Gathering around the bonfires to appreciate the party pieces that were pleasant to the eyes and ears, they basked in a rare mood of happiness. While they were still applauding warmly the Soviet Union sailors' dance performed by Li Bozhao, Xu Teli sauntered onto the stage in a tattered cap, wearing his sheepskin jacket inside out.

Planting himself at the centre of the stage, Xu Teli didn't say anything but stuck his two hands into his sheepskin jacket to scratch up and down with a serious face. Twisting left and right with a puckered brow, he hunted out something and popped it into his mouth. After a *pop* noise, he yammered with a wrinkled nose: "Yeah, this one is fat." A similar performance was put on repeatedly and the facial expression that lice was skittering up and down and the victim was feeling unbearably itchy was shown to the fullest; the others were amused to laugh with their hands clasping over their bellies.

Suddenly he stopped performing and said very seriously: "The Monkey King was fearless. He was afraid of neither the heavens nor the earth nor the monsters and demons. We should learn from him and vanquish the present difficulties."

After a pause, he continued: "But monkeys pay no attention to hygiene and their bodies are infested with lice. They have to hunt them out one by one and send them into their mouths to chew up. We shouldn't learn from them in this respect. We should pay attention to personal hygiene. We should wash our faces, comb our hair, take baths, change our clothes and wash the laundry so that lice won't grow on us. Lice are blood-suckers and carriers of disease. They should be wiped clean away."

Now the others knew that Xu Teli was not just trying to amuse them but was using his turn to boost their morale and offer them some ideological education.

"Never Forget the Annihilation of the Enemy; Keep Busy Teaching Others Every Day."

Throughout the strenuous Long March, Xu Teli, as a senior educator, never lost sight of his duty to impart knowledge and educate the people. He grasped every possible opportunity to teach the soldiers in the Red Army.

On their way, he thought out many ways to instruct the soldiers to read. He wrote several words on the conical bamboo-strip hats worn on the heads of the soldiers marching at the front. These served as moving blackboards for the troops behind to learn from. Days passed by. The soldiers were thereby able to read more words. He told the advance forces that the words written on the placards by the road to propagandise and boost the morale should be big so that the soldiers could discern them conveniently on their way.

Moreover, Xu Teli taught the soldiers *pinyin*. Some young women soldiers declined mischievously: "These are foreign words. We won't learn them!" He explained patiently: "These are *pinyin* letters created by ourselves. They belong to us. We should learn them. Later when our circumstances are better, we should still learn them even though they are foreign languages and words!" He encouraged the female soldiers to not only be revolutionary role models but also mistresses of culture. Only by this means could they gain outright liberation in various respects, including politics, economics and culture.

When the army stopped to take a break and set up camp, he requested that the soldiers write on the ground using tree switches as their writing brushes and the earth as paper. He commented humorously: "These materials are in inexhaustible supply!"

Zhu De and Kang Keqing later wrote a poem to praise him. It read: "Never Forget the Annihilation of the Enemy; Keep Busy Teaching Others Every Day."

Under such difficult circumstances, Xu Teli never forgot his duty as an educator because he was filled with the confidence that victory was at hand and convinced that all difficulties were temporary and that after the revolution succeeded the knowledge they had learned would prove its worth.

Coming Back to Hunan to Propagandise the Anti-Japanese War

"Paper! Paper! Please read how Mr Xu Teli the representative of the Eighth Route Army has come back to Changsha to assume office."

The newspaper boys' sounds of sonorous hawking broke the silence of the city. Passers-by, enticed by the important news, circled in.

"Give me a copy!"

"Give me a copy, too!"

"Give me a copy!"

People vied against each other to buy. Some read out happily on the spot: "Having been away from home for a dozen or so years, Xu Teli the Hunan educator came back to Changsha at two pm yesterday. His sideboards and hair are now completely white. He was wearing a short grey-cloth upper garment and looked spirited. He is still his former self …"

What was going on? The story went like this: After the Xi'an Incident in 1936, Chiang Kai-shek was forced to accept the injunction of the CPC: "Abandon the civil war and fight the Japanese in a united front." Chiang cooperated with the CPC against their foreign foes. In order to motivate the people more widely and strengthen the Chinese united front against Japanese invasion, the CPC set up offices and communications services in Chongqing, Xi'an, Wuhan, Changsha, and Guilin and other cities. At the end of this year, Xu Teli came back to Hunan to preside over operations at the Communications Service of the Eighth Route Army in Hunan as the senior councillor and representative of the Eighth Route Army (The name was changed into the Eighteenth Group Army later on).

At this time, seen domestically, the biggest city in the nation Shanghai had been occupied by Japan and Nanjing the seat of the KMT government was also plunged into a critical situation. On knowing how war was tearing apart the country and households were being massacred, the hearts of people in Hunan burned with anxiety. Many were far from confident that the Japanese invaders could be defeated. Therefore, when they heard that the Eighth Route Army had sent a representative here, they felt a glimmer of hope, like a ship in the fog that spies a lighthouse. What is more, the representative was their respected old educator Mr Xu Teli. How could they not be in raptures? They rushed about to spread the news and thronged to where the communications service stood – Number 2, God of Longevity Street. Among them there were workers and peasants, as well as teachers, young students and reporters; some came from the city proper and some from the distant counties under the jurisdiction of the provincial government. From morning to evening, Longevity Street was flooded with visitors and became as boisterous as a temple fair.

When they spotted Xu Teli, who they trusted so implicitly, the people were cordial towards him as if they had met their respectable teacher. All kinds of questions were fired away.

"The Communist Party and the Nationalist Party have been locked in a long-running feud. Will you cooperate to fight Japan?" one reporter enquired.

"We will. Both the Communist and Nationalist Parties are Chinese. We are all offspring of the Yan and Yellow Emperors. As long as we refuse to be slaves without a motherland, we should pull together and fight foreign invaders. As to if the Communist and Nationalist Parties will split again after their cooperation, I don't think the current of history is regressive but progressive. People won't accept the split. Whoever turns to division again is courting self-destruction!" a beaming Xu Teli answered.

"Even though the Communist and Nationalist Parties can join together to fight the Japs, surely Japan is too powerful for us to beat them?" This time it was a young student who posed the question and those around him obviously took this as the burning issue.

"We can! We definitely can!" Xu Teli replied. Referring to "On Protracted War" he used Mao Zedong's theoretical ideas to analyse this problem in detail: "We say we can win not because of the reasons listed by others: Japan has no coal and no iron. The enemy will turn up their toes after the Anti-Japanese War has lasted six months. Neither of these statements accords with the reality. We say we can win because it is a protracted war. We will fight the enemy slowly for several more years. We can boast a large population. Gradually the enemy personnel and materials will be consumed up and our strength will grow. By then, it will not be the case that they triumph over us but the other way round! The Anti-Japanese War is a struggle concerned with life or death, the survival or extinction of the country and nation. As long as people from all walks of life pull together to form a firm united front against Japanese invasion and carry the Anti-Japanese War to the end, victory will be ours."

"Will the CPC truly fight the Japs?" another doubtful student asked loudly.

Xu Teli replied: "We CPC will fight the Japanese to the bitter end and we mean unity sincerely. There is no doubt about this. Now a nasty enemy is at our gate. 'Brothers might quarrel at home, but they will unite to ward off foreign invasion.' The Nationalist and Communist Parties have united to fight the Japanese. That is an inescapable trend that echoes the will of the people." He listed many further facts to prove that the more altercations the Eighth Route Army had fought, the stronger they would become. He continued confidently: "Guerrilla warfare has been the masterstroke of the Red Army under the leadership of the CPC. If one hundred guerrilla battles must be fought, the Red Army will win one hundred times. Some have already queried: 'Does the CPC have weapons and munitions factories?' We answer: 'Yes!' They ask again: 'Where?' We reply: 'In Nanjing in the past, but in Tokyo now. Through guerrilla warfare we will grab the enemy's weapons to arm ourselves and occupy the enemy's backyard to be our base areas.'"

The longer he harangued, the more passionate he became. While delivering his speech, he gesticulated. He had captured the attention of every listener. His sincere attitude and good-humoured, vivid, eloquent and forceful speech unlocked their minds and kindled the flames of hope in the depths of their hearts.

When he was in Changsha, Xu Teli often went to schools and government units and so on to give speeches. On every occasion he addressed packed audiences. One day he delivered a speech on the "Ten Guiding Principles" to fight the Japanese and save the country at the Silver Palace Cinema. The listeners amounted to three to four thousand. The whole venue was crammed so solid that not even one drop of water would be able to trickle out. Not a single foothold was available outside the gate. Many people had to climb up to the windowsills to listen.

In order to spread anti-Japanese propaganda so that more people would know the message of the CPC was correct, Xu Teli ensured that newspapers publicised his speeches. He often wrote articles for newspapers such as *Anti-Japanese War Weekly* and *Salvation Daily*.

Owing to the outstanding work of Xu Teli and the other comrades, a new high tide was rising among the people of Hunan in their fight against the Japanese invasion. They formed many organisations aimed at saving the nation from the Japanese, including the women's national salvation association, the peasants anti-Japanese association, the workers anti-Japanese association, the students anti-Japanese association and so on. Thousands of hot-blooded young men went to the frontline to take on the Japanese invaders; some rushed to Yan'an and trod the revolutionary road.

"He Has Snatched Away the Trade of Many Story-tellers."

There was a Fire Palace in the city proper of Changsha, which had always been the favoured haunt of story-tellers, entertainers and snacks vendors. Every day many people from the lower strata of society, for example wharf porters, cart-drawing coolies and rickshaw-pullers gathered together there for entertainment and food. The spot started to buzz with life.

One day, Xu Teli arrived at this place. First he sat down there sipping his tea quietly. Seeing that a growing number of people were gathering together, he planted himself on a borrowed wide long bench and declaimed his speech in a loud tone. He started with the CPC's proposals for combatting the Japanese and went on to expound the bright outcome he perceived for the Anti-Japanese War; beginning from the national united front against Japanese invasion, he went on to expose the crimes of how some diehards in Hunan sabotaged the anti-Japanese efforts.

He proclaimed: "Now some vagabonds are scraping at people for their riches, declaring that they will be used to purchase bombers to fight the Japs and build up air defence facilities. But where are the bombers and air defence facilities? I am telling you: the people's money has all been used to build mansions. We should cry out loudly at them: stop wantonly profiting from the crisis faced by our country under the anti-Japanese banner and take out the money to buy bombers and artillery pieces."

Making a stand for what was right and just, his oratory was consequently stern. Barely stopping for breath, he reeled off a speech lasting several hours. Those story-listeners, leisure-seekers, tea drinkers and diners had all been attracted here and changed the whole clamorous Fire Palace into a huge meeting place.

On that day, one newspaper in Changsha gave a very vivid description of Xu Teli's speech: "Don't belittle this place. The old educator Mr Xu Teli has now delivered a speech here! He has dived in the depths of civilian life. With his vivid tone of voice, he explained state affairs in detail and snatched away the trade of many story tellers. More and more listeners gathered around and Mr Xu's oratory went on and on. At noontime, the audience invited him for lunch. This showed how concerned they were with the fate of the nation,"

"I Had to Put the Future of the Country and the Liberation of the Nation First."

Securing the release of political prisoners was an important item on the cooperation agreement between the Nationalist and Communist Parties during the Anti-Japanese War period. While he was working in the Communications Service of the Eighth Route Army in Hunan, Xu Teli had negotiated with the KMT authorities for many times and required the release of detained political prisoners.

One day, he received news from reliable source: More than thirty comrades including Qiao Xinming (1909 – 1963) the former Chief of Staff of the 20th Division of the Anti-Japanese Advance Troops of the Chinese Workers' and Peasants' Red Army had been marched to Changsha Military Prison from a KMT prison in Jiangxi. He decided to go and visit them as soon as possible.

When Xu Teli reached the prison, the prison governor knew that he enjoyed high prestige among the people and was also the representative of the Communications Service of the Eighth Route Army in Hunan. According to his reasoning, if he didn't allow him to see the political prisoners, he would never quit from asking. Therefore, he was forced to show respect to Xu Teli and ordered the gate of the prison to be opened to welcome his arrival.

Xu Teli paid no attention to the rules in the KMT prison. Planting himself in there, he shouted loudly: "Political prisoners, fall in!" Qiao Xinming and the other comrades walked out of their cells slowly. They must have never expected that they could meet Xu Teli, Chairman Mao Zedong's teacher and a high-ranking CPC leader in a KMT prison. Xu shook hands with them one by one and extended his cordial concern to them. The political victims were so moved they shed hot tears. Xu Teli delivered a speech before them with a beaming face. First he explained how the Nationalist and Communist Parties had cooperated again to fight the Japs and then expounded the CPC's guiding anti-Japanese lines and policies. Finally he wrapped up his impassioned oration with: "Comrades, the sun is coming out and the day is breaking! Don't worry. Take good care of yourselves. Summon up your fight and strengthen your confidence. New battles await you."

After coming back to the communications service, he immediately drew up a list that included the names of Qiao Xinming and more than thirty other comrades and requested that the Nationalist Party free them as soon as possible. Nonetheless, not only did the KMT diehards refuse to release them but they marched them secretly to a junior high school in the rural area of Taoyuan County in Hunan and attempted to murder them.

Upon hearing the news, anger burned in Xu Teli's belly and he went directly to the provincial government to seek out and negotiate with Zhang Zhizhong the Chairman of the KMT Government of Hunan Province.

"All the political prisoners should be freed. This has been written and signed in the cooperation agreement between the Nationalist and Communist Parties on the negotiation table. Why not be as good as your word and release the political prisoners?" Xu Teli questioned.

"Mr Xu, there is no need to lose your temper, there is no need to lose your temper. If there is any problem, let's talk about it well," Zhang Zhizhong persuaded.

"If we can talk about it, you should free them ASAP." Xu Teli didn't give an inch.

"Free them? As far as I know, there are no members of your honourable Party in the prison. The list drawn up by Venerable Xu doesn't originate from hearsay?"

"What hearsay! They have just been marched here from a Jiangxi prison. I already went to see them long ago. I never expected that Chairman Zhang will be so ill-informed!"

Zhang Zhizhong was a comparatively open-minded personage among the KMT ruling group. Under the resolute requirement of Xu Teli, he agreed to release the incarcerated comrades, including Qiao Xinming. Thanks to Xu Teli's rescue, several batches of comrades left jail one after another, saving many key members of the Party.

While Xu Teli was rushing about day and night in order to save Qiao Xinming and the other comrades, his younger son Xu Houben contracted typhoid fever on his way to Changsha from Yan'an and needed emergency treatment in the hospital. But Xu Teli had no time to visit him. When Qiao Xinming and the others were freed finally and he hurried to the hospital, he was confronted with one person dead and another wounded. His son had died from the disease without having the chance to see his father for the last time. Overcome with grief, his daughter-in-law Liu Cuiying had collapsed and fallen head-first down the stairwell. From standing on the second floor she landed on the first floor and lost consciousness.

Finally, Liu Cuiying survived but with a concussion that lasted a dozen or more years. Xu Houben was by that time Xu Teli's youngest and only surviving son. His eldest son Xu Duben had sacrificed his life for the Great Revolution in 1927. Xu Teli was in his sixties back then. His grief was unimaginable!

Later when his granddaughter Xu Yuqiang asked about this, Xu Teli explained in a pathetic state: "How great a sum of wealth those more than thirty comrades were for our Party! 30 versus 1, I had to put the future of the country and the liberation of the nation at the first place. When I rushed to Xiangya Hospital, what I saw was one dead and one wounded – your father had passed away and your mother was lying on a sickbed with her head wrapped up with bandage. My grief knew no bounds."

Chapter Five

His Family Style and Education Still Benefit Subsequent Generations

Growing Old Together with His Wife He Had Been with Since Childhood

Xu Teli's wife Xiong Licheng stepped across the threshold of the Xu family aged only eleven and served as their daughter-in-law from childhood until she passed away at eighty-two. For seventy years, they respected and loved and supported each other. Though living in humble circumstances, they helped one another like two fishes in a dried-up spring which need each other's saliva to survive. Both parties always remained loyal to the other. In December, 1957 when Old Lady Xu celebrated her birthday, someone sent her a horizontal scroll, which read: "Growing Old Together since Childhood." All present exclaimed that it was well-written and that it was a true reflection of the couple of old people.

As a professional revolutionary and educator, Xu Teli was often away from home for a long time. Therefore, their family life was characterised by hardships and long separations rather than being a peaceful idyll.

In order to pursue his personal ideals and faith, Xu Teli left his hometown as early as 1905 and went out to establish schools and engage in educational work. Few and far between were the days when he could stay at home. More often than not, he was compelled to rush about outside. In 1919, in the quest for new knowledge, he travelled far across the oceans to France to enrol on a work-study programme. During that time he was separated from his wife for fully five years. In 1927, he became a CPC member and threw himself into the revolution. He then went to Jiangxi to participate in the Nanchang Uprising, to the Soviet Union to be trained in Marxism and Leninism and to the Soviet areas under the direct leadership of the CPC Central Committee to involve himself in cultural and educational work. Later he followed the Red Army under the direct command of the CPC Central Committee to embark on the Long March and dedicated himself to cultural and educational work at the revolutionary base area between Shaanxi, Gansu and Ningxia Provinces after they reached Northern Shaanxi. For ten years he and his wife did not once hear from each other. At the beginning of the Anti-Japanese War period, he came back to preside over the work at the Communications Service of the Eighth Route Army in Hunan. The husband and wife were finally reunited, but this was to last for little more than one year. However, from 1940 they were cut asunder once again. Not until 1949, when the whole country was liberated, could they reside together in Beijing.

Even though the separations became more and more protracted, husband and wife were always joined in their hearts and bound together by their affection.

Xiong Licheng went to the Xu family at eleven and helped to manage the household chores from an early age. Later she supported Xu Teli in his efforts to read even though that entailed insolvency, she supported him in running schools at the price of sacrificing their home. She even more readily supported him in embarking on the revolutionary road. She received little schooling but was far-sighted and bold and supported Xu Teli to read, establish schools and take the revolutionary road at any cost. Xu Teli was always filled with gratitude and love towards her. His granddaughter Xu Zhou recalled that her maternal grandfather often talked about their grandmother's virtues in front of his grandchildren and always cared for and loved their grandmother. In those days when he was outside, he always missed his wife and children. When he was free from his busy duties, he grabbed any available break to write to them.

In 1939, Xu Teli wrote to his younger daughter Xu Moqing, who was by then staying at home, and drilled it into her that she must show her filial gratitude to, care about and take care of her mother.

The letter read: "Your mother is already seventy. She has not only managed to run this family but also helped me run a senior primary school for a total of thirteen years and nurtured many students. She received no education, but has made a contribution to the local educational cause. Many literate women are not as good as she. She has my respect. She gave birth to you and so should warrant your special filial devotion towards her. If you as a husband and wife can do anything to alleviate the difficulties faced by this family, please try your best. If you can't be of any assistance yourselves, you can sell some of our farmland."

The words were terse, but the affection in that short letter was obviously deep. From this we can discern Xu Teli's great concern for his wife and family.

Because Xu Teli lived alone for a long time, many kind-hearted comrades persuaded him in private to find a mistress, but he put his foot down.

"I am a man of blood, flesh and affection," he explained. "I love my family and my wife and children. ... My wife married me when she was still a child. She is not well-educated, but she has shared my weal and woe since we were young. I have constantly had to go outside to engage in education and revolution. She stayed at home bringing up the children, labouring and helping me with the running of my schools. She supports and helps my cause. Throughout my life I have advocated the liberation of women. If I discarded her, wouldn't that mean there was another victimised woman in this world?"

All the listeners were moved by his words.

Soon after the establishment of the New China in 1949, Xu Teli brought his wife to Beijing. By then, the pair was already both in their seventies and finally had the chance to live together again. During those days, Xu Teli was extremely considerate and often spoke to his staff like this: "You don't need to give me any special consideration, but you must take good care of the old lady. She is an illiterate housewife. It is easy for her to get an inferiority complex. She should be relieved of her spiritual burden." Every time when he went outside to recuperate, he would always bring his wife with him. When they dined together, he would set aside the dishes that were of slightly better quality for her. His own clothing was simple and plain, but from time to time he would buy a little good cloth for his wife to make some new clothes. Several springs of their spring bed at home were broken. He then lay on the caved-in side and left the intact side to his wife.

After Xiong Licheng passed away, Xu Teli felt very grief-stricken and missed her very much. He always kept a group photo which featured him and his wife in his pocket and frequently took it out to have a look so that the photo became creased in the middle.

His faithful love and consideration towards his wife embodied his noble character and moral sentiments.

You Should First Think About How to Make a Contribution to the Society

Xu Teli spent an exceedingly long time away from home immersed in educational and revolutionary work. Often he was left with no time to take care of his family. But his educator's professional consciousness again made him pay much attention to the education of his children.

He pointed out that "As senior revolutionaries, as parents and as heads of our families, we should never forget our duty to educate our children because in this society, our children are not only our relatives and descendants but also members of society and of the whole revolution. Whether they are good or bad should not simply be a concern for our families but for society as a whole." Accordingly, "if we want to turn our offspring into the Red successors of the revolution and hope that 'those later comers can surpass the old-timers,' we should care about and aid them in every respect, whether this be ideology, study, daily life or anything else. We should care about their lives. They should have sufficient food to eat and enough clothes to keep warm so that they are able to study and work energetically. This is naturally very important and necessary. But what is more important is that we should care about their ideological state and political lives."

Xu Teli and Xiong Licheng produced a total of eight children but only four reached adulthood, namely: the elder daughter Xu Shouzhen, the elder son Xu Duben, the younger daughter Xu Moqing and the younger son Xu Houben. He was very strict with them and taught them earnestly.

He frequently instilled it in them that young people must take others into consideration more readily and make more of a contribution to society but never be overly-obsessed with themselves and their families.

Born in 1906, Xu Duben was Xu Teli's eldest son. By then Xu Teli was playing out his ideal of saving the country through the promotion of education. He had left his home at Wumei Village and was teaching at schools such as the Zhou Family Girls School (The name later was changed to the Zhounan Girls Junior High School), Xiuye School and so on. Later, Xu Duben went to study at a junior high school in the city proper of Changsha. Someone introduced him to a girlfriend. He also wanted to accept her. After hearing about this, Xu Teli enjoined his son gravely: "You are still young. You should study hard for the revolution, lay a solid foundation for your cause and become a person that benefits society. You should first think of how to contribute to society, not how to arrange your little family. If everyone were selfish, how would any progress be made in society?"

His father in effect dismissed his idea of dating the girl and starting a family. Xu Duben then threw himself into his study and work. He studied very hard, approached tasks meticulously and cared about the problems of society and the pains and difficulties of the people. He joined the CPC when still in junior high school and became one of the earliest members of the Party. During the first Great Revolution, the nineteen-year-old Xu Duben actively participated in the peasant movement and took the post of Chairman of the Liling County Peasants Association in Hunan. Under his leadership, the peasant movement there soared like a raging fire. When his father Xu Teli asked him about his marriage again, he answered: "Now I have no time to talk about this. The struggle is so intense. I don't even have enough time to cope with revolutionary business." In this way, Xu Duben threw all his energy into the revolutionary cause.

The sheer enormity of the dogged revolutionary work left Xu Duben chronically fatigued and soon his condition worsened into a disease. In 1927 he died in Changsha Renshu Hospital. His demise was felt acutely by the Organisation and they held a solemn memorial meeting for him.

Many escorted his coffin back to his home village, where he was buried.

He was only twenty-one and unmarried when he passed away.

Children Should Go Where They Belong

Born in 1917, Xu Houben was Xu Teli's younger son. When he was two years old, Xu Teli travelled all the way to Europe for a work-study programme. Father and son were separated for five years and did not meet again until Xu Teli came back in July, 1924. After returning to his motherland, Xu Teli continued to pursue his ideal of saving the country through promoting education and immediately threw himself into the establishment of schools. First he established Changsha Girls Normal School and later took on the posts of Headmaster of Changsha Normal School and Headmaster of Hunan First Girls Normal School. His workload was so gruelling that he seldom had time to stay together with his family. Nonetheless this kind of tight-scheduled life was also soon to be interrupted. In 1927, the KMT rightists betrayed the revolution. He joined the CPC and took the road of a professional revolutionary from then onwards. This time he was separated from his kin and children for a decade.

During those ten years, Xu Houben first completed his primary education and then went to middle school. In 1935, he dropped out of Changsha County First Junior High School (The name was changed into Changsha County Junior High School the following year) owing to the straitened financial circumstances at home and went to Changsha Big Vehicle Repair Shop to be an apprentice. In December, 1937, Xu Teli came back from Yan'an to preside over the work at the Communications Service of the Eighth Route Army in Hunan as the senior councillor of the Eighteenth Group Army of the National Revolutionary Army and representative of the CPC Central Committee. One of his jobs was to organise and mobilise progressive young people to go to Yan'an to participate in the revolution. His heart swayed, Xu Houben shared his ambition with his father. Xu Teli had suffered the pain of losing his elder son during the first Great Revolution, but considering that there was a crying need for vehicle mechanics in Yan'an, he agreed without hesitation. He felt that his younger son and daughter-in-law ought to head to Yan'an to throw themselves into the Anti-Japanese War.

However, Old Lady Xu was unwilling to part company with them; she later came to a compromise, insisting that her daughter-in-law should stay behind.

Xu Teli tried to talk her round: "Our son and daughter-in-law are going there to study and do revolutionary work. They should go there together. How can we tear them apart?"

He continued: "We should love them both, but if we always tell them to stay beside us, their promising future will be put off kilter. If the parents truly love their children, they should allow them to go to where they belong to and fulfil a particular cause for society …"

With Xu Teli's backing, Xu Houben and his wife set out for Yan'an in the spring of 1938. They studied for six months in the Northern Shaanxi Public School and were then dispatched back to Changsha by the Organisation in July, 1938. Quite unexpectedly he contracted typhoid fever on his way and the disease grew more intense after he reached Changsha. Medical treatment proved to no avail and he passed away tragically. How heavy a blow this was for Xu Teli, who was already sixty-one years old!

You Should Consider the Difficulties Faced by the People and Government More Frequently

Xu Teli's love and concern and help towards his children were never expressed through indulgence and satisfying material desire. Always using his lofty goal that "Revolution comes first, work comes first and the other people come first" as a lodestone he taught them skilfully, patiently and affectionately through a combination of personal example and verbal instruction.

Born in 1904, his elder daughter Xu Shouzhen liked painting from an early age. With her father's support, she studied in the mixed school – Yueyun School.

After graduating from junior high school, she sat exams and was admitted into the Shanghai Xinhua Art School to learn painting in 1927. She was an activist in the Red workers union under the leadership of the CPC. In 1928, she was arrested because she took part in activities arranged by a peripheral organisation of the CPC and lost contact with her family. Soon after she was discharged from prison, Shanghai was occupied by the Japanese troops. Thanks to a personal introduction, the jobless Xu Shouzhen found a gate-keeping and letter-forwarding post in a certain work unit of the Japanese puppet regime in Shanghai. Thereafter, she lost contact with Xu Teli.

In 1949 the New China was established. When she knew her father was a high-ranking leader in the new government, Xu Shouzhen went to Beijing in a state of elation. Father and daughter who had been torn asunder for more than two decades were reunited. After hearing of his daughter's hard life in the intervening years, Xu Teli felt heartbroken and hoped that his daughter could stay beside him. But the New China had barely been established. Many things were waiting to be done. The country faced countless hardships in the spheres of politics, the economy, culture, and education, to name just a few. He then persuaded his daughter that she should not be obsessed with her personal difficulties but rather consider the difficulties faced by the government more frequently. Xu Shouzhen originally thought that her father, being a high-ranking CPC official, would allow her to come to Beijing to work. Hearing him out, she went back to Shanghai at ease.

In a letter written to his daughter, Xu Teli explained: "I am already seventy-four but still work eight hours every day. The government will cover my living expenditure as much as it can, but the situation is tough. I am unwilling to spend unnecessarily. Therefore, I don't want to see you come up north. ... If you want to become a member of our Party, you should work harder than the others to prove that you are the kinsfolk of a communist."

Later, he wrote to Xu Shouzhen and her husband many times and encouraged them to make progress politically and care about the revival of the nation.

He said: "You are still not communists. The problem doesn't lie with the Organisation but first and foremost with your actions and ideology ... I hope that you don't spend every hour of every day obsessed with just your own personal benefits. You might think of your own hard situation in the first half of the night, but in the second half you should consider the difficulties faced by the people, by the government and by the officials in charge of the government units. If you conduct your life in this way, your personal vexations will be gone, your mind will be broadened and you will change into a progressive."

With the unrolling of the "left-leaning" movement, Xu Shouzhen, who was working peacefully and striving upward actively, was again affected. In 1957, implicated by the Pan Hannian Judicial Case, she was convicted as a "counterrevolutionary." After knowing of this, Xu Teli was put on a knife-edge and immediately told Xu Zhou to go to Shanghai to make enquiries. Xu Zhou sought out the local Organisation and gained the answer that it was true. On the one hand, Xu Teli was adamant in his belief that his daughter was no counterrevolutionary, but on the other, he was duty-bound to accept the Organisation's verdict. Torn between his kin and the Organisation, he patiently persuaded his children to believe in the Organisation. Xu Shouzhen accepted the reformation through manual labour silently and died with unresolved grievances in 1973. Not until 1983, following the Third Plenary Session of the Eleventh Central Committee of 1978, was the wrongful conviction of Pan Hannian overturned. Xu Shouzhen's reputation was posthumously rehabilitated in 1985. The historic injustice was finally righted and at long last Xu Shouzhen's name was cleared. Xu Teli, who by then was already under the Nine Springs of the Underworld, ought to have at last been able to close his eyes at ease.

"Work Honestly and Always Be an Asset to the People"

Born in 1916, Xu Moqing was Xu Teli's younger daughter. This was a child who shouldered the burdens of the household from an early age. In the autumn of 1927, after the first Great Revolution ended in failure, Xu Teli's elder son Xu Duben sacrificed his life. Xu Teli, who was already over fifty, followed the CPC to leave home. The elder daughter Xu Shouzhen was arrested and went missing. The drastic changes that befell the family dealt repeated blows to Xiong Licheng. She almost lost her mind. Xu Moqing was only eleven by then and Xu Houben was only ten. Facing these disasters, the eleven-year-old Xu Moqing bore the strain. She needed to cook, wash laundry, grow vegetables, raise pigs, take care of her unhinged mother, escort her younger brother to school and watch over her niece Xu Zhou who by then was only four and didn't know any better.

Consequently, she didn't even complete her primary education and whiled away her childhood and adolescence doing heavy household chores. Sustained by her efforts, her younger brother finished junior high school and married Liu Cuiying when he was sixteen. From then on, the household had the added support of her sister-in-law, but their life was still very hard. She developed asthma at an early age – probably on account of overwork – but there was no money to spend on treatment.

In 1937, the full-scale Anti-Japanese War broke out. Xu Teli came back to Changsha and without a jot of hesitation encouraged his younger son Xu Houben and his daughter-in-law to go to study in Yan'an. Xu Mouqing also wanted to go there. But her sixty-one-year-old mother Xiong Licheng would then have nobody to take care of her. She dismissed the thought out of hand. Following her father's advice, she decided to learn medicine in order to assist the Anti-Japanese War. She went to study at the nurse's class in Changsha Self-disciplined Girls School. After graduating she went to work at Changsha Serious Injury Hospital. This hospital received many grievously wounded soldiers sent back from the frontline and the workload for nursing staff was arduous. Xu Moqing studied and worked hard. She finally became an honourable white-clad fighter dedicated to healing the wounded and rescuing the dying. Here she became acquainted with Lu Zhensheng, a learned able-handed surgeon who was always ready to make a contribution to the Anti-Japanese War and national salvation. Later they got married.

During the Anti-Japanese War, Xu Teli twice dispatched people with letters written by him to collect his wife and granddaughter to Yan'an; he also told Xu Moqing and her husband to go together. Xu Moqing thought that her father was very busy, her mother was disease-stricken and her niece needed to be taken care of by someone. She therefore followed her mother's advice and stayed in her hometown to keep the household afloat.

During the War of Liberation between 1945 and 1949, Xu Moqing from time to time received information about her father Xu Teli and her sister-in-law Xu Qian (i.e., Liu Cuiying) from the Organisation as well as silver coins to serve as her living allowance. She took care of her mother and niece more devotedly at home so that her father and sister-in-law could fight the revolution with their minds at ease.

After the liberation of the whole country in 1949, Xu Teli settled down in Beijing and arranged for hands to collect his family from Wumei. Xu Moqing was given a job at the Beijing Railway Hospital. Originally she was able to live together with her parents. Reasoning that her father was a CPC Central Committee leader and she was only a common citizen, she thought it sensible to live somewhere else. Her family duly moved to a two-bedroom house in a tenement compound, bought some old furniture and still lived an assiduous frugal life. Her neighbours didn't even know that she was Xu Teli's daughter.

When they were in Beijing, Xu Moqing and her family were subject to the overall rationing system. She actively took part in the study arranged by the Organisation for the cadres. In 1952, she was transferred to the Beijing Railway General Hospital affiliated to the Ministry of Railways of the PRC. In 1956, she joined the CPC. She worked quietly and made a silent contribution on her nurse's post until her retirement in 1977.

Throughout her life, Xu Moqing followed her father's admonition and lived a diligent, thrifty, plain life on the basis of her own honest work. She never put forward any unreasonable requests towards the Organisation even if it were for something she deserved and the Organisation hadn't considered or had difficulties in doing that. She often upbraided her children: "As the offspring of the old man, we should work honestly and always be somebody who will benefit the people. Only in this way will we not fail him. We shall never sully his face!" These words were as precious as pieces of gold and jade bouncing back up from the floor.

Xu Teli's granddaughter Xu Zhou was correct in her observation: "Throughout her life, my younger aunt neither accomplished anything that startled the heavens and shocked the earth nor gained a string of eye-catching 'titles.' She only worked honestly, lived a plain life and treated others kindly and with tolerance."

One passage from "Comrade Xu Moqing's Life Story," compiled by the Beijing Railway General Hospital, reads: "(Comrade Xu Moqing) for several dozen years never cared whether her post was high or low and whether her pay was good or bad but always obeyed the arrangements of the Organisation and did whatever the Party told her to do. She never put forward any difficulties or requests towards the Organisation but always did her nurse's work willingly. She displayed consummate self-discipline and a quiet devotion. She lived up to her name as a good daughter of the proletarian revolutionary Xu Teli …"

You Should Have Your Own Life

Xu Teli's intensive care and teachings towards his daughter-in-law, whom he later adopted as his daughter, showed more clearly his broad-mindedness and touching feelings as a revolutionary and educator.

His daughter-in-law Liu Cuiying was also a native of Changsha County. In 1933 she married Xu Houben. By then Xu Teli was presiding over the educational work in the Soviet areas under the direct governance of the CPC Central Committee in Jiangxi Province and had lost contact with his family. Therefore, the marriage was arranged by the old lady Xiong Licheng. After her marriage, Liu Cuiying helped her mother-in-law Xiong Licheng and her younger sister-in-law Xu Moqing to manage the house; her husband Xu Houben apprenticed himself to the Changsha Big Vehicle Repair Shop. In 1936, she gave birth to her daughter Xu Yuqiang.

In 1937, the Anti-Japanese War erupted. The Nationalist and Communist Parties cooperated for the second time. At the end of the year, Xu Teli came back to Changsha from Yan'an to preside over the work at the Communications Service of the Eighth Route Army in Hunan. He was very busy back then and had no time to come back home at all. Liu Cuiying brought her daughter and followed Old Lady Xiong to the city proper to look for her father-in-law. Not until then did she come to know the old man. Because the communications service was newly established and they were short of serving hands, Wang Lingbo (1888 – 1942) the Director of the Communications Service asked her to stay there to do some logistical work.

In the spring of 1938, with Xu Teli's support and blessing, Liu Cuiying left her daughter, who by then was only a little more than one year old, to her mother-in-law and went to Yan'an together with her husband. After studying in the Northern Shaanxi Public School for six months, she graduated and was dispatched by the Organisation to come back to Hunan to work together with her husband. Unfortunately, her husband Xu Houben contracted a disease on the way, and passed away in hospital in Changsha, having failed to respond to treatment. He left behind a widowed mother and an orphaned daughter. The heavy spiritual blow made Liu Cuiying, who was only 23 years old, sink into perpetual grief. She took a nasty tumble in the hospital and was left with a chronic headache. The pain resulted from losing her husband and the headache that attacked her intermittently tortured her until she lost the will to live. She thought of death and wanted to seek release through committing suicide. One day she hardened her heart and tried to hang herself. Luckily, someone interrupted her and she was saved in time.

For one thing, Xu Teli had to wrestle with the intense agony of losing his son; for another he had to console his daughter-in-law and help her find a way out of her misery at the earliest opportunity. What is more, in order to prevent his old partner from sliding into the depths of grief, he needed to keep her in the dark about his younger son's death with the help of his daughter-in-law. He wrote to Liu Cuiying many times to console her and encourage her to build up a new life.

In one letter he wrote in the summer of 1938, he said: "You are a member of our family. Your child is the blood and flesh of our family. You are still young. You should have your own life. After you have remarried, it is improper for us to address each other as 'father-in-law' and 'daughter-in-law'. You can be my daughter and it is good as well if we address each other as 'comrade.' But before you remarry, I hold myself responsible for your life."

In order to help alleviate Liu Cuiying from future worries, Xu Teli decided it was best for him to look after her and watch over her as if she were his own daughter. After the Changsha Conflagration in November, 1938, Xu Teli brought his old spouse, granddaughter and widowed daughter-in-law to Guilin in Guangxi Province through Hengyang and Shaoyang cities together with the Communications Service of the Eighth Route Army in Hunan. In Guilin, a man wooed Liu Cuiying and wanted to marry her. Liu Cuiying thought it over and over and still couldn't straighten out her thoughts. She thus felt vexed, lonely and helpless.

After perceiving this, Xu Teli at once wrote three pointed letters to her, showing his care and instructing her as if she really were his daughter. In the letters, he outlined some principles when faced with the prospect of marriage: "What makes an ideal partner for a young woman? First, he should be honest and kind and virtuous and not be in the least inclined to abandoning his wife. What is more, your ages should be well-matched." He then helped Liu Cuiying to analyse: "He (referring to that man) is a politically progressive CPC member. In a revolutionary army, you choose a mate not for money or position but because he is progressive. Also under his help you can make progress further and see the hope of joining the Party."

He encouraged Liu Cuiying to seek out a new life bravely. His heartfelt love and concern and teachings soon helped her struggle free from her misery and vexation.

"The old man's earnest concern moved me very much. But how could I find the heart to leave this benign amiable and highly respected fellow? … I declined this proposal and requested to go to Yan'an to study and work. The old man understood and trusted me and agreed with my request."

Therefore, Liu Cuiying again took the road to Yan'an.

Changing Liu Cuiying's Name to Xu Qian

While sincerely caring about Liu Cuiying's life, Xu Teli also spared no efforts to support her revolutionary aspirations. This was a rather painful process: First, he should do his best to keep it a secret from the old lady Xiong Licheng. In order that Xiong Licheng wouldn't be too grief-stricken because her daughter-in-law would be far away from her for a long time, he made an appointment with Liu Cuiying that they should withhold the full truth from her. They only told her that she and her granddaughter would go back to Hunan temporarily while Liu Cuiying would be left behind in Guilin. Secondly, Xu Teli racked his brains to find a new name for his daughter-in-law. On that day when he should see off the old lady and his granddaughter, he especially went to the compound where Liu Cuiying was boarding.

"You are leaving," he said cordially. "Let me give you a new name."

He took out a sheet of paper and wrote down the two words "Xu Qian" on it. Liu Cuiying couldn't understand the connotations of the name, but she felt the old man's deep love. She had many words to confide to him. But the moment she opened her mouth, she was choked with sobs.

With the understanding and support of Xu Teli, Xu Qian took the road to Yan'an in January, 1940. She went to study first in the Northern Shaanxi Public School and then in the China Women's School, formally planting her feet on the revolutionary road. In the autumn of that same year, Xu Teli came back to Yan'an. He wrote a short piece with the expressed purpose of explaining to Xu Qian what *qian* meant.

"Every day a gentleman is striving forward (*qian*)," he expounded. "From morning to evening he is on full alert as if he is confronting some danger. Only in this way can he shield himself from disasters and make smooth progress. Such will be his concentration and spirit that he is sure to have a promising future."

It only takes half an eye to be able to perceive that Xu Teli changed his daughter-in-law's name not only out of love, but also out of the great expectations a father harbours towards his child. Precisely as Xu Qian said: "A name has no significant connotations. The matter of whether a person's name is elegant or vulgar has no bearing on whether they have high or low ideology. But through changing my name, I felt that my old father was extending his thoughtful kindness to the next generation."

Chapter Six

"An Exemplary Teacher of His Generation and a Role Model for the World"

Two Deep-fried Glutinous Rice Cakes

Xu Teli had a rare quality – "Always putting other people first." Li Weihan commented: "Never be selfish but always be altruistic. Take it as a pleasure to help others and care about other comrades. This has always been a virtue of Venerable Xu. He is the type of person who always has others but never himself in his heart. Whenever anything happens, he will always think of others, shouldering the difficulties himself while trying to make matters convenient for others."

In December, 1934, the Red Army under the direct command of the CPC Central Committee occupied Tongdao City in Hunan Province. There, the CPC Central Committee summoned an emergent meeting, studied which direction the Red Army should march forward and decided that they would quit their former plan of going northwards and out of Northern Hunan to rendezvous with the Second and Sixth Army Groups but instead march towards Guizhou Province where the enemy forces were weak.

It was already early winter, though the South of China was still experiencing its rainy season. Xu Teli followed the army for one whole day, marching through a downpour. During that time, they scaled mountains while chewing on raw rice kernels and conquered one great eminence after another. At long last, they reached a small market town at dusk and everyone felt cold, starved and exhausted.

"Now we should have a good rest and cook a hot meal to eat!" they thought.

However, the Company Commander relayed the order from the Headquarters: "Take a brief break here and then continue on our route."

Even though it was a short break, they still wanted to seize this rare opportunity and buy some well-cooked food to eat. With people shouting merrily and horses neighing, the small town became a scene of hustle and bustle. The only two small shops were immediately packed solid until water couldn't leak out. If one was slightly slow, they could only stand outside the human walls worrying helplessly.

It took one guard great efforts to buy two glutinous rice cakes deep-fried in oil. He hurriedly sent them over to Xu Teli. "Venerable Xu, hurry and eat them!" While speaking like this, he crammed them into his hands.

"Everyone's stomach is grumbling. Why should I be any exception!" Xu Teli declined no matter how the guard persuaded.

Seeing that he was unwilling to take the food, the others all persuaded him:

"Venerable Xu, you are advanced in years and haven't enjoyed anything hot for several days. Since the food has already been bought, please accept it!"

…

Seeing that there was a stretcher by the road, Xu Teli recalled that the wounded on it had caught a high fever and nothing had passed his lips for days. One flash of inspiration hit him. He said to the guard: "Then one for each of us!"

He took over the deep-fried glutinous rice cakes and ran to the stretcher before the guard could bat an eyelid. He bent down and benevolently took a look at the wounded. He then ripped the deep-fried glutinous rice cakes into shreds and crammed them all into the man's mouth.

Two Sheepskins

The following story occurred when the Red Army reached the Mountain Jiajin on the border region between Sichuan and Xikang Provinces – the first great snow-crowned rarely-trodden mountain encountered during their Long March.

It was frigid in the snow-buried world, but they had discarded their clothing to travel light before going across the River Dadu. Now no longer did they have any other pieces to put around them. At this time, the advance forces sent them two sheep. This was rare delicious food.

They slaughtered the animals, ate a square meal and again lay the two sheepskins out to dry near the bonfire.

"Venerable Xu and Venerable Xie are both advanced in years and not healthy enough. They have so little on them. How can they brave the snow-capped mountain?" Li Jianzhen suggested: "Let's send the sheepskins to them to ward off the chills!"

The others cheered in agreement.

"Venerable Xu, come and drape this sheepskin around you!" The comrades walked to him with one sheepskin and ropes and got ready to bind the sheepskin around him.

"No, no, I can still hold on. Give it to Venerable Xie! He is weaker than me," Xu Teli waved his hands and declined.

"Venerable Xu, drape it around you! Here is another fleece for Venerable Xie," someone raised the other sheepskin and persuaded.

"One piece is not enough. His front may be protected, but his back is exposed. He is weak and suffering from a disease. He should have both!" Xu Teli insisted.

Seeing that he was so resolute and sincere, the comrades had to send the two sheepskins to Xie Juezai[1].

"Since Venerable Xu doesn't want it, you should send it to another comrade! How can I feel comfortable always having him take care of me!" Xie Juezai also declined.

---

1   Xie Juezai (谢觉哉, 1884 – 1971) was born in the county-level Ningxiang City, Hunan Province. He was an excellent member of the CPC, a prominent jurist and educationalist, an outstanding social activist, a forerunner in the jurisprudential circle and one of the founders of the people's judicial system. In 1933, while serving as Minister of Internal Affairs in the Soviet Areas under the governance of the CPC Central Committee, he presided over and participated in the drafting of the early laws and ordinances of the Red regime such as the *Labour Law*, the *Land Law* and so on. After the establishment of the PRC, he served variously as Minister of Internal Affairs, President of the People's Supreme Court, and President of China University of Political Science and Law.

"Juezai, we are comrades-at-arms that are as close to each other as the hands to the feet! Why still bother about who takes care of whom? Don't let it trouble your mind and always feel uneasy at heart," Xu Teli consoled him calmly.

The others watched how the two old people deferred to each other and, moved by the deep friendship between them, didn't know to whom they should listen.

"Why still stand here but not help Venerable Xie bind the sheepskins in place?" Xu Teli hit on an idea at the spur of the moment.

The others crowded around Xie Juezai and bound the two sheepskins around him in a melee.

Xu Teli stood nearby watching and chortling.

Moved to hot tears, Xie Juezai smiled too.

The moving friendship between these two tested aged revolutionaries who would live or die together soon spread out among the Red Army and became a spiritual force that encouraged the soldiers to yield to no hardships and strive forward.

"Is Now the Time for Us to Be Courteous to Each Other?"

In the summer of 1935, the Red Army started to trudge across the boundless desolate grassland.

When traversing such a wilderness, having ample supplies of food spelled the difference between life and death. For every soldier of the Red Army, being able to muster sufficient rations was a most pressing problem. However, the local Tibetans had gone to ground long before because they were uncertain what kind of a force the Red Army was. Not a soul was to be seen.

The highland barley stood ripe in the fields but hadn't been harvested yet. The Headquarters ordered that they should reap it to solve their food problem and leave behind silver coins and brief explanatory notes. As there were no scythes in the stockade they had to tug it up with their bare hands.

Xu Teli followed the others to pull cluster by cluster. The stems of the highland barley were slippery, thick and tough. Tugging at it only a few times, his hands became scratched. But he acted nonchalantly as if nothing at all had happened. Talking in a jovial mood, he persisted in finishing the work together with the others.

After the highland barley was lifted, they were unable to locate a big stone mortar or a pair of grinding stones to remove the husks. They had to rub it with their hands.

"Your Honour is at an advanced age. Days of pulling barley has left scars all over your hands. So please stop rubbing." The other comrades persuaded him to stop rubbing the barley grains.

"Why try and stop me? Do I not have to eat too?" Xu Teli pretended to be angry with a long face. "If I need to eat, I am duty-bound to rub of course. If you forbid me, does that mean you want to starve me to death?"

The other comrades on the Long March were by now familiar with his temperament. Knowing that it was impossible to dissuade him, they had to pick up speed so that the work could be completed as soon as possible and he could have a rest.

After the highland barley was winnowed, Xu Teli pressed the others to rest. He, however, took it on himself to forage along the ground for any stray grains and dropped them into a bag. "A few extra grains might help one more comrade get out of the grassland and thus save one more pair of hands for the revolution!" he reasoned.

In order to cope with the constant threat of a food crisis, Xu Teli was unwilling to consume his share of highland barley. Instead, he scavenged as best he could for wild vegetables, grass roots and tree bark that might appease his hunger.

One day, he found out that the highland barley of his disease-stricken good friend Xie Juezai had been eaten up. Xie's deathlike pallor and bony frame struck him with alarm. Without a moment's hesitation, he tipped all the food he had fought hunger to save into Xie Juezai's rations bag.

At such a critical time and under such circumstances, everyone knew it clearly in their heart what food meant. What is more, Xu Teli also happened to be battling dysentery.

Xie Juezai declined: "Venerable Xu, you are older than me. Since we hit the road, whether we were on foot or in camp, more often than not it had been you who took care of me. During these days since we came to the grassland, I've seen you gnawing at wild vegetables and grass roots without ever accepting any proper food. Now how can you give all your food rations to me? You had better keep them to yourself!"

"Juezai, Is now the time for us to be courteous to each other? I am stronger than you are. I can get by on a few wild vegetables. But if you go hungry, that's another story. I don't have the heart to see you fall down!"

Xu Teli's words caused crystalline teardrops to roll out of the corners of Xie Juezai's eyes.

Xie Juezai could never forget this kindness. He later recalled: "But for the food rations given to me by Venerable Xu, which revived my spirit and built up my strength, I would have been left as a goner on the grassland. So many years have passed by, but I can never forget that."

In 1937 in Yan'an, the CPC Central Committee celebrated the sixtieth birthday of Xu Teli. In his poem "Congratulations to Comrade Teli on His Sixtieth Birthday, " Xie Juezai wrote:

Boundless is the marshy grassland.
Cold are those towering hillocks.
Who is that aged gentleman who tightens his waistband?
He tips his bag upside down when he gives me a hand.
Yet is as nimble as a monkey when scaling rocks.
And as speedy as a bird when dodging roadblocks.

His clothes and caps were mended by his own hands.
But better needlework it demands.

"Let Me Get Down and Try it out First"

When faced with benefits, advantages, fame and interests, Xu Teli always adhered to the principle of "always putting others first." However, there were also times when he would "take the lead." That was when they faced difficulties and dangers!

As their struggle across the grassland had almost come to an end, the soldiers for once wore an expression of reassurance. However, new difficulties were apt to crop up anytime and anywhere. One zigzagging river suddenly darted out of the waist-high grass and spread out horizontally in front of them. Capped with black foam, the water babbled forward through clusters of putrid grass. They were taken aback.

One voice suddenly broke the silence. "Let me get down and try it out first!" The others looked to see where those words were coming from and found that it was Xu Teli – the oldest one among the company. Barely had those words been spoken when he rolled up his trousers legs, removed his upper garment and strode over to the river.

"Venerable Xu! You can't get down there. It is too dangerous!" the soldiers chorused.

"The current is too rapid and it is so cold. What is more, you are old … Let us wade through it first," while speaking like this, several young men hurriedly stripped off their clothes.

"Won't it still be dangerous if you wade through it first?" Xu Teli asked in reply. Before the young men had chance to jump into water, he had already leaped in with a loud splash. While treading water, he tried to gauge the depth of the river and finally found out a relatively shallow waterway. The wounded riding on horseback and the women comrades tugging at the horses' tails, they all wade through the river safely. Every comrade wore a victorious smile.

Saving a Grandma and Granddaughter with No Care for His Own Safety

On 19th October, 1935, Xu Teli reached Wuqi Town, under the jurisdiction of Jingbian County, in Northern Shaanxi together with the CPC Central Committee. When he reached the back streets of the town, he encountered an unexpected incident.

The River Luo flowed past Wuqi Town. Its waters were torrential and rapid. That morning, a grandma and her granddaughter were acting carelessly and slipped into the river. They cried out loudly for help. The water was deep and fast-flowing. Many stood on the bank but could do nothing to help. The situation was critical. After hearing of this, Xu Teli rushed to the river and leaped into water without any regard to his own safety and saved the grandma and her granddaughter. Thereafter, Xu Teli's selfless rescue became an oft-told tale that spread far and wide.

"Marx Is Protecting Us"

Be it at work, in daily life or when engaged in the revolutionary struggle, Xu Teli was always filled with revolutionary optimism. This he used both to encourage himself and rally other comrades when fighting bravely against hardships and dangers.

In 1934 on their way to break the enemy's third blockade line, the Cadres' Recuperation Company halted on a mountain slope to have a break. Dong Biwu, the Secretary of the CPC General Branch, wanted to boost their morale and so took this opportunity to convene a meeting of the CPC General Branch. It was a bald mountain standing within the enemy's blockade line. They sat down together and argued vehemently. Suddenly an enemy bomber flew over, wheeled several circuits above the mountain and dropped a bomb, which exactly landed at the centre of their circle. The bomb plunged to the ground head-on, causing the top soil to be spattered anywhere, smearing their heads and faces all over with dirt. Fortunately, it didn't explode.

Xu Teli showed great presence of mind and remained as calm as calm could be. Shaking the dirt off of his clothes, he commented humorously: "Marx is protecting us. He tells us to carry on with our work because our task hasn't been accomplished yet!"

Xie Juezai smiled until his eyes narrowed into mere slits.

Dong Biwu was a poet. Wiping off the dirt that had dropped into his eyes, he concocted a jingle on the spot: "The bomb landed but didn't blossom like a flower. We should all thank Old Marx's protecting power …" The others lent him a ready ear for the rest part, but he continued: "The following two lines can't be cooked up in an instant."

While edging sideways they continued their meeting.

"I Am Still Young at Heart"

The Long March was extremely strenuous. A young soldier in his twenties frequently found it taxing. Xu Teli was already pushing sixty, but, still feeling young at heart, he showed even more vitality than much younger comrades.

In order to avoid the enemy's encirclement, pursuit, obstruction and interception and especially to avoid the bombardments of the enemy bombers, the army often marched at night. Despite adopting all kinds of precautions, troops would still go missing in the dark. Therefore, the army often took advantage of the safe breaks in the daytime to do military training – to practise bayonet charges and to learn self-defence skills such as how to distinguish directions and turn-offs at night. Thinking that he was rather long in the tooth and needed his rest, the Organisation did not inform Xu Teli about this training.

One mid-morning, the enemy planes had barely flown past when a soldier in leggings and wearing a hat woven out of tree twigs for disguise trotted out of the trees to participate in the training. The instructor took a look. It was Xu Teli.

"Venerable Xu," the instructor persuaded. "You were on the go all of last night and so should go back for a rest."

Slapping his chest, Xu Teli replied: "Everyone did the same and was spent and broken. But the comrades are all training here now. I of course shouldn't be made the exception. Do you want to disqualify me as a soldier of the Red Army?"

He continued: "You judge only on appearance and that is wrong! I am still young at heart!"

While speaking like this, he planted himself spiritedly among the ranks.

Delivering Eggs Three Times

The Government of the Shaanxi-Gansu-Ningxia Border Region received a batch of eggs. They decided to take care of the old and weak comrades and distribute a little "old-age allowances" to them.

A woman comrade took charge of delivering the "old-age allowances" to Xu Teli – a dozen or so eggs. After making it clear through enquiries, Xu Teli declined sincerely: "Thank the Organisation for their deep concern, but I am fine and don't need this stuff. Please bring them back and send them to comrades who are weak or sick."

After learning of this, the Organisation again dispatched the woman comrade to deliver the eggs to him. Xu Teli again declined.

The lady insisted: "Venerable Xu, you are already in your sixties and are different from the young and middle-aged. You must have some nutritious food. This is what the Organisation has decided …"

Before she had finished speaking, Xu Teli laughed out loud. "Ha – ha – I might be three times as old as you and should be counted as an old man, but I won't be thought of as weaker than you. Look, how many items of clothing have I put on? How many are you wearing?"

While speaking like this, he rolled up the legs of his unpadded grey-cloth trousers that had been patched and re-patched.

"Look, I'm wearing only unpadded trousers. What about you? Yours are cotton!"

His words silenced the woman comrade. But, struck by a flash of inspiration, she put the eggs on the table and said: "It is one thing how many pieces you have flung on but it is another thing how old you are. Please take them."

With these words, she turned around, strode out of the door and ran down the mountain.

She had never expected that soon after she came back, the eggs were again sent back together with a letter written by Xu Teli in person. In the letter, he explained why he couldn't accept the eggs. After reading through the letter, the others racked their brains and hit upon an idea finally – write a letter to him in the name of the Organisation.

After the letter was completed, the same woman comrade returned in high spirits with the letter and eggs to the cave house where Xu Teli lived. "Venerable Xu, I am back again!"

On catching sight of her, Xu Teli said with a smile: "Good child. Take a seat!" While pouring her a cup of tea, he queried: "Why are you in such a good mood? Here to discuss my 'old-age allowances' problem again?"

The woman comrade was prepared this time. She took out the letter written by the Organisation in a leisurely manner and handed it to him, replying: "Today I am not here to discuss that. Just to forward a letter."

After Xu Teli had read through the letter, she asked on purpose: "Venerable Xu, this is a decision made by the Organisation. You won't tell me to bring the stuff back again!"

With no other options available, Xu Teli had to say: "Since it is a decision made by the Organisation, I should obey. OK, I will accept them."

Having fulfilled her task finally, the woman comrade went back hilariously. However, after taking over the eggs, Xu Teli ate none of them but sent them all to sick comrades.

The Stable-hand-like Minister of Education

For the sake of his cause, Xu Teli always practised thrifty living. He never took this as a privation but thought it a pleasure. For, as he had said: "Having grown accustomed to a frugal plain life, I hold that only frugality and plainness can bring spiritual happiness."

In October, 1935, the Red Army under the direct command of the CPC Central Committee completed the Long March of twenty-five thousand *li* and reached Northern Shaanxi. In November, the Northwest Office of the Central Provisional Government of the Soviet Republic of China was established at Wayaobao and Xu Teli took the post of Minister of Education.

In order to familiarise himself with the local educational situation, Xu Teli went to the only primary school in the town – the Lenin Primary School, which was established by the city government. One morning, while a heavy snow was falling, he audited their classes. Wang Zhiyun happened to be teaching Chinese language when he realised that all of a sudden some of his pupils had shifted their eyes to look outside the classroom. He followed their gaze. An old man whose tattered clothing was tied about his waist with a black wool rope was standing at the door listening to his class. He looked the very image of a stable hand.

The pupils darted their curious glances outwards every now and then. Afraid that their attention might be diverted, Wang Zhiyun wanted to drive him away. But, looking at his very sincere and intelligent eyes and expression of concentration, he felt that doing that would cause embarrassment. Who was this fellow? In a puzzled mood, he finished this Chinese language lesson. The old "stable hand" didn't leave until the end of the lesson.

The next day, the old "stable hand" came again together with three other comrades who were also in tattered clothing. One tall intellectual-looking man stepped forward to make the introductions.

Pointing at the old man with an honest serious face, he said: "This is Comrade Dong Biwu, Secretary of the Disciplinary Inspection Committee of the CPC Central Committee and President of the Party School of the Central Committee of CPC."

Pointing at another one, he said: "This is Comrade Cheng Fangwu, the Academic Dean of the Party School."

Finally, pointing at the old "stable hand" that had come the day before, he continued: "This is Comrade Xu Teli, Minister of Education of the Soviet Central Government. I am Feng Xuefeng."

Wang Zhiyun was startled: These were all leading officials of the CPC Central Committee! The old "stable hand" was in fact the teacher of Chairman Mao – Venerable Xu. How plain and common he was! However, his greatness and uncommonness were epitomised through his plainness and commonness.

The "One-hundred-treasure Gown" during the Long March

During the most arduous Long March, Xu Teli gave fullest play to his frugal style of life. Materials were in extremely short supply at that

Chapter Six "An Exemplary Teacher of His Generation and a Role Model for the World" 261

time. In order to solve the difficulties in the respects of food, clothing, boarding and everyday use and so on, he invented many "masterpieces." For example, a Trottiera clock was hung around his neck to be used as a "pocket watch;" rough cloth was sewed into an octagonal cap with the top and beak and five-point red star all being made meticulously … Among all his genuine "handiworks," the most unforgettable one in the minds of the officers and soldiers must be his "one-hundred-treasure gown."

During the Long March, Xu Teli owned a long gown, which he wore in the daytime and used as a quilt at night. However, he made some "modifications" to ensure it was as useful as possible. Whenever he laid his hands on a piece of cloth in any colour – be it big or small – he sewed it onto the long gown to form big or small pockets. These stored any sort of miscellaneous items, separated according to type. For example, there were stamps and inkpads, grandpa's glasses as well as official documents, books, and odds and sods. Those which needed to be used regularly were put in convenient pockets and those which were seldom used found their way into "remote" spots; important articles were dropped into important positions and those unimportant ones also had a place to "settle down" … One can visualise how peculiar this long gown must have appeared. As time elapsed, the number and variety of items in storage grew.

Few set any store by his "one-hundred-treasure gown" at the very beginning. Hou Zheng, the Commander of the Cadres' Recuperation Company to which Xu Teli belonged persuaded him several times and hoped that he would simplify his "equipment" in the gown to travel light. However, Xu Teli only smiled but didn't follow his advice. After the army occupied Tongxing, some items belonging to capitalists – including cigarettes, sweets and grain – were confiscated. Hou Zheng thought that since he couldn't change the capacity of Xu Teli's long gown, he could change its contents anyhow. Therefore, he persuaded Xu Teli to discard some "useless" things and change them into food. But the obstinate Venerable Xu stuck to his old ways. What is more, he gathered the nails, iron wires and a hammer he got in Tongxing into an iron box, which was then incorporated into his "one-hundred-treasure gown." This was all well and good, but when they marched again it was to the accompaniment of a new "jingling" music.

A particular incident changed Hou Zheng's attitude towards the "one-hundred-treasure gown." One day, Xu Teli caught up with Hou Zheng from behind. Hou Zheng was standing beside the stretcher of Zhong Chibing the Political Commissar of the 12th Regiment and worrying in vain. Zhong Chibing's right leg had been wounded during the Battle of Loushanguan and was then amputated with a sword. But the wound was infected and his high fever would not subside. Zhou Enlai instructed the recuperation company especially that they must carry Zhong Chibing to march. However, exactly at this time, the stretcher was broken. It was impossible either to repair or to buy another one in the middle of nowhere. Distressed and at the end of his wits, Hou Zheng broke out into a cold sweat on his forehead.

Catching sight of this, Xu Teli teased him: "Hurry up. What are you waiting for?"

A raging fire was attacking Hou Zheng's heart. He lost control and shouted brusquely: "Hey, you old codger – how come you haven't made tracks yet. Stop hanging around here where you're neither use nor ornament."

Xu Teli didn't take offence at his words but replied in a leisurely manner: "Don't panic. I can find a solution. Bring me one of the poles that are used to carry the medicine boxes."

Since this was the situation, Hou Zheng had to do what he was told to. After the carrying pole was brought to him, the treasures in Xu Teli's "one-hundred-treasure gown" started to do their stuff. Like magic, he brought out ropes, nails and a hammer from inside and made quick work of repairing the stretcher. Bystanders watched with admiration and Hou Zheng was utterly convinced. The fame of the "one-hundred-treasure gown" spread out since then.

"Health is the Seed Money of Revolution"

Among the ranks of the revolutionary army, Xu Teli was not only the oldest but also the longest lived. This had everything to do with the value he attached to physical exercise and the way he cherished his health. He often said: "Health is the seed money of revolution. The more revolutionary seed money the better. The healthier one is, the more work they can do for the society and people." Despite being in his eighties and nineties, he could still study and work energetically. Several dozen years of persistent physical training had borne fruit.

Xu Teli learned how to swim at the age of fifty-two when he studied at Yat-sen University in Moscow in the Soviet Union. He felt that it was very useful. After leaping into water with a splashing sound, he could relax his sinews and bones freely and wash his skin clear and clean whether he dived to the bottom or floated in the water surface – it was so refreshing.

In Yan'an, Xu Teli joined the "leaping fish swimming team" that was mainly composed of young comrades. At that length when the River Yan was the deepest at the foot of the Mountain Qingliang (meaning "refreshing and cool"), he often jumped into water to swim together with the others, laughing heartily. His strokes were graceful, and he would dive down or float on the surface freely. What is more, few younger men could match his speed.

One year, Yan'an held a sports meeting, with the 100-metre swimming race being one event. Before the race began, a white-haired, white-bearded but ruddy-faced competitor stood among the line of young and vigorous athletes – that was Xu Teli who was already pushing seventy. The judge gave the order and they plunged forward together. Xu Teli tried the backstroke, his hands paddling and his legs kicking out, and ploughed his way forward. His headful of silvery hair floated on the surface and followed the waves to move forward like a cluster of silver silk. Inspired by the elderly yet energetic Xu Teli, the audience clapped their hands to cheer and the atmosphere was electric. After this event, Xu Fanting the renowned educator in Yan'an wrote a poem:

I still remember that one August the autumn wind was cold.
Soldiers and folks gathering along the River Yan were so bold.
A seventy-year-old gentleman danced in the water.
With gawking eyes how many young people could only behold.

Going on Foot Rather Than Riding in a Sedan-car

Material conditions improved somewhat after the establishment of the PRC. The CPC Central Committee allocated a sedan-car for Xu Teli's personal use, but he seldom rode in it except when there was an emergency or he had to attend a meeting.

One winter afternoon in 1949, he went to Beijing Hospital to see a doctor and ran into Peng Wenlong, who was also there waiting in line for the same reason. It had been a long time since they had last seen each other. They had numerous topics to talk about.

At this moment, Xu Teli's guard ran over and asked for directions: "Venerable Xu, I will go and see if your sedan-car has come or not. If it hasn't, I will make a call, tell them that you are in Beijing Hospital and ask them to come and collect you."

Xu Teli replied: "There is no need to make the call. Wait a minute and see what happens. It doesn't matter though the car doesn't come. If it means hitching a ride from another comrade I'll still be able to get home."

Hearing them out, Peng Wenlong asked in surprise: "What? Venerable Xu, you came here on foot?"

Xu Teli nodded his head: "I have got accustomed to that. Walking is a very good physical exercise."

Another time, Xu Teli left home in the afternoon but still hadn't come back home by nightfall. His family asked around at various places but didn't found him and were on tenterhooks. He was nearly eighty by then. What if something had happened to him? His family reported it to the CPC Central Committee. After knowing of this, Premier Zhou Enlai was concerned and immediately made a call to Luo Ruiqing the Minister of Public Security of the PRC, requiring him to do everything he could to find Xu Teli as soon as possible. At 9 pm, the Ministry of Public Security called back and reported that Xu Teli was found. Not until then did everyone's heart find peace.

This was what had happened. That day, Xu Teli took a bus to Xishan or Western Mountain and came back in the evening. Because there were too many passengers and not enough buses, he waited in line together with the others. It was nearly nightfall. Seeing that he was white-haired and very advanced in years, people invited him to get aboard first, but he declined their kindness and persisted in waiting. Not until the comrades from the Ministry of Public Security found him did he leave.

Xu Teli seldom went out by car. This gave his guard a bellyful of complaints. He sometimes grumbled: "The other people's guards always go everywhere in a small vehicle, but, I have to leg it here there and everywhere after the leader Venerable Xu. I need extra pairs of shoes!"

His words reached the ears of Xu Teli. One day, he called him to a halt and enquired amiably: "Your family is a middling peasant one? How much grain does your family bring back home? How is their life?"

The guard replied: "My family lives in the Mountains Taihang, where the land is barren. Every year everyone brings back home no more than five hundred *jin* of rice grains – six hundred if the harvest is bumper but no more than five hundred if it is meagre. During February and March when last season's crops have almost been eaten up and the new ones are not yet ripe, we must supplement that with wild vegetables. But our life is still much better than that before the Land Reform Movement of '47 – 52!'"

Xu Teli asked again: "Do you know where the petrol that fuels the car comes from? How much petrol will be consumed to go to the city proper for once and how much it's worth?"

The guard didn't know and shook his head.

Xu Teli explained to him patiently: "Our country is newly liberated and can't produce petroleum yet. Now our cars and petrol are all exchanged from abroad with gold and other materials. One gallon of petroleum costs several dozen thousand people's currencies (old), which might fuel a car to ride for about thirty *li*. Just imagine: it is several dozen *li* from Xishan to the city proper. If you were to take a sedan-car to go there and back several times, that's as much as a peasant's annual income. Now people still live a hard life. How can I take a car alone to waste petroleum freely! If the gap between our lives and theirs was too glaring, the people would complain!"

The guard listened and listened and gradually ducked his head.

Xu Teli stroked his shoulders kindly and continued his lecture: "Young man, there are three advantages to walking rather than riding in a car: First, you build up your body. Second, you save expenditure. And third, you strengthen the relationship between the officials and the people. Hasn't the best of three worlds been made?"

Convinced by Xu Teli's patient education, the guard never complained again but followed him to train the soles of his feet into a pair of iron ones.

"Your Time Is Precious. Does That Mean That Others' Time Is Worthless?"

As a senior revolutionary and educator, Xu Teli never took advantage of his seniority but always regarded himself as a common citizen, abiding by the rules and regulations of society obediently.

One day, he went to the Beijing Hospital to see a doctor. The waiting room was packed solid and the patients were all sitting on the long chairs that had a back rest waiting for their serial numbers to be announced.

Seeing that there were so many people, his guard became worried.

"Venerable Xu cherishes his time best," he thought. "If he waits for his turn like this, how much time will be wasted?" He therefore went over to him and enquired quietly.

"Venerable Xu, there are too many people. I will go and inform Director Zhang so that you will see the doctor first. What do you think?"

Xu Teli hurriedly waved his hands and refused: "No, no, don't inform him. We'd better wait in line. It doesn't matter if I wait a little while."

The guard cast a glance at the wall clock and grumbled with pouted lips: "Then that is rather a long while to wait …"

Finding out that the guard was a little unhappy, Xu Teli beckoned him to sit down and, patting his shoulder, explained to him patiently: "Your time is precious. Does that mean others' time is worthless? If we don't wait in line to see the doctor, the others will have to wait longer. Whatever we do, we should always take the others into consideration but not think only about our own convenience. What is more, if you go to look for Director Zhang, we are given special care and don't need to wait in line because we are acquaintances. If acquaintances all don't follow the rules, how can order be maintained here?"

Feeling that Xu Teli had a point, the guard then waited patiently together with him for his serial number to be called out.

"This Is Talking Blindly with Your Eyes Wide Open!"

Xu Teli boasted a very noble ideological quality. That was his work style of "seeking truth from facts." He said: "Seek truth from facts – this is my motto as well as the essence of Marxism." "Be it in the study or at work, be it the leaders or the led, everyone should seek truth from facts in doing anything." "If we don't seek truth from facts, our revolution, construction, work and study will deviate and be threatened by the danger of taking a crooked road."

In 1958, the "wind of boasting" and the "communist wind" characterised by extreme equalitarianism were in vogue in the society. Some people wantonly practised fraud and deceived their superiors and deluded their subordinates. In the autumn of that year, Xu Teli took a southern tour and passed by Henan Province. Escorted by Wu Zhipu, the First Secretary of the Party Committee of Henan Province, he went to a commune to visit the cotton field. It was late autumn. A light frost set in and they experienced a series of cloudy rainy days. The cotton balls mostly hadn't popped open yet, but the speaker was full of heroic words and declared that the yield of cotton could amount to several hundred *jin* per *mu*.

Xu Teli retorted: "I don't believe this. This is talking blindly with your eyes wide open! On my way back I shall drop by again to check it out and see how many *jin* the yield is."

The speaker also boasted that the yield of rice could be more than ten thousand *jin* per *mu* because the rice stalks grew so densely even wind couldn't blow through.

Hearing this, Xu Teli became more unhappy. "This is impossible! How can rice grow if it is not well-ventilated? This is common sense," he said to the comrades around him.

After coming back to Beijing, he sank into a bad mood. Later the related departments informed him to go to Xushui to visit. He declined.

He said: "We should learn from Lenin for his revolutionary spirit to fulfil a cause through painstaking efforts and from the Americans for their down-to-earth spirit. When the Americans manage the economy, they always set greatest store by rationality. But our country sees too much feudal stuff: red tape, blind directions, waste of manpower and materials! Waste is a crime more serious than corruption! …"

His secretary Xu Qian persuaded him: "You should be careful when you speak outside. The others might say that you oppose the Great Leap Forward."

He meditated awhile and said: "It is easier said than done to seek truth from facts. But every CPC member should abide by this principle!"

He continued: "It is easy to talk big, but people will suffer eventually!"

The later reality proved that his worries were not unfounded. The practice of being boastful brought serious consequences to society. He was very indignant.

"Those boasters want to hoodwink the others but end with sacrificing the social credit," he said. "They themselves are isolated, fall from power and lose their last scrap of human dignity. Every so-called smart guy that lacks the down-to-earth style of work will leave a harmful legacy to the society and their offspring!"

Keeping Up the Fight as Long as He Still Lives

On 1st October, 1949 when the founding ceremony of New China was being held, Xu Teli mounted the Tian'anmen Rostrum, witnessed how Chairman Mao hoisted the first red five-star flag, listened with his own ears to how Chairman Mao Zedong solemnly announced to the world that the Chinese revolution had achieved the great success, and celebrated the final realisation of the revolutionary ideal that the Chinese people had fought for more than one hundred years.

In that year, Xu Teli was already seventy-two. In the eyes of the ordinary people, he should be enjoying his twilight years at leisure, but he never slackened due to old age. After the celebration, what he thought of was not how to enjoy his easy and carefree life since the revolution was accomplished but how to fulfil the arduous tasks in our economic and cultural construction. In his poem to celebrate Wu Yuzhang's seventieth birthday, he wrote:

…
Colonialism dominated China for more than one hundred years.
But now we have wiped clean our tears.

Our future is arduous.
The key lies with the people and engineers.
Don't be over-optimistic, please.
Success never comes with great ease.
You and I are both in the autumn of our lives.
But our lifeblood is committed to the travail.

The poem demonstrated his acute vision, his strong sense of responsibility towards the revolutionary cause and his grand aspiration that "a noble old steed might have to crouch down beside the trough, but he still aspires to run one thousand *li* a day."

In order to learn new knowledge and make more contributions to the construction of New China, Xu Teli never gave a thought to his old age but made an ambitious plan that he would learn and work for another twenty years. As long as he was still alive, he would learn and work. He told his good friend Xie Juezai that a man hasn't grown old as long as he is still making progress. But he is old if he has stopped making progress.

In this way, Xu Teli energetically threw himself into the cultural and educational cause of the New China regardless of his old age. He led a batch of propaganda personnel and historians to engage in the compilation of the general history of China, the revolutionary history of China and the history of the CPC. Meanwhile he continued caring about and giving directions to educational work through all kinds of means: explaining with reports, expounding with articles, investigating and inspecting, receiving visitors, communicating through letters, and writing inscriptions at people's invitation … He dedicated his light and heat to the socialist cultural and educational cause. The adamant veteran was fighting as long as he was still alive.

His Last Days

Xu Teli passed his last days in the tempest of the Great Cultural Revolution.

After the Cultural Revolution was set in motion, he encountered abnormalities in political life and society became turbulent. Several loudspeakers near his dwelling place took turns to roar every day that we should "rebel," that we should "conduct revolution" and that a great number of distinguished meritorious senior revolutionaries should be overthrown. Xu Teli, who was bright-minded and fond of chatting smilingly at ordinary times, sank into a very agitated mood. Pointing at the door and windows with his walking stick angrily, he ordered his family to shut them so that the sound from outside wouldn't float in.

He became taciturn. Sometimes he summoned his family to his side and seemed to have many words to say to them, but, his lips quivering, he again swallowed them. Frequently he paced to and fro alone in the room and gagged his mouth at length. When he really couldn't hold on, he would blurt out to himself: "This is strange. How could he have become our enemy? ... But how? No, I don't believe ... I, I really can't make head nor tail of it ..."

He had many words to say to Chairman Mao from the bottom of his heart. He phoned him many times, but couldn't get through. Sometimes, in great agitation he wanted to take a vehicle to go to Zhongnanhai directly, but was dissuaded by the workers nearby. Worry and gloom tortured the old man. One day, he said to his good friend Xie Juezai quietly that he wanted to go to the countryside to raise pigs. After hearing of that, Xie Juezai, touched greatly, composed a poem:

He is ninety but remains a live wire.
When he stays idle what does he admire?
Being envious of those farmers and scholars,
Raising pigs in mulberry shade is his true desire.

On National Day in 1966, Xu Teli came to the Tian'anmen Rostrum early and wanted to have a word with Chairman Mao. Before the military review, he hid in one room beside the elevator. When he saw that Chairman Mao was coming, he wanted to step forward to welcome him, but a large group of people had thronged to Chairman Mao's side long before. How could the old and weak Xu Teli squeeze in? He could only wave at Chairman Mao from afar and then watch how Chairman Mao walked past. Unwilling to watch the military review any longer, he went back home early. He had never expected that this would be the last time he would see Chairman Mao …

In November, 1968, Xu Teli's state of health became critical. Premier Zhou Enlai seized a break from his gruelling schedule to visit him in the hospital and required that the hospital must throw every resource they had into rescuing him. But doctors are also powerless before what have been predestined by Heaven. On 28th November, Xu Teli died from a disease and departed from this world forever.

Zhou Enlai asked Xu Qian, who had always been standing by serving Xu Teli: "What were Venerable Xu's last words?"

Xu Qian answered: "He said, after he has passed away, his body should be left to medical science."

Hearing her out, Zhou Enlai couldn't speak for long and his eyes were sparkling with tears.

After Xu Teli passed away, the CPC Central Committee held a solemn memorial ceremony for him. The CPC Central Committee and Chairman Mao both presented a wreath. Premier Zhou participated in the memorial meeting in person. Teng Daiyuan represented the CPC Central Committee to read the eulogy. In the eulogy, Xu Teli was highly praised, "His life being a glorious, great and revolutionary example!"

A common man but a crusader for Marx and Lenin to boot,
The enlightener of a generation; an educator to the young.
Ten thousand generations will recall his words and virtues immortal,
An exemplary revolutionary, fully deserved of his repute.

This poem was entirely apt in its praise of Xu Teli. He lived up to his reputation as an exemplary teacher of his generation and a role model for the world.